W9-CFC-580

MULTICULTURAL EDUCATION SERIES

James A. Banks, *Series Editor*

(continued)

Teaching and Learning on the Verge
Democratic Education in Action

Shanti Elliott

TEACHERS COLLEGE PRESS

TEACHERS COLLEGE | COLUMBIA UNIVERSITY
NEW YORK AND LONDON

Published by Teachers College Press, 1234 Amsterdam Avenue, New York, NY 10027

Library of Congress Cataloging-in-Publication Data

Elliott, Shanti.
Teaching and learning on the verge : democratic education in action / Shanti Elliott.
   pages cm
  Includes bibliographical references and index.
  ISBN 978-0-8077-5641-6 (pbk. : alk. paper)
  ISBN 978-0-8077-5642-3 (hardcover : alk. paper)
  ISBN 978-0-8077-7372-7 (ebook)
     1. Democracy--Study and teaching. 2. Democracy and education. I. Title.
  LC1091.E545 2015
  370.11'5—dc23   2015010156

ISBN 978-0-8077-5641-6 (paper)
ISBN 978-0-8077-5642-3 (hardcover)
ISBN 978-0-8077-7372-7 (ebook)

Printed on acid-free paper
Manufactured in the United States of America

22 21 20 19 18 17 16 15   8 7 6 5 4 3 2 1

Contents

We may have reached a moment in our history when teaching and learning, if they are to happen meaningfully, must happen on the verge.

—*Maxine Greene*

Series Foreword

Horace Mann and other early constructors of American education viewed citizenship participation as one of the essential goals of the common or public schools. A widely shared belief among American educators prior to the harsh critiques of the schools by revisionist historians and sociologists during the 1970s was that public schools fostered democracy and promoted social and economic equality. In 1972, Colin Greer published a scathing critique and revisionist interpretation of schools that argued that the belief that schools taught and exemplified democracy was the "great school legend." The schools not only did not teach or promote democracy argued Greer, they perpetuated social-class stratification and reinforced the class divisions within the larger society.

Schooling in Capitalist America: Educational Reform and the Contradiction of Economic Life by Samuel Bowles and Herbert Gintis (1976)—an erudite and complex Marxist analysis of U.S. schools—reinforced and extended Greer's thesis. Bowles and Gintis argued that the social organization of schools was similar to the capitalist workforce structure and that schools reproduced and mirrored the hierarchy of capitalist institutions. Consequently, schools socialized different classes of youth for their adult roles and statuses in life. In 1978, Diane Ravitch published a searing critique of the revisionist interpretations of U.S. schools and argued that they distorted the historical record. The schools, she argued, have facilitated the social mobility of immigrant and low-income students.

In this illuminating and timely book, Shanti Elliott reveals a keen awareness of the critiques and counter-critiques of schools that have been developed by scholars such as Greer, Bowles and Gintis, and Ravitch—as well as of the limitations and possibilities of schools. She describes the contradictions that exist when schools try to educate for citizen participation and democracy within social, political, and economic contexts—including schools—that violate democratic values. However, Elliott believes that schools can advance democratic citizenship within the contradictory social, political, and economic contexts in which they exist. She formulates a conceptual framework and describes examples that illustrate how teachers can involve students in meaningful civic action projects. Such projects enable students to internalize democratic values and practice civic action skills in school and community activities in which they acquire critical consciousness, a better understanding of oppressive systems, and take actions that help to make their schools and communities more just and equitable. *Self-reflection, questioning power,* and *dialogic hunger* are linchpins of Elliott's framework for teaching democratic values and civic action. One of the major goals of this book is to describe ways in which teachers can help students to raise their level of consciousness and to become social critics and effective civic actors in their local communities, state, and nation.

An essential component of Elliott's conceptualization and thinking is that adults—including teachers—must participate in and become part of the process of democratic change for citizenship education to be effective and authentic for students. Elliott's conceptualization and ideas about democracy and civic education mirror the ideas of democracy in John Dewey's (1938) classic book, *Experience and Education.* He states that "all genuine education comes about through experience" (p. 13). Elliott believes that for civic educational experiences to be effective and meaningful for students, adults must participate in them with students as collaborators and co-learners. They must also raise the level of consciousness of students about the social, economic, and political contexts in which they live. In formulating her concepts of democratic education and civic action, Elliott draws thoughtfully upon the ideas of transformative educational theorists such as Michael Apple, Henry Giroux, Paulo Freire, and Mikhail Bakhtin to create a framework for teaching democracy and civic action that is teacher friendly, classroom tested, and visionary.

Elliott's conceptual framework for teaching democratic education and civic action is especially timely because of the growing population of students from diverse racial, ethnic, cultural, linguistic, and religious groups who are attending schools in the United States and in other nations. The racial, ethnic, cultural, and religious polarizations in the United States and in other nations are revealed by the tensions between police and communities of color in cities such as Ferguson, Missouri, and Pasco, Washington; as well as by the violent events that occurred in Paris after the publication of a contentious cartoon of Muhammad by the satirical magazine *Charlie Hebdo.* The growing income gap between adults (Stiglitz, 2012)—as well as between youth that are described by Robert D. Putnam (2015) in *Our Kids: The American Dream in Crisis*—is another significant reason why it is important to teach democracy and civic education in schools. As Elliott points out, schools should help youth from diverse groups learn to live together and to create communities that are characterized by civic equality, democracy, and social justice. The increasing and complex dimensions of diversity within U.S. schools and in schools around the world make her argument especially compelling.

American classrooms are experiencing the largest influx of immigrant students since the beginning of the 20th century. Almost 14 million new immigrants—documented and undocumented—settled in the United States in the years from 2000 to 2010. Less than 10% came from nations in Europe. Most came from Mexico, nations in Asia, and nations in Latin America, the Caribbean, and Central America (Camarota, 2011). The influence of an increasingly diverse population on U.S. schools, colleges, and universities is and will continue to be enormous.

Schools in the United States are more diverse today than they have been since the early 1900s when a multitude of immigrants entered the United States from Southern, Central, and Eastern Europe. In 2014, the National Center for Education Statistics estimated that the percentage of students from ethnic minority groups made up more than 50% of the students in prekindergarten through 12th grade in public schools, an increase from 40% in 2001 (National Center for Education Statistics, 2014).

Language and religious diversity is also increasing in the U.S. student population. The 2012 American Community Survey estimated that 21% of Americans aged 5 and above (61.9 million) spoke a language other than English at home (U.S. Census Bureau, 2012). Harvard professor Diana L. Eck (2001) calls the United States the "most religiously diverse nation on earth" (p. 4). Islam is now the fastest-growing religion in the United States, as well as in several European nations such as France, the United Kingdom, and The Netherlands (Banks, 2009; Cesari, 2004).

The major purpose of the Multicultural Education Series is to provide preservice educators, practicing educators, graduate students, scholars, and policymakers with an interrelated and comprehensive set of books that summarizes and analyzes important research, theory, and practice related to the education of ethnic, racial, cultural, and linguistic groups in the United States and the education of mainstream students about diversity. The dimensions of multicultural education, developed by Banks (2004) and described in the *Handbook of Research on Multicultural Education* and in the *Encyclopedia of Diversity in Education* (Banks, 2012), provide the conceptual framework for the development of the publications in the Series. The dimensions are content integration, the knowledge construction process, prejudice reduction, equity pedagogy, and an empowering institutional culture and social structure. The books in the Multicultural Education Series provide research, theoretical, and practical knowledge about the behaviors and learning characteristics of students of color, language minority students, low-income students, and other minoritized population groups, such as LGBTQ youth (Mayo, 2014).

Elliott's book is especially timely and needed because educational initiatives and developments such as the Race to the Top competitive grant for states and school districts and the Common Core State Standards Initiative—because they focus on high-stakes tests and hold teachers and schools accountable for the performance of their students on standardized tests—have resulted in an alarming neglect of the teaching of social studies and civic education in U.S. schools. The focus has shifted to a heavy emphasis on subjects such as math and reading, which make up a disproportionate share of the items on high-stakes standardized tests.

A recent report on civic education, *Youth Civic Development and Education* (Malin, Ballard, Attai, et al., 2014)—published jointly by the Stanford Center on Adolescence at Stanford University and the Center for Multicultural Education at the University of Washington—lament the declining importance of civic education in U.S. schools. The report states:

> Despite the clear urgency of this mission, civic education as practiced in schools throughout the United States is not preparing students for effective participation in civic life. Few young people are sufficiently motivated to become engaged in civic and political activity. . . . Not surprisingly, sectors of the population from low-income and marginalized communities have been most affected by what has been called "the civic engagement gap." (p. 7)

Elliott's cogent voice about the need to make democratic education an important mission of schools echoes the sentiments of civic education scholars since the turn of the century—including George Counts (1932), John Dewey (1938), Amy Gutmann (2004), Walter Parker (2002), James Banks (2007), and Joel Westheimer (2015)—who have described why democratic education is essential for the perpetuation of a democracy. As Walter Parker insightfully argues, democracies are fragile and must be continually reconstructed and renewed in order for them to survive. With this book and its practical and imaginative suggestions for schools and communities, Elliott makes an important contribution to the litany of compelling voices that remind us that democracies and democratic citizens must be continually created and reinvented if democratic societies and nations are to survive.

—James A. Banks

REFERENCES

Banks, J. A. (2004). Multicultural education: Historical development, dimensions, and practice. In J. A. Banks & C. A. M. Banks (Eds.), *Handbook of research on multicultural education* (2nd ed., pp. 3–29). San Francisco, CA: Jossey-Bass.

Banks, J. A. (2007). *Educating citizens in a multicultural society* (2nd ed.). New York, NY: Teachers College Press.

Banks, J. A. (Ed.). (2009). *The Routledge international companion to multicultural education.* New York, NY and London, UK: Routledge.

Banks, J. A. (2012). Multicultural education: Dimensions of. In J. A. Banks (Ed.), *Encyclopedia of diversity in education* (Vol. 3, pp. 1538–1547). Thousand Oaks, CA: Sage Publications.

Bowles, S., & Gintis, H. (1976) *Schooling in capitalist America: Educational reform and the construction of economic life*. New York, NY: Basic Books.

Camarota, S. A. (2011, October). *A record-setting decade of immigration: 2000 to 2010*. Washintgton, DC: Center for Immigration Studies. Available at http://cis.org/2000-2010-record-setting-decade-of-immigration

Cesari, J. (2004). *When Islam and democracy meet: Muslims in Europe and the United States*. New York, NY: Palgrave Macmillan.

Counts, G. S. (1932). *Dare the schools build a new social order?* New York, NY: John Day Company.

Dewey, J. (1938). *Experience and education*. New York, NY: Macmillan.

Eck, D. L. (2001). *A new religious America: How a "Christian country" has become the world's most religiously diverse nation*. San Francisco, CA: HarperSanFrancisco.

Greer, C. (1972). *The great school legend: A revisionist interpretation of American public education*. New York, NY: Basic Books.

Gutmann, A. (2004). Unity and diversity in democratic multicultural education: Creative and destructive tensions. In J. A. Banks (Ed.), *Diversity and citizenship education: Global perspectives* (pp. 71–96). San Francisco, CA: Jossey-Bass.

Malin, H., Ballard, P. J., Attai, M. L., Colby, A., & Damon, W. (2014). *Youth civic development and education: A conference consensus report*. Palo Alto, CA: Stanford University, Stanford Center on Adolescence & Seattle, WA: University of Washington, Center for Multicultural Education.

Mayo, C. (2014). *LGBTQ youth and education: Policies and practices*. New York, NY: Teachers College Press.

National Center for Education Statistics. (2014). *The condition of education 2014*. Available at http://nces.ed.gov/pubs2014/2014083.pdf

Parker, W. C. (2002). *Teaching democracy: Unity and diversity in public life*. New York, NY: Teachers College Press.

Putnam, R. D. (2015). *Our kids: The American dream in crisis*. New York, NY: Simon & Schuster.

Ravitch, D. (1978). *The revisionists revised: A critique of the radical attack on the schools*. New York, NY: Basic Books.

Stiglitz, J. E. (2012). *The price of inequality: How today's divided society endangers our future*. New York, NY: Norton.

U.S. Census Bureau. (2012). *Selected social characteristics in the United States: 2012 American community survey 1-year estimates*. Available at http://factfinder2.census.gov/faces/tableservices/jsf/pages/productview.xhtml?pid=ACS_12_1YR_DP02&prodType=table

Westheimer, J. (2015). *What kind of citizen: Educating our children for the common good*. New York, NY: Teachers College Press.

Acknowledgments

Teachers are my tribe, so I have a whole lot of teachers to thank for their help with this book. Beginning with the literary sisterhood of women in my immediate family: my mom Frances, sisters Maria and Marjorie, and cousin Christina, all of whom read my book and nourished me with good advice, keen questions, and inspired cooking. My husband, Mark, and my dad, Bruce—also teachers!—cheered me on with their love and wisdom. I also thank my other parents, Paul and Sara, my brothers Matt and Mig, and my Tunisian family, who sustain and inspire me.

Other educators and friends who have read this book, encouraged me, and helped me to clarify my thinking include: Bill Ayers, Harry Boyte, Joan Bradbury, Randolph Carter, Mary Dilg, Jay Featherstone, Rachel Fiske, Andy Kaplan, Mark Larson, Avi Lessing, Meira Levinson, Kim Richards, Carol Rodgers, Brian Schultz, and Douglas Sharp. I am grateful to each of them for their generous support and intelligent critique.

My colleagues at Francis Parker School have taught me and collaborated and conspired with me, and I am endlessly grateful for them. Lisa Williams has stood steadily by me in the day-to-day work of developing civic education at Parker. My deep thanks to the Civic Engagement leaders, who see their support of students' civic learning as a fundamental part of their teaching, no matter what discipline they teach. In particular, I want to recognize the current 11th-grade team, Jeanne Barr, Andy Bigelow, Theresa Collins, Stacy Gibson, Matt Laufer, and Mike Mahany. Each of these teachers nurtures the great human capacities of their students, and models the vision, imagination, and determination of sustainable civic education.

Thanks to my administration: Dan Frank, Damian Jones, Ruth Jurgensen, MaryAnn Manley, John Novick, Tom Rosenbluth, Joe Ruggiero, and Kimeri Swanson-Beck, who have supported my work, including a sabbatical year that gave me the time and funds I needed to travel, research, and write this book. I appreciate the trust they placed in me, both in my work on the ground and in my writing. These educators exemplify the respect, vision, and courage needed in leading education for democratic society.

I am also grateful to my colleagues at partner schools, who believe in the power of young people and base their practice in respect, creativity, and love. These include: Kate Balogh, Xian Barrett, Jill Bass, Tiffany

Childress-Price, Robyn D'Averso, Eric Davis, Christine Diaz, Rick Diaz, Kelly Fischer, Alejandra Frausto, Miguel Guevara, David Harris, Adam Heenan, Geoff Hiron, Carrie Kelso, Anton Miglietta, Danny Morales-Doyle, Nate Ramin, Kim Richards, Sue Rucker, Sarah Saïd, Brian Schultz, Craig Segal, Kelli Tepastte, Heather Van Bethuysen, Jeanne Walker, and Patty Whitehouse.

At Parker, I encountered a number of social justice mentors, without whom this book would not have been written. These parents and faculty include Mark Aymer, Mike Brayndick, Gary Childrey, Kevin Conlon, John Donahue, George Drury, Alice Ducas, Tania Giordani, Darlene Gramigna, Pat Handlin, Sunnie Hikawa, Maryanne Kalin-Miller, Marilyn Katz, Katie Haskins, Prexy Nesbitt, and Flint Taylor. I am also grateful to my former students Kara Crutcher, Agnotti Cowie (from Parker), and Fanny Diego (from Farragut), who have developed into powerful social justice leaders in Chicago.

I also want to recognize the influence of people and organizations whose embodiment of democratic leadership has been important for this book. In Chicago: members of Teachers for Social Justice, Chicago Teachers' Union, Caucus of Rank and File Educators, Project Nia, Kenwood Oakland Community Organization, Mikva Challenge, Chicago Youth Initiating Change, and Chicago Grassroots Curriculum Taskforce. At a national level: North Dakota Study Group, Matrix Leadership, Institute for Democratic Education in America, FairTest, Voice of Witness, and the Institute for Descriptive Inquiry. Special thanks to Jitu Brown, Jasmin Cardenas, Rico Gutstein, Ann-Louise Haak, Jessica Havens, Carol Jungman, Mariame Kaba, Amina Knowlan, Pauline Lipman, Cliff Mayotte, Tom and Anne Pigman, and Bob Thompson—each who have been guides for me with an impact that reaches far beyond the pages of this book.

Thanks to participants in Teachers' Inquiry Project programs and especially TIP leaders Joan Bradbury, Joby Gardner, Jeanne Kim, and Tina Nolan. Thanks to Francis Parker School for funding the Teachers' Inquiry Project so generously. Thanks to Ellen Belic, Kelli Covey, Adam Davis, Tim Dohrer, Mary Gajewski, Mary Goosby, Sophie Haroutunian-Gordon, and Tem Horwitz for supporting the work of the Teachers' Inquiry Project.

I visited a number of schools in writing this book. Special thanks to the students, teachers, and administrators of Rudy Lozano Leadership Academy, Urban Academy, and June Jordan School for Equity, for allowing me to come into your school and document what I learned there.

Thanks to my editors and readers at TC Press: James Banks, Brian Ellerbeck, Jennifer Baker, Carol Rodgers, and my anonymous readers, for your generous and thoughtful support.

A final word of gratitude to my students, who are my inspiration, my enchanters, and my puzzle. Any light that shines through this book comes from them.

This book is dedicated to my children Eleanor, Theodore, Katherine, Elizabeth, and Mateen.

Introduction

Playing with Power

They're playing a shell game. We're not going to play their game; we're going to kick over the box!

—Jitu Brown

Young people are experts at recognizing contradiction, hypocrisy, and subterfuge. Subject to being placed in positions that range from awkward to untenable, they have good noses for sniffing out injustice. Young people have a vantage point and a set of capacities that position them perfectly to help adults work through a problem that is increasingly taking over headlines: What is democratic education in a country with rising inequality?

As a social covenant declaring dignity and self-determination for all people, democracy demands collective struggle against inequality. However, inequality blocks collective struggle. Some of our young people go to schools where they learn to be thinkers, philosophers, leaders. Others go to schools where they learn to follow rules. For the most part it is family wealth and race that determines which kind of education young people will receive. Jonathan Kozol's (2005) portrait in *The Shame of the Nation* gets right at the heart of the problem: He shows us New York City public schools with crowded and dilapidated classrooms and sets them in contrast with mansions where wealthy people shrug resignedly and write checks to charities that try to patch up both inadequate social supports and people's uneasy consciences. The conflict between democratic values and unjust realities makes for a split world where, like the two entirely separate but overlapping realities that China Miéville (2009) describes in his novel *The City & The City*, people are conditioned to "unsee" the other world. This is a confusing and immobilizing situation for people to be in: It suits the power holders but not democracy.

Though schools often teach "unseeing," with education that avoids addressing the actual conditions of students' lives, many young people are not fooled. Kozol (2005) describes his conversation with 15-year-old Isabel from Harlem, who says of her experience in an all-Black school and neighborhood, "It's like we're being hidden. . . . It's as if you have been put in a garage where, if they don't have room for something but aren't sure if they

1

should throw it out, they put it there where they don't need to think of it again" (p. 28). Segregation systematizes unseeing; when it hurts kids and degrades democratic life, why do we still tolerate it?

Habits of relational distrust block many White Americans from recognizing the bigger issues of systemic racism, even when they stare us in the face. In her book *Talking to Strangers: Anxieties of Citizenship since Brown v. Board of Education*, Danielle Allen (2004) examines the failure of integration in America. She blames cultural patterns of distrust of "the Other" in American society that enabled segregation and that will perpetuate segregation until these attitudes are transformed: "Democracy depends on trustful talk among strangers and, properly conducted, should dissolve any divisions that block it" (p. xiii). Allen also describes a young person's refusal to "unsee" segregation as she describes an interchange about his opportunities for college:

> Thirteen-year-old Malik Burnett lived in a housing project in Chicago until his building was demolished and his family was forced to move to a run-down part of the West Side. Malik loves his teachers, he's proud of being third in his class. . . . "You know all those famous universities all over Chicago? They want you to come and they have great financial aid packages to make sure you'll have the money to go. You just keep concentrating on your reading and math." [Malik responds:] "The white people who won't come live in my neighborhood, or even visit it, will welcome me in theirs? Why should they feel any differently about my coming to live with them than they do about coming to live with me?" (pp. xiii–xiv)

In Allen's telling, she sees (or "unsees") Malik through the lens of meritocracy: If he works hard enough, he will be rewarded. Malik, however, knows that "they," the distributors of success, have faces, and those faces are White. The White faces he has seen remain in neighborhoods far, far away from his. Thus, the formula his mentor offers does not compute with his experience.

Malik's questions point to an unspoken rule in the geography of segregation: People from African American and Latino neighborhoods in Chicago must enter and exit through a gate that is overseen by predominantly White elites. And the gate does not go the other way. The map is laid out to reinforce inequality and imbalance.

Can young people handle talking about this? Are their teachers— themselves raised, as D. Allen (2004) observes, "not to talk to strangers"— capable of addressing questions like Malik's? If not, why not? And what does it mean for democratic society if we cannot learn and teach about inequality?

This book is about seeing both worlds, and learning in the dynamic space of the contradictions. I find that Maxine Greene's expression "teaching and learning on the verge" captures the possibility and the challenge of experimental work that strengthens democratic life. Our schools are like fishbowls of democratic society: They show us who we are as a people, and they have the capacity to advance our social intelligence. Throughout the United States, people in schools are developing democratic education, but the vision and the energy they generate, which should be deepening our society's social capacity, are ignored and repressed. In part this is due to an abstract and ideological concept of "democratic" as concerned only with voting and campaigning, rather than relationships, thinking, perception—the thoughtful everyday communication and expansive creative energy that allows for the health of society.

Instead of listening to what young people have to say to us about the world they are inheriting, our country complains about "terrible schools," "bad teachers," and the "broken school system." This is the language of "unseeing." In this book, I highlight the democratic work young people are doing—students from high-income families and low-income families and in between, and from a range of public and private schools—as they grapple with the contradictions of democratic society and proffer insight and solutions.

While democratic education can include processes of voting, governance, rights and representation, in this book I focus on more informal democratic processes. The central problem of democratic education, as I conceive it, is inequality. When inequality is addressed only within individual schools as a program, or in individual classes as an academic topic, the educational scope is distorted. Focusing on educational inequality apart from its real-life contexts is like running an athletics program but having no sports teams to apply athletic skills on the field. This book aims to support educational equality between and outside of schools, based in real work with kids.

Local Contexts

Democratic education insists on viewing student achievement within a broader context of relationships, environment, and social progress. It demands accountability of the public, not of individual students and teachers.[1] Beginning with the assumption that, as Maslow's hierarchy of needs posits, achievement depends on a foundation of safety, democratic education embeds learning within the demand that society provide the surrounding supports without which progress cannot happen at either an individual or a societal level. Especially for traditionally marginalized students, academic achievement is closely connected to the teacher–student relationship and the teacher's belief that the young people are capable of high achievement—but this relationship depends not only on the action or training of the teacher.[2] Democratic education addresses the *context* that makes culturally relevant pedagogy possible.

This is not a book for adults who want to make their kids better. It is a book for adults who want to learn with, from, and for kids to make the world better. I agree with George Counts (1934), who urged people who care about democracy to include children in it—not with simulations or lesson plans, but in real life: "A genuine society is composed of neither children nor adults, but of persons of all ages living together in close interdependence, it is in such a setting that life goes on" (p. 561). Democratic education, then, establishes schools as think tanks of sustainability and respects young people as leaders of social change.[3]

Democratic education requires rethinking the frame of the adult–child hierarchy, whereby young people are as a class dismissed from adult concerns and decisionmaking. Many books about children assume that adults need to "do something" to and for young people. This assumption undermines democratic education. This book is primarily about *the work adults do on themselves and with one another* in order to strengthen democratic education. The mantra "It's all about the kids" is a dangerous oversimplification that has blinded many of us to the complex relational, political, and intellectual work of education. I am arguing for paying attention to young people and the contexts they are in—not to add yet another tool to the arsenal of the complex project of shaping children, but in order to study what we as adults need to understand and change about ourselves if we want to be part of making a better world.

We know, after all, that inequality in education is not just a matter of supplies, teacher quality, or even safety. The sorting process that happens in and around the schools suffocates democracy. In the face of the dilemma that there is "no room at the top for the masses," this country has accepted a rigged process of elimination. "Schools are the mechanism used to resolve this messy social conundrum, which was previously accomplished through overtly racist and classist social policies" (Duncan-Andrade & Morrell, 2008, p. 3). High-stakes testing, training in obedience, and school and district policies that destabilize rather than support, produce "stratified knowledge, skills, dispositions, and identities for a deeply stratified society" as Pauline Lipman writes. In neoliberal American cities, children of the wealthy are welcomed as innovators and players on the world stage, who "work hard" and deserve their good fortune, while their low-income peers "are reduced to test scores, future slots in the labor market, prison numbers, and possible cannon fodder in military conquests" (2003, p. 179).

Which leads us in short order to the school-to-prison pipeline: The students who are denied high-quality education—predominantly people of color—are the ones filling our country's prisons. The legal, legislative, and economic systems of this country have provided the terms and mechanisms to leave White privilege intact even while many White people believe racial progress has succeeded.[4] "The New Jim Crow," in Michelle Alexander's powerful analysis, is a system that promotes mass incarceration, especially of African American men, masked by an official language that makes this racist reality seem inevitable and neutral. Such language aids the process of "unseeing," much like when I hide by covering my eyes: If we do not name race, segregation, and White supremacy, maybe they do not exist.

Given this state of affairs, democratic education involves struggle and conflict that is as generative as it is serious.[5] Youth resistance is vital to democracy, which I see as a nonlinear process of *becoming* rather than a set of acts or achievements. Democratic relationships involve constant movement, tension, and change:

> Community cannot be produced simply through rational formulation nor through edict. Like freedom, it has to be achieved by persons offered the space in which to discover what they recognize together and appreciate in common; they have to find ways to make inter-subjective sense. Again, it ought to be a space infused by the kind of imaginative awareness that enables those involved to imagine alternative possibilities for their own becoming and their group's becoming. (Greene, 1988, p. 39)

This is an intellectual description of *play*. The civic activity that develops young people's capacities as socially active human beings in democratic society is a natural continuation of the playing they did as little children.

I will be talking about democracy not as a political system but as a *current* that forces powerful institutions to stay limber and not stiffen. This current streams from many places. School can be one of these places—but only if the people in the school find ways to be tunnellers, held by the system but always sniffing out the cracks that let the light in. When people approach their relationships with institutions as *public play*, they can fill the current of democracy with the creative energy that counters business as usual. This is what education for democracy looks like—it is not about voting or running for office, but about designing lenses to see through "the crap" (Postman & Weingartner, 1971)—lenses that bring into view the stories of people who are often sidelined by institutional power and that clarify the possibilities for changing oneself.

Inequality Versus Breathing

Perhaps the trickiest set of relationships challenging democratic life in this country is between two groups: people who are systemically empowered, by virtue of their education, race, or class, and people who are disempowered in any of these areas. Growing numbers of schools are developing partnerships between student groups from different economic strata, as an educational approach to the problem of inequality. But the complexity of this work is not matched by the supports available to these teachers and their students. Thus it is vital for educators learning to build such partnerships to have access to records of field-testing. How can democratic education engage the challenges of relationships across fields of inequality?

If "unseeing" perpetuates a divided world, critical consciousness is the active work of *seeing*. By analyzing systems of power, people learn to climb out of assigned roles and hierarchies and into democratic relationships (Young, 2004). This is a particularly important process for people with privilege. Phrases such as *"we need to do something about our broken school system,"* carry unspoken political, class, and racial weight. "Doing" involves a "doer" and the doer's objects. In today's United States, the "doer" is usually a White male; the subjects are usually lower-income people of color. The individualism that comes with an emphasis on doing—and the paternalism that comes with "doing *for* others"—breaks down with an emphasis instead on "doing *with* others." In order for people of privilege to be *with* people experiencing marginalization or oppression, they need to change their footing, their perspective, and their aims.

This is part of the development of critical consciousness, as Brazilian educator Paulo Freire describes it in his foundational book of education philosophy, *Pedagogy of the Oppressed*. People from opposite sides of power—students and teachers, people and leaders—change inequality through study of "reality" in which *both are subjects*, coming to know reality and reshaping it (Freire, 2000). When people work together to understand how systems of power are tied to models of knowledge that legitimate inequality, they start to transform them. Such awareness enables people to freely choose their identity—which means dismantling the identity that was socially prescribed. "Only when individuals are empowered to interpret the situations they live together do they become able to . . . locate themselves so that freedom can appear" (Greene, 1988, p. 122). Dismantling socially prescribed identity is a highly relational process. While *Pedagogy of the Oppressed* provides important theoretical framing for this work, practice is needed, too—this is what Freire calls *praxis*: reflection and action.

Democratic life grows in *dialogue*, the interchange between people and between people and the civic, corporate, and governmental powers that affect their lives. The more this interchange takes public, active, and reciprocal forms, the healthier democratic society is. Like conscious breathing, education for democracy involves heightened attention to intake and output. This makes the learning process energetic and dynamic—and, like breathing, continuous.

Breathing in: Facts and situations are not just accepted at face value but met with *questions* such as these: Why are things this way? Whom do they benefit? Who is claiming authority in this matter, and what right do they have to this authority? What do I need to look into more deeply if I want to understand?

Breathing out: Education for democracy is based in *movement*, pushing beyond the bounds of what is expected of us. This is less about action or outcomes than about the movement of crossing borders that highlight identity, difference, and limits.

In civically engaged learning, internal movement is matched by physical movement: leaning in to listen, spending time in unfamiliar places, marching alongside. In this movement, drawing more on the presence of the body and soul than the will, I see an antidote to do-gooder expressions of privilege and power. The Civil Rights Movement multiplied the number of paths for public relationships across difference; this book will focus on how people in schools can access and extend these paths.

Private School, Public Vision: A Vital Ambivalence

> The notion that intelligence is a personal endowment or personal attainment is the great conceit of the intellectual class, as that of the commercial class is that wealth is something which they personally have wrought and possess.
>
> —John Dewey

The tempo of my story is set by my class, gender, and racial identity as a White woman who grew up middle-class, teaching in a predominantly White and privileged progressive independent school, Francis W. Parker School in Chicago. Like many teachers at this school, I am fascinated by the contradiction that we inhabit, where the mission focuses squarely on democracy—and the students by and large come from the ranks of the elite.[6] It is a school where we are encouraged to explore these contradictions. Working with the contradictions that are closest to home enables Francis W. Parker School to be the kind of laboratory for democratic education that its progressive founders of 100 years ago meant it to be.

I run a civic engagement program, which lives in the tensions between democratic values and a reality of privilege and entitlement that pollute democracy. This is shifting, challenging ground. Approaches to civic education highlight the differing cultural values of a socially stratified society.[7] Some schools do not teach civic education. On the other hand, social justice–oriented programs in communities of color take aim at systemic social change—through projects such as living wage campaigns and countering the school-to-prison pipeline. Community service programs are more common in dominant culture communities. Often these programs address symptoms rather than causes—serving food at a soup kitchen, for instance, without a context of inquiry into public policies and social conditions that make people more housing vulnerable (Boyte, 2005).

Dynamics of race, class, and power shape relationships. If community service takes place without attention to context, it can widen the divisions between people of different classes. Volunteerism and charity often distract well-meaning people from the analysis of social problems and contribute to avoidance of politics.[8] As Meira Levinson (2012) argues, "By centering responsibility on individual citizens and exempting social, economic, and civic structures and institutions—governments, corporations, legislation, economic regulations, and so forth—service learning implicitly fosters a political ethic that favors the status quo and reduces activism for social change" (pp. 223–224). Addressing injustice through "service" promotes an individual rather than communal view of action, diverting public engagement from political issues.

When they encounter inequality without learning frameworks for understanding systems of oppression, young people may withdraw from civic life (Westheimer & Kahne, 2004). Furthermore, unless they learn practices of critical reflection, White affluent students (and teachers) unknowingly reproduce dominant culture expectations about people of different races, classes, and cultures from themselves (Goodman, 2001). Even learning the language and concepts of social justice can serve people of privilege as a tool for reinforcing power (North, 2009; Swalwell, 2013) and deepening injustice.

This critique applies to my book as well: Like any product or process emerging from a person with dominant culture privilege, it can be read as a justification for the status quo. Consciousness of this tension heightens the urgency for dialogue. To strengthen opportunities for reflection and dialogue and to challenge our participation in asymmetrical power relationships, at Parker, we participate in different modes of social engagement. This book represents a "lab report" on this continuing process of what I call, following Dewey and Addams and other progressive thinkers, "social learning."[9] It lays out the theory behind our experiments, observations on experience, comparison with designs and experiences in contexts different from our own, and ongoing questioning, reflection, and recalibration.

It is my hope that this experimental process will hold space for other educators to engage in the active dialogue that drives education for democracy. The heartbeat of this book is the belief that, through asking questions, expanding the imagination, and joining in struggle, people can change patterns of injustice that diminish everyone.

DEMOCRATIC EDUCATION: CONTRADICTIONS, BOUNDARIES, IDENTITIES

> The good we secure for ourselves is precarious and uncertain, is floating in mid-air, until it is secured for all of us and incorporated into our common life.
>
> —Jane Addams

At the heart of democratic education is trust in human capacity—both that of the individual human being and that of people who join in learning, acting, and loving. Democratic education includes and intersects with progressive education, social justice education, critical and feminist pedagogy, civic education, antiracist education, and service learning, so those pedagogies will be central to this book. However, I am not laying out an educational program, but posing questions and telling stories to invoke thinking, experimentation, and action. How else do we counter social imbalance that raises up the privileged and pushes down the marginalized?

Schools are where the public comes into being. As Benjamin Barber (1997) emphasizes, we learn to be a public in our schools; we learn the skills and the vision for building a common life. The "public" doesn't exist on its own but gains shape through struggle. As a movement centered around the development of the public in the face of threats from private interests and corporate powers, progressive education has acted as a steward of public life and democratic capacities over the last century.

Progressive education seeks balance between individual freedom and collective consciousness.[10] The person grows in a web of interaction, not on a linear path of individual action. Many other relationships intersect with this basic social one: the relationship between teacher and student, between academic subjects and between academics and real life, and between learning about power and learning to create and exercise power.[11] These relationships are the loom of democratic education.

Relationships involving knowledge are relationships of power, and imbalance is the default. Creating the balance expressed in Dewey's concept of democratic education—"the widening and deepening of conscious life"—requires deliberate effort. It is through the ongoing collective work of creating the public that the soil is prepared for healthy human life. When the public is not always asserting itself, profiteers "eclipse" the public, as Dewey (1954) writes: "When the public is as uncertain and obscure as it is today, and hence as remote from government, bosses with their political machines fill the void between government and the public" (p. 120). In the United States today, an idealization of the private sphere has even more successfully eclipsed faith in public institutions. Weakened public trust is "skillfully manipulated . . . by legislators, policy analysts, and entrepreneurs who want to restrict funding to public education, subject it to market forces, and ultimately, privatize it" (Rose, 1996, p. 4). An embodied public—people who demand inclusivity, transparency, and honesty in matters that affect the collective body—watches out for the uses and misuses of power.

On the other hand, a public that does not know itself to be a public is "uncertain" and, hence, powerless: "Unless local communal life can be restored, the public cannot adequately resolve its most urgent problem: to find out and identify itself" (Dewey, 1954, p. 216). "The public" is invisible—taken for granted and exploitable—until it is *named*. In Chicago, John Dewey, Jane Addams, Col. Parker, and other progressives talked fervently about the public, for in being named, the public gains weight and value. It was important to them that people understand "public" neither as a product of state processes, nor solely in terms of who owns what. To have meaning—indeed, to exist—the public must be *locally embodied*. Global citizenship encourages broad social awareness, but if they are not anchored in the reality of the local, travel and focus on large-scale human problems may actually weaken people's capacities for living in community.

Like love, the public lives in action, in give and take, in struggle. This activity is particularly concentrated around our schools. Progressive education grew out of a vision of the school as a meeting ground where America learns the communicative, relational, and imaginative capacities required to fulfill its democratic heritage. Dewey emphasized that education must be concerned above all with understanding the events, power structures, and identities that affect people's actual lives. "The tools of social inquiry will be clumsy as long as they are forged in places and under conditions remote from contemporary events" (Dewey, 1954, pp. 179–181). And yet, the powers that were arrayed against America's democratic promise remained unchanged by progressive education—or perhaps indeed their powers were *strengthened* by it since many people in power benefited from progressive education practices in the course of their own education (Bowles & Gintis, 1977).

Dewey's more radical colleague George Counts challenged progressive educators to "build a new social order." Avoiding the fight, he argued, handicaps education.[12] But subsequent generations of progressive schools have focused on child-centered pedagogy—and avoided the social and political implications of progressive education.

Since Dewey's laboratory schools (my school being one of them) failed to sustain the struggle against entrenched undemocratic power systems, we have to look elsewhere for models of education that interrupt "unseeing" complicity with power and strengthen the embodied public. Dewey recognized that the settlement houses provide this model, by building up public space, or what Evans and Boyte (1992) call "free spaces."[13] As a space where learning and political life melded among people of different ethnicities, generations, and classes, the settlement house is a touchstone of democratic education.

The Play of Self-Invention in Community

If I can't dance, I don't want to be part of your revolution.

—Emma Goldman

The story of Hull-House, the first settlement house in America, could be told as an epic of place and democratic power: Public space grows through the ongoing effort of human beings confronting the vise-grip of inequality in America, and exploring how to break it. The people of Hull-House worked to base public policy and social theory in local, specific people and changing situations. Keeping human beings front and center, they directly resisted the business and political interests that, like the iconic runaway engines in Charlie Chaplin's *Modern Times*, reduce human beings to cogs in the wheels of the system.

Along with other Progressives, the people at Hull-House were committed to the principle of self-determination, and in their work they gave expression to the great American story of self-invention—not that of the lone frontiersman, but of a more sustainable life: self-invention in community. Public space enables people to choose who they want to be rather than being shaped only by the authority of familial and institutional influence. Maxine Greene (1988) refers to public space as "in-between" space, forged by people who "felt and named a gap between what they were and what they desired to be; and, making an intentional effort to cross the gap, knowing it was an alternative to remaining where they were, they felt provisionally free" (p. 95). Public space is neither impersonal nor institutionalized: It nurtures creative self-determination.

Self-invention in community is an incredibly vibrant and dynamic process, so it is no wonder that it led directly to one of the liveliest forms of American culture, improvisational theatre. Bear with one more note on Chicago history, to set the scene for a genealogy of public space with both local and global dimensions.

Viola Spolin developed improvisational theatre out of her work with immigrants at Hull-House. Spolin worked with Neva Boyd, collecting and leading games that immigrants who came to Hull-House had brought with them. Improv theatre continued to evolve in the work of Spolin's son Paul Sills, who founded Chicago's now-famous The Second City theatre.

Powerful intersections were characteristic of Hull-House: The historical and scholarly work of archiving folk culture from around the world was at the same time the social practice of connecting people from different cultures with one another. The play transcended boundaries of function even while it bridged cultures and generations. There is a beautiful continuity in the development of improv theatre.

Paradoxically, *disruption* is an inherent part of that continuity. In considering the social tensions underlying democratic education, it is relevant to note that Spolin's work with immigrants—which developed so fruitfully in the diverse matrix of Chicago—was a clear break from the values and life of her father, whose work was capturing and deporting immigrants. Spolin's father, Make Mills, was a leader of the Red Squad on the Chicago police force, which sought to weaken the labor movement by terrorizing the immigrant community (Coleman, 1991, p. 29). Spolin's work was a creative embodiment of the phrase "beating swords into ploughshares." The play that nourished and flourished in Spolin's work countered the forces of fear and hostility that her own father propagated.

This aspect of Spolin's life story illustrates how a person can re-create her identity for herself through the equalizing, dynamizing, social force of *play*. Spolin (1999) writes, "True improvisation re-shapes and alters the student-actor through the act of improvising itself. Penetration into the focus, connection, and a live relation with fellow players, result in a change,

alteration, or new understanding for one or the other or both" (p. 37). Spolin's life and work help to establish play as a force for democratic power, in
which the individual re-creates himself or herself.

Play in the public space of Hull-House has a democratic charge that must
not be underestimated. The creative force of play faces down established
power and clears out space for more voices, more possibilities. In a society
that has not yet learned an effective analysis of power, play offers experimental frameworks. After all, the ordinary language of classroom and workplace
ignores the complex, nuanced, and multilayered field of power dynamics.[14]

Play in public space activates a reciprocal relationship of people with
the surrounding environment. In her foundational work on game theory,
Spolin's teacher Neva Boyd emphasizes the importance of play as a function
of community, "Traditional games were not consciously created by adults
for the amusement or instruction of children but are, rather, human nature
socially patterned" (1934, p. 48). Noncognitive contexts of learning—body,
space, voices, feelings—shape the individual's intellectual development and
also shape the life of the collective.[15]

Boyd's game theory respects the wholeness of the individual. The interaction of the person and the environment, the individual and the group,
brings forth new capacities in all. In games, as in Hull-House activities in
general, boundaries between people and between disciplines break down.
Boyd is talking about education that fosters leadership for change.

In this book I pay tribute to this heritage of democratic education that
is subjective, local, and playful, first and foremost by honoring my readers'
own minds, their own powers of truth making. I engage with philosophers
and offer my own experiences and responses to the stories I encounter, not
by way of a methodology but as a voice in dialogue. This dialogue questions
the separations between generations and roles in our schools, so it includes
students and teachers as well as people in diverse out-of-school contexts.[16]
The projects I describe are purposefully open-ended: They are meant to support readers' own experimentation in seeking out and forging public space.

This story of relationships in and around schools, relationships that cross
lines of class, race, and generation, can serve as a case study for social learning not only within schools but also in other contexts such as community
organizations and cultural institutions. People in and out of schools daily
actualize the progressive idea that education is not just for adapting people to
the world as it is but for helping to transform the world into a more just and
peaceful place. Recognizing this daily work deepens democratic life.

I argue that fostering the kind of equality and reciprocity needed for democracy depends on three dispositions: *self-reflection, questioning power,*
and *dialogic hunger.* These are not values such as empathy or altruism.
They are felt more than understood or intended.[17] Though values and good
character may intersect with democratic dispositions, putting character education at the center can confuse processes of democratic education. The
experiential nature of democratic education means that adults and young

people are journeying together; both are in intensive learning conditions. Throughout the book I cross the lines between adult and child learning. In the next pages I outline democratic dispositions with some initial examples.

Questioning Power

> This is not class warfare, this is generational warfare. This administration and old wealthy people have declared war on young people. That is the real war that is going on here. And that is the war we've got to talk about.
>
> —James Carville

The first corner of the triad that I call democratic dispositions is *questioning power*. This means first of all stepping outside the familiar paradigms of education—and exposing the hierarchies it is embedded in, starting with adultism. Adultism presumes and systematizes the superiority of adults over children in terms of knowledge and rights. However, when young people bring older people into dialogue, they illuminate our limits. They challenge the accumulative premise of learning, the assumption that the more educated you are, the more right you have to determine the value and direction of others' learning. Learning about education requires paying especially close heed to what people who have not had much access to it have to say about education.[18]

Chicago educator Brian Schultz (2008) offers an example of democratic education that illuminates *questioning power*. He tells the story of his 5th-grade class: African American students in an under-resourced school, who develop a powerful civic identity in the course of fighting for a new school. The students and their teacher deal with the overwhelming challenges of the project through dialogue that stretches them, highlights difference, and fosters community.

One scene demonstrates particularly clearly the disposition I call *questioning power*. A political candidate who hears about the students' campaign for a new school offers to come and speak with the students and draw media attention to their cause. He wants to donate $500 to the class. Schultz puts the question to his students, Should they invite him to come? The students initially respond with enthusiasm, chatting excitedly about classroom PlayStations and pizza parties—but one student, Crown, speaks up against the proposed visit. Crown challenges his classmates to analyze the politician's motives. He insists on researching the candidate, pointing out that if he isn't going to be a winning candidate, he's not going to be able to help them. The students' research yields the finding that the candidate probably won't win. Crown then returns the class's focus to the end goal. He compares the candidate's visit to a record deal: A smart recording artist won't automatically jump at the first record offer but will pause and consider who offers him or her the best deal. He reasons as follows:

We don't want to go down with his sinkin' ship. If we get seen with him we might never get a new school. . . . If we take that loser's money it might hurt our chances. I say we hold out for the better deal . . . wouldn't you hold out for the better record deal? . . . I think this guy is just using us to get in the news heself. . . . He is just wantin to help out now because it could help him, but lemme tell—ain't nothing gonna help him win his race! (Schultz, 2008, p. 73)

Crown is taken in by neither the financial bait nor the promise of celebrity. He questions the power of money, attention, and adult authority and translates the "deal" in terms that enable his classmates to take a principled stand. The students listen to Crown and decide to take a pass on the candidate and his offer.

However, the further they push their campaign, the more complex the political landscape becomes. The students learn through a newspaper article featuring the students' struggle that instead of committing to building a new school as the students have been urging, Chicago Public Schools administration decided to close their school. The students are devastated. They agonize, feeling responsible. They wonder if the highly public nature of their campaign precipitated this disastrous end. But in their research they discover that the school board had slated the school for closure before the school year had even begun.

At this moment, Schultz was facing the very real possibility of a tragic backfire: His youthful activists were positioned to become embittered, perhaps permanently civically disengaged. However, in the midst of their disappointment, the students received letters of support from the public. These letters reframed their struggle. Unknown adult allies highlighted the legacy that belongs to young people: to question power. One letter, for example, compared the students to the young Student Nonviolent Coordinating Committee (SNCC) leaders in the Civil Rights Movement, who "helped youth and adults learn about their rights as citizens." The letter from this stranger goes on, "These young people worked hard and sometimes felt like giving up but they were determined to make a difference and stand up for what was right. So stay strong, young warriors your ancestors would be very proud of you!" The students took heart as they saw that their struggle was part of a venerable line of civil rights activism.

Reggie, for instance, responded by connecting the adult supporter's words with attention to his own feelings:

Now I am going to fight for what is right to get a new school. We are not going to give up the fight for nothing. We can be brave for a new school like the SNCC. . . . We were like young warriors and our ancestors would be very proud. This makes me feel much better because I want to keep fighting. I was upset and mad yesterday because of what was written in the newspaper [but] your letter makes me want to go on. (Schultz, 2008, pp. 85–86)

Years later, Crown and other students attributed their subsequent academic success to the skills and motivation this project fueled in them in 5th grade. *Questioning power* is generative: The questions grow, across issues, communities, and generations.

Schultz's students point to a gap in knowledge, power, and relationships that they see as harmful to themselves and dangerous for the democratic society they are poised to enter. Through their civic campaign, the young people step into this gap, constructing a dialogue that reaches across race and class lines—and across generational lines. Adults are part of this dialogue, as guides and models, but *also as perpetuators of an unjust social order that the young people are resisting.* Schultz shows us that when adults listen to young people, they create space for all of them to stretch beyond what is expected of them and break through the boundaries they are circumscribed by—especially the ones they did not know about. Studying these limits allows for *shared* struggle, *shared* possibility.

The capacity for *questioning power* is heightened by dialogue, across contexts and across generations. The letter connecting the 5th-graders to the SNCC leaders suggests a genealogy of resistance that builds through the experiences and stories of people fighting for justice. This questioning helps the students to shape themselves consciously and critically; by doing so, they join in the democratic work of reshaping the world.

Dialogic Hunger

> I am conscious of myself and become myself only while revealing myself for another, through another, and with the help of another.
>
> —Mikhail Bakhtin

Democratic education makes space for people to *question power*, and also for engaging their human need for difference and awareness of interdependence—what I call *dialogic hunger*. I use the term *dialogic* in the spirit of the Russian philosopher Mikhail Bakhtin, who connected dialogue with relationship, process, and resistance to authority.

According to Bakhtin, dialogue takes place along and across borders; threshold space invokes surprise and transformation. As spaces for youth—people in transition—schools are a quintessential border space, closely connected to change in society. In her book *Crossing Boundaries*, Valerie Kinloch (2012) takes note of the many borders associated with schooling and the energy that comes from crossing borders. Challenging the hierarchies that subordinate young people to adults and lived experience to textbook knowledge, Kinloch describes 12th-graders in a Harlem high school, trying to make sense of democratic practices in a lived context of racialized inequality.

Rather than describing *what* or *how* she is teaching students, Kinloch emphasizes what she is learning *from* her students. Young people—less

invested in and less corrupted by systems of oppression—are good at pointing out inconsistencies. This capacity is an indispensable resource for fighting
inequality. She describes her students reading Jonathan Kozol's book *Shame
of the Nation* and discussing the question "Do we live in a democracy?" Her
students' responses offer precise interpretations of democracy. Damya says,
"You gotta have that working-together, living-together, growing-together
combo to have democracy, or at least to have values that point to being
democratic. That's what I think for today." Damya stresses being *together*—
this condition of togetherness is a more basic foundation for democracy than
what a person does, chooses, or cares about. When she adds, "That's what I
think for today," Damya also wisely signals that defining something as large
and unwieldy as democracy has to be tentative at best.

I call Damya's notion of interdependence "dialogic" to emphasize the
person-to-person encounter that deepens understanding. I call it "hunger"
because it is a feeling. It is not about calculation or ethics but about the human connection that people need, especially the connection with "the Other." Dialogue is a reaching toward the "in-between" space of interchange
between people dealing with one another—and themselves—consciously,
in a world where otherness is often feared. *The Other* is an awkward term,
reflective of the disconnections that prevail in a world where segregation
and injustice are "unseen." "Dialogic hunger" is an ongoing condition and
a productive pain. It holds the outrage and mobilizes the courage to fight
for a world of dignity for all people.

Democratic education requires adults—teachers, parents, and the wider
public—to engage in a great deal of deconstructing and reconstructing of
knowledge. As progressive education philosopher George Counts (1934)
points out, "An educational program that is the product of bewilderment will
itself beget bewilderment. The more difficult problems of society will not be
resolved by passing on to children facts whose implications are beyond the
comprehension or courage of adults" (p. 534). In conditions of uncertainty
and contradiction, it is important for people to be able to discern—and to
learn what is hard for them to discern. Especially within themselves.

Self-Reflection

> Patricia: Reflect on your choice. Why you did what you did. Ain't
> that right, Miss? C'mon, Miss, you know that's (pause) DEM-O-
> CRA-TIC!
>
> —Valerie Kinloch

When Kinloch (2012) asks her students "Do we live in a democracy?" her
student Patricia responds with the words of this epigraph. Patricia points
to the metacognitive work that is at the heart of democratic education. Democracy, in this view, is not concerned with choice so much as thinking
about what influences your choice. Another student, Stephen, has a pretty

good idea of what tends to influence people's choice: power. "What we got is like [pause] pretend-to-be-democracy, like a we-want-y'all-to-believe-this-a-democracy. This thing we got hurts people who ain't got power . . . people who poor, Black Brown, and some White people. That's on the real. Maybe this ain't 'bout democracy as a system, but as ideas and values" (Kinloch, 2012, pp. 54–55). Stephen is calling for honesty, breaking through the clichés, assumptions, and hypocrisy that swarm around the idea of democracy and obscure it. This requires consideration of one's own complicity in "unseeing." Attention to the relationship between systems of power and one's own power, in relation to the power of other people, is what I mean by *self-reflection*.

Kinloch's African American high school students meet up with her White teacher education students for a discussion on equity in education. The White teacher candidates express hesitation about talking about inequality across race lines. The students urge them on, saying, "you gotta try;" "teachers put students out there all the time. Put yourself out there and see what happens" (Kinloch, 2012, p. 22). These students are challenging teachers—and themselves—to take the risk of thinking hard about themselves and the society they are part of, to engage together in the ongoing process of *self-reflection*.

Heightened focus on the power imbalance between younger and older generations leads to a tension that is both uncomfortable and generative. When people engage in dialogue about the boundaries that separate them from others, they create access to transformative learning—learning that balances stronger self-awareness with collective consciousness.

Kinloch's students, like Schultz's students, have the benefit of adult allies who are engaged in questioning power, dialogic hunger, and self-reflection. Unlike patronizing adult supporters who praise young people *individually* at the expense of the youth *community*, teachers, community leaders, and parents who develop as youth allies share a belief in and support for the power of young people to create social change.

Questioning power, dialogic hunger, and self-reflection are all ongoing states: They do not resolve, but they do help people deal realistically with the uncertainty of life and relationships.

EXPERIMENTS IN DEMOCRATIC EDUCATION

I offer this book as a supplement to civic education, a dialogue with service learning, and a challenge to progressive education, none of which has yet evolved into a reliably sustainable model for democratic relationships. I do not claim to offer such a model either: Democracy in America has not yet developed enough for such a model to exist. We live in an unequal, deeply segregated society, and until that changes, all approaches are at best provisional, small steps in the long march for justice.

Before groups, programs, and individuals can create democratic relationships, they must engage in processes that clarify the ground they stand on. When they illuminate the hidden controls around and within them—and when they feel the web of connections beneath them—people come closer to democratic relationships, in part because they come to realize how difficult truly democratic relationships are.

To reiterate, I am not aiming to provide a comprehensive program for education in America—I am, indeed, arguing, that there is not and should not be such a thing. Blanket statements about schools, teachers, and students oversimplify and miseducate in dangerous ways. Systematic education is an outdated concept—perhaps it never was useful. It implies that there is an established domain of received knowledge, a canon; and as a result of both deliberate and accidental processes, the reality most public school students live in does not make it in there.

Playing with Power: Conceptual Framework

Progressive education supports democratic development by means of what I call *"playing with power."* Founding progressives like Jane Addams, Francis Parker, and John Dewey insisted that democratic progress depends on not only political processes like voting and fair laws, but also rigorously developed social education processes. These processes include but are not limited to cognitive work: They also include play, intuition, and interest in other people. Democratic dispositions grow in the interchange between the individual's inquiry and meaningful encounters with the social and political world around him or her. Choreographing this process is an art that teachers learn over time and in tandem with their students.

Other philosophical bases for this work include more recent thinkers in the progressive tradition like Maxine Greene and Patricia Carini. These educators teach a relationship of curiosity and respect toward learners, in opposition to deficit-based approaches that prevail in current education policy.[19] In addition to these philosophical influences, my outline of democratic dispositions has taken shape amidst several overlapping fields:

- **Civic education**, notably, my work is indebted to Joel Westheimer's and Joseph Kahne's (2004) focus on the justice-oriented citizen; Harry Boyte's (2005) theories and practices of public work; and Lani Guinier's and Gerald Torres's (2003) model of "power-with" cross-race, cross-class coalition building. These civic education frameworks have led me to connect *dialogic hunger* with public and political work.
- **Place-based education** is concerned with the particular, the local, and the interactive dimensions of education. My exploration of *self-reflection* as a practice for ecological and social literacy is rooted

in a focus on body, voice, and place. It is informed by feminist thinkers such as bell hooks (1994) and Sharon Welch (1990), the pedagogy of place outlined by David Gruenewald (2003a, 2003b) and Greg Smith (2002), and the dialogic philosophy of Mikhail Bakhtin (1993).

- **Critical pedagogy** such as Paulo Freire's (2002) emphasis on dialogue and praxis and Henry Giroux (2005) and Peter McLaren's (2007) approaches to power analysis in contemporary contexts informed my inquiry into the role of *questioning power* in democratic education. Critical race theory and critical pedagogy are important to me in heightening awareness of race, culture, and systems of power in education contexts. I apply Richard Delgado's (2011) description of counterstorytelling—naming dominant narratives and creating counternarratives that resist and transform—to specific education contexts.

The chapters of this book unfold three dimensions of democratic education, which I identify as self-reflection, questioning power, and dialogic hunger. My inquiry plays out against the overlapping backgrounds of classrooms of diverse public and private schools, and the streets of Chicago. A number of relationships define the scope of the book: the relationship between public and private education; the role of political and social analysis in education; and the social, cultural, and geographic borders that shape identities and communities in this country.[20]

Chapter 1: Social Action as Ritual

The ecology of personal and interpersonal processes at the base of democratic education lead me to focus on *self-reflection* in Chapter 1. In this chapter I tell a story of environmental justice activism that leaked out of a classroom and crossed both disciplinary and neighborhood boundaries. Riffing on the connection of person, place, and action expressed in place-based education theory, I propose that adolescents' intuitive sense of *ceremony* helps them to resist fragmentation in schools and communities. Rituals and play, deliberately invoked, enable young people to register the patterns that convey the connectedness of life and people. Markers of community—in Leslie Marmon Silko's (1986) novel *Ceremony* and in organizing for environmental justice—provide a legend connecting adolescent rites of passage with deepening understanding of race, class, and cultural identity.

A story of cross-neighborhood social action enables me to frame the book in questions that crop up around boundaries. For instance, "How can people who are not affected by a problem take part in addressing it, without imposing their cultural values, power, or biases?" In this chapter I also introduce my own process of self-reflection by foregrounding questions that accompany my inquiry into democratic education, such as, "How can adults support young people to develop their own approaches to social responsibility?"

Chapter 2: Leadership in Love and Struggle: Learning to Be Allies

Chapter 2 grounds youth leadership for social justice in what I call *dialogic hunger*, a human desire to connect with people who are different in terms of race, class, and generation. I argue that cultivating this disposition helps in developing "power-with" frameworks of social justice work: an emphasis on collaboration over charisma and investment in relationships over efficiency. Dialogic hunger spurs realization of how much more one has to learn, and it ends not in conclusions but in questions and intensified thinking. It brings "in-between" space into being.

I discuss oral histories as a curricular practice for deepening students' intellectual engagement while strengthening their capacities for coalition building. I offer Myles Horton's story of Highlander Folk School (Horton, Kohl, & Kohl, 1997) as an example of living oral history that fosters *leadership-in-alliance* in young people. In contrast with management models of leadership development, which generally involve goal setting and sequenced tasks, Highlander's stories base leadership in community practices. Civil rights leaders like Myles Horton, Ella Baker, and the networks of allies surrounding them, offer concrete models of shared power based in questions, experiences, and solidarity. These stories illuminate sustainable practices for working across class, race, and generation lines.

Chapter 3: Unruly Teachers: Collective Reflective Resistance

Chapter 3 foregrounds *conflict* in education. I continue to explore oral histories as a practice of democratic education, available to students in diverse school and out-of-school settings and suggestive of the dialogic and many-voiced bases of learning that strengthen democratic society. In this chapter, I pay particular attention to how oral histories enable teachers and students to understand and work productively with conflict. This focus has interpersonal applications, but I am equally interested in how students learn experientially about the contested nature of knowledge.

Teachers provide resources for *questioning power* through exposing students to contradictions—including teachers' acknowledgment of their own biases and fears—and through developing practices of reflection that ground inquiry in attention to political, racial, and cultural contexts. Through cross-context intellectual work, educators resist education that compartmentalizes and dehumanizes. This chapter tells stories of teachers who, in crossing borders to collaborate, actualize the philosophy Paulo Freire (2000) describes in *Pedagogy of Freedom*:

When we live our lives with the authenticity demanded by the practice of teaching that is also learning and learning that is also teaching, we are participating in a total experience that is simultaneously directive, political, ideological, gnostic, pedagogical, aesthetic, and ethical. In this experience the beautiful, the decent, and the serious form a circle with hands joined. (pp. 31–32)

By making connections, between people and between different academic subjects, teachers craft models of education for the common life. Democratic education lives in webs of diverse partners and allies that support young people. When teachers and students make these webs visible, they are able to hold the public accountable for their part in nurturing the common life.

Chapter 4: Public Play: On Hull-House, Theatre of the Oppressed, and Other Democratic Spaces

Museums, arts, and theatre have the potential to be "in-between" spaces for examining oppression and liberation at individual and collective levels. Educators across education contexts understand such "extracurriculars" as valuable extensions of (and sometimes counterpoints to) classroom learning. Functional, task-driven approaches to learning miss these liminal spaces. Standards-based education oversimplifies the world—and dismisses young people's capacities for engaging with the complexities and challenges of reality. Arts, on the other hand, support the growth of democratic dispositions of self-reflection, questioning power, and dialogic hunger.

In focusing on the role of arts in democratic education, I highlight Theatre of the Oppressed play as a way to deal with the horror and tension that can surface in real-life learning. I tell three stories of conflict that engage self-reflection, dialogic hunger, and questioning power. The frame of theatre makes it possible to explore conflict and social responsibility in ways that are accessible to young people. In one of the stories I focus on, students grapple with the issue of femicide in Juarez; the second piece unfolds a dialogue about oppression, conflict, and identity; and the third represents families experiencing the dismantling of communities associated with school closings.

Chapter 5: On Accountability and the Educating of Counternarrators

This chapter reflects on outcomes we can both see and work toward in democratic education. People in schools and communities can overturn hierarchies of accountability. An educated public means a public who is, whether it inhabits the offices of government, the boards of corporations, or the homes in our neighborhoods, accountable for the education of all of its children. It means a public who is learning from, alongside, and for its children.

Since much of the experience of education is concerned with assessment of students, teachers, and schools, in this chapter I focus on assessment from a democratic education standpoint. Instead of a comprehensive study of alternative assessments, I focus on how *counternarratives* change the terms of accountability to community-based ways of understanding responsibility and power.

I focus on three schools, June Jordan School in San Francisco, Rudy Lozano Leadership Academy in Chicago, and Urban Academy in New York. I observe how they approach the relationship between individual learning and the needs, pressures, and possibilities of society. This exploration yields models of assessment that are both more generative and more rigorous than traditional assessments. From the work of these schools, I identify pedagogical approaches that transpose democratic education practices that target pressure points in education policy.

Chapter 6: Building Sustainable Education: A Dissenting Democratic Countertradition

When schools are understood to be centers of social power for everyone, they shift their footing from a disjointed, competitive, individualistic orientation to one that is integrated, challenging, and affirming. In this chapter, I look at the work of coalitions who recognize and fight for the environment needed for students to learn. I feature the conversations of education activists who show how the incessant focus on the schools and a narrow view of achievement is distracting this country from looking at the real problem of forces of inequality that harm the surrounding environment of too many young people.

These leaders think about the broader life of the human being, over time and in relation to the life of the collective. Education leaders-in-alliance both famous and not have been working over the course of many generations to sustain a focus on the dignity of children and their families and to help the wider world learn and grow alongside them. Chapter 6 focuses on some of these leaders, not as heroes but as representatives of our common life, who model approaches to educational sustainability that people in any community, any context, can grab hold of and integrate into their work.

***

Creative resistance is inherent to democratic education. While political struggle has a place in the book, my emphasis is more on the intellectual work of reflection, inquiry, and dialogue that challenges prescriptive ways of thinking. Strong currents of democratic intelligence course through many schools, including those in highly stressed communities, and recognizing these currents enlarges democratic life for everyone. The tools this book offers are not methods of teaching or learning—or activism. They are not external to individuals and schools. They are ways of looking, exploring, and appreciating. Democratic education begins with the premise that people have within them powers, and that processes that tap these powers are necessary to democracy.

So, instead of talking about outcomes, skills, methods, and value-added measurements, in this book I tell stories about *processes*. This is a book about education, for people in education, and I aim to offer readers space for thinking, wondering, and learning, which methodological models too often do not. These chapters are meant to honor the work and the play of human beings engaged in ongoing change.

CHAPTER 1

Social Action as Ritual

A Living Response

Muscles aching to work, minds aching to create—this is man.

—John Steinbeck, *The Grapes of Wrath*

It is a warm October night, and I am standing in the middle of a circle of desks with the wrong people in them. My students' parents are crowded in, many two to a desk, 40 big folk perching on the blue plastic chairs with an alacrity that contrasts jarringly with the slouches and jittering that mark their children's occupation of this space. As I spin around to meet the eye of each parent, I tell the story of Am Lit through the texts we read. It hits me that all of our texts break into our lives *from the margins*, whether we are riding along in the old jalopy of migrant farmworkers or in the glittering ephemeral Rolls Royce of an upstart who will never be admitted to upper-crust society—perhaps all American Literature is from the margins. Is that part of what makes it American, or is a borderline status inherent to art in general?

"Liminality, marginality, and structural inferiority are conditions in which are frequently generated myths, rituals, philosophical systems, and works of art" (Turner, 1977/1995, p. 128). Does walking on the borders through American literature help adolescents to recognize their own powers and vulnerabilities as they make their passage through a threshold space that calls for study in itself?

My thoughts are interrupted by a tall dad with gray hair and suspenders and a baritone voice: "Couldn't you teach some texts that are *not* marginal, that anchor our kids at the center?" I laugh lightly and sidestep—I am not about to get into an argument about the canon in the 10 minutes I have with the parents tonight. I am not going to ask: Who gets to decide what is at the center, and what are the margins? By what criteria?

Though I bite my tongue, this parent's suggestion appalls me. The books I teach are sacred to me. They call forth our shared humanity. They are the looms on which we weave our individual and our collective stories. I do not choose them to communicate a political or moral message, or as an exemplar of a literary genre or period. I choose them as companions for human beings making their way through a world that is electric, disappointing, dull, demanding. I choose them as vehicles for relationship, to build our muscles of solidarity and resilience, and for expanding the borders of what is true.

The books we read spark things within us and between us. Every time I teach a text, what it invokes in my students and in me is different. In a world of rush and requirements, shared reading is a ceremony that drops us into a changed time, heightened perception, expanded sense of presence:

> Out of the corner of his eye Gatsby saw that the blocks of the sidewalk really formed a ladder and mounted to a secret place above the trees—he could climb it, if he climbed alone, and once there he could suck on the pap of life, gulp down the incomparable milk of wonder. (Fitzgerald, 1925/1994)

There are moments that transport me beyond the confines of my role as teacher; often they are like this, hovering at the corner of my eye, too fleeting to settle into or even register. I reckon students' learning moments are often like this too—sneaking up on them, catching hold, and flitting away, leaving behind snags of insight and questions.

One of the toughest things about teaching is handling the evanescence of understanding. The moments of intellectual illumination and of human connection that break through the walls of routine, pressures, and hierarchies flash, then disappear. I am willing to accept that understanding is not permanent and connections may come and go, but I believe that not taking account of the insights and questions that are born in the shared space of the classroom suffocates a great source of energy in our world.

So, I explain to the assembled parents, in my classes I organize students in a *living response* to their reading, a response that gives body to their learning. This kind of response is generally known as *social action* (though I use other terms for this also). What is important is that this response allows us to solidify and extend classroom connections, and it builds a foundation of learning that expands the available range of self-awareness and engagement in the world around us. The other premise here is that the young people in our classrooms are capable of and needed for intelligent leadership in civic life.

In this chapter I discuss how social action brings together social, intellectual, personal, and civic learning. I begin with my own process as a White, able-bodied, middle-class female teacher in a private progressive school, learning civic engagement through trial and error, with colleagues inside my school and in other schools and community organizations. From this beginning in my school, subsequent chapters extend out to consider oher school community and political contexts. I tell this story to illustrate an unpredictable aspect of democratic education, centered in the present moment and unfolding over time as people pay attention to what is happening in the here and now, inside and around them. I did not set out to engage in democratic education; my students led me to it through their interest in social action in response to what they were learning in my class.

Here and at all points throughout this book, when I talk about democratic education, inherent in "democratic" is the understanding that (1) relationships, processes, and learning are what I mean by democratic; I am not talking about the more formal dimension of voting or the ideological political issues (though these are important, and perspective, differences, and conviction are very much part of the relational field of democracy I consider); and (2) *everyone* is engaged in the learning process; it is not something that adults set up for young people in order to train them in good conduct or attitudes. How can adults teach young people to "make the world a better place" when the adults themselves have not learned it? Democratic education depends on constant reflection, study, and openness to change on the part of adults, and when they engage with young people in social action, these practices can bloom in older and younger folk alike.

Social action involves analysis of immediate context in relation to the broader society. It is rooted in the rigorous work of self-reflection and honesty. Matthew Knoester (2012) notes in his study of Mission Hill School, a public progressive school in Boston,

> a school that hopes to be democratically inclusive and responsive . . . must continually strategize and find ways to counteract the forces of inequality and suppression—which are rooted in capitalism, racism, and patriarchy and dehumanize the people that attend and work in schools. (p. 25)

At Mission Hill as at Parker, attending to race, class, and gender dynamics among parents, teachers, administrators, and students must accompany social analysis of and action in the wider world. I discuss this ongoing attentiveness in terms of *witnessing*. As we saw in the work of Brian Schultz's students in the Introduction, social action involves relational intelligence.

I draw the notion of social action as a constant struggle for equality, enacted in analyzing, acting, and reflecting, from theories of critical pedagogy developed by Paulo Freire and other thinkers. In his seminal book *Pedagogy of the Oppressed*, Freire (2002) writes as follows:

> To surmount the situation of oppression, people must first critically recognize its causes, so that through transforming action they can create a new situation, one which makes possible the pursuit of a fuller humanity. But the struggle to be more fully human has already begun in the authentic struggle to transform the situation. (p. 47)

Though oppression hurts people in different ways, it is a "situation" that must be confronted by all people; in this confrontation humanity is deepened.

When students and teachers work together to understand how they are affected by the reality they have inherited, they start to construct a new reality that is based in human dignity and intelligence.[1]

Our social reality rests on a bedrock of inequality that poisons the potential for democracy; these poisons are sealed in when people ignore or justify injustice. As a school committed to democracy and a community that is aware of inequality, Parker tries to create ways to flush out these poisons. The hierarchies that affect schools—adultism, classism, racism, sexism, ableism—have their counterparts in every area of society. My hope is that the experiments offered here, on the stage of *playing with power*, will contribute to the aeration that allows for authentic democratic life. Schooling (and working life in general) in the United States today offers little support for the intellectual work, social creativity, and collective audacity inherent to the activity I call "playing with power." Freedom—challenging prescriptive ways of thinking and being—requires building up such supports wherever possible.

Too often we pass by the walls of schools without asking questions about what they are closing in and out. Schools cloister young people. With their isolation from the doings of the world comes a disregard for their capacities to contribute. An accumulative model of knowledge dominates: Those who haven't gathered years of information are inferior, deficient. What are the ways of knowing that get buried—or never even allowed to be born—by this model? The assumption that education is only what a person knows outside of himself or herself is consummate disrespect.

As progressive philosopher John Dewey (1902/1987) reminds us, for education to matter, it must remain in motion and in tension: "We have taken democracy for granted; we have thought and acted as if our forefathers had founded it once for all. We have forgotten that it has to be enacted anew in every generation, in every year and day, in the living relations of person to person in all social forms and institutions" (p. 416). Democracy takes form in the ongoing work of specific human beings analyzing systems of power and coming to understand one another across differences; it takes place in real time and real space. "Democracy" as a universal term, separate from context, detracts and distracts from these living relations.

However, student-centered education, the hallmark of progressive education, only deals with part of the problem of the exclusion of young people from the world. Progressive schools honor students' knowledge, but for the most part they keep the students carefully protected from the social and political world of democratic life. In 1932, George Counts lamented, "Perhaps one of the greatest tragedies of contemporary society lies in the fact that the child is becoming increasingly isolated from the serious activities of adults" (Counts, 1978, p. 15). Although Dewey and other leaders of the progressive education movement believed in teaching for social action, they eschewed this riskier face of progressive education in favor of the more comfortable terrain of student-centered education.[2] In so doing, they accepted that our children—in progressive and nonprogressive schools alike—will remain underdeveloped and our schools unequal.[3] In turning away from the dangerous world of political struggle, progressive education failed to develop its potential as a force for democracy.

"Turning the Soul"

There are notable exceptions to this history of failure in democratic education, like teacher education programs that resisted the separation of education from public life. For example, The Putney School in Vermont was a teacher education program based in experiential learning centered on political, racial, and economic questions.[4] Another important pioneer in democratic education was the Bank Street teacher education program developed by Lucy Sprague Mitchell and running from the 1930s through the 1950s. Mitchell believed that democratic learning—identifying with others—"came not from sitting in a classroom but by getting out into the world and being a part of what was happening—by going to the street corner, the factories, the train stations, the union halls, and the coal mines" (Vascellaro, 2011, p. 113). In the course of week-long bus trips to different regions of the country (called "long trips"), Mitchell's students witnessed compelling injustices, from environmental devastation, dangerous working conditions, and health problems caused by strip mining, to hateful Jim Crow laws in Georgia.

The trips showed participants that political issues were not so much a matter of voting, ideology, or even conviction as they were a question of relationships between human beings and their relationship to their communities. In his study of the Bank Street experiential education curriculum, Salvatore Vascellaro (2011) writes as follows:

> Labor became the miners who, at great risk, dug their own mines so that their families would have food; the vitality and humor of the miners as they welcomed and engaged with the students; the slag heaps that dominated the company towns and filled the air with coal grit; the miners' wives and children; the steelworkers, their skill and bravery as they endured the searing heat and danger of the mill; the camaraderie at their union meeting the danger they felt for themselves at the picket line of striking steelworkers; and Zilphia Horton teaching labor songs to striking workers across the South. Labor became raw materials vividly transformed before their eyes into essential aspects of the material world through the time and energy of the workers, all taken for granted and rarely seen. (p. 144)

Mitchell's students explored a wide range of human work and art and struggle as interconnected and not as separate domains. Shifting the frame of reference, from social issues to the more textured domain of the stories of individual human beings in relationship to the history, institutions, and patterns of society, heightened students' ability to see "them" as continuous with "us."

Through such "social learning" programs, not only are participants' views of other groups changed but their own sense of themselves changes. In her history of the Putney School, a model of teacher training based in "reconstructionist" principles developed through experiential learning, Carol Rodgers (2006) comments, "This, it seems to me, speaks of the real work of turning the soul: putting students in relationship with others different from themselves, within the context of compelling places and events (outside the classroom), and ultimately with themselves" (p. 1289). Social responsibility is less a moral commitment than a reflex; it develops through relational and spiritual experience that goes beyond the safe cognitive limits of conventional education (Berman, 1997). Both Bank Street and Putney education programs exposed the radical possibilities of teachers and students changing conditioning, acknowledging their assigned roles and seeing how they might play with those.

Teacher education programs that emphasize teacher research continue this progressive emphasis on connecting personal experience, reflection, and dialogue with social transformation: "inquiry is an intellectual and political stance rather than a project or time-bounded activity . . . as part of an inquiry stance, teacher research is a way to generate local knowledge of practice that is contextualized, cultural and critical" (Cochran-Smith, 2004, p. 12). Teacher research engages relational thinking rather than impersonal transmission of knowledge. I will discuss the work of "turning the soul"— which involves both pedagogy and teachers' personal development—at more length in Chapter 4.

The Social Action of Witnessing

In recent years, social justice educators have developed Freire's focus on praxis—critical reflection and action—in many different contexts. In tandem with related research into civic engagement, their studies and stories have strengthened the possibilities for democratic education.[5] I will draw on these insights throughout this book, but in this chapter I name collective action for the common good as "social action." In social action, the basic unit of *experience* is distinguished from the wider field of social justice curriculum.

Discerning social action as a combinable unit of democratic education allows me to emphasize its relationship to *place*. Social learning is the purposeful interaction among concrete places, people, and activities. Yet schooling structures limit experience and perception when they isolate people *in* schools from places *outside of* schools. "By regulating our geographical experience," place-based educator David Gruenewald (2003a) writes, "schools potentially stunt human development as they help construct our lack of awareness of, our lack of connection to, and our lack of appreciation for places" (p. 7). Knowledge disconnected from personal presence cannot foster the generative activity I will describe as *witnessing*.

Place-based education emphasizes local knowledge: Whether in a neighborhood or a field or a room, people learn by paying attention to the ground they stand on, and, as their circles of awareness widen, continuously returning to and renewing this ground. Drawing on this framework, I argue that social action, learning that is tied to specific places and real situations rather than abstract facts, encourages questioning. When we ask students to participate in the complex and difficult and grand and detailed work of the world, we are trusting them, taking them seriously. They rise to the occasion. This does not necessarily mean that they do it well, or that they make the world a better place—but the same must be said of the adults who are running things.

Education that integrates social action involves questions, uncertainty, setbacks to be dealt with, and celebration of small triumphs. Social action is an area of authentic learning—where teachers and students are pushed out of our comfort zones, where we do not know. It is a part of civic education that provides particularly fertile opportunities for teachers to learn and to process learning out loud for students. Civic educators shift the paradigm of helping, of making a student do something—the transitive form of education—to partnership, collaboration, making sense together—perhaps less *intransitive* than *intratransitive*.[6]

Social action taps capacities of young people in ways that a purely textual or disciplinary focus cannot. When we read *The Grapes of Wrath* (Steinbeck, 1939/2002), for instance, my American Literature class learned about day labor in Chicago and attendant problems of homelessness, illness and disability, exploitation and prejudice, and erratic education for the children of migrant workers. Students attended town meetings on day labor, participated in rallies for workers' rights, and wrote and distributed information about labor issues in Chicago. The stories they heard and the power dynamics they saw playing out before their eyes gave rise to questions about social responsibility and human relationships that book reading alone could not have sparked.

Social action is an ongoing process, not a result. It is perhaps better understood less as an one-time act that effects direct change, and more as an activity of *witnessing*. Like a ritual, social action enacts a shift in the routine order of the world, change that may be felt more than seen. In this shift, new perspectives and feelings can come forth. In social action, people step outside of their usual roles and practice occupying space, words, and interactions in more connected, less linear, and singular ways: ways that acknowledge the being of other people. When people affirm the value of the collective for itself, not just for what the collective will accomplish, they give expression to democracy in ritual form.

I want to emphasize that I am not talking about character, intentions, or morality here. I agree with Westheimer and Kahne's (2004) caution:

To the extent that emphasis on . . . character traits detract from other important democratic priorities, they may actually hinder rather than make possible democratic participation and change. For example, a focus on loyalty or obedience (common components of character education as well) works against the kind of critical reflection and action many assume are essential in a democratic society. (p. 6)

Thus, social action is not character education or service. For too long, social action has been loaded down—and distorted—by baggage of *goodness, guilt, and gratitude*: what I think of as *the Grim Gs*.

Though there is a moral dimension to civic engagement and multicultural awareness, it is unwieldy—abstract associations with goodness and rightness confuse and divide people, obstructing good thinking rather than advancing it. People are more willing to engage in discussions about race and power and justice if they are able to personalize the conversation without judging themselves or others with regard to being good people.

Civic engagement is not a vehicle for bringing students into different communities to "help people," to "give back," or to "appreciate what we have." The stale clichés and weighty obligations associated with social service strangle the learning that our students need to be able to do in the world—and that the world needs them to do. Civic engagement aims for students to develop sensitivity to place, situation, and context, in their own experience and that of others and in larger societal domains. Its connection to physical place and local knowledge counters the neutral knowledge of dominant culture. Rather than seeing each book they read as part of a contrived curriculum, civically engaged students see themes that thread through from work to work—and from generation to generation in American life.

Ceremony and Counternarrative

The more I engaged my students in social response to literature, the clearer my own questions about social responsibility became. They involved three intersecting currents: border crossing, dialogue, and knowledge, in the form of these questions:

1. How do people of different levels of inherited power, wealth, and privilege forge equity in and through work together? What helps them to resist inherited patterns of racial, class, and cultural inequality?
2. What is the relationship between social action outside the school and face-to-face relationships within the school?
3. How can participation in social action support young people making their way through adolescence? Correspondingly, how can young people's participation help to develop the field of social action as a whole?

These questions, and the paths they created, are at the heart of the story of one class's engagement with the novel *Ceremony*, by Leslie Marmon Silko (1986). The novel explores different kinds of power: political and racial, spiritual, and communal. It also critiques conventional Western education and contrasts it with indigenous American learning processes. The novel is a ceremony that challenges Western expectations of what a novel does. I am interested in drawing upon its power to invoke the liminal elements of human challenge and change.

Thus, my story of teaching *Ceremony* introduces themes that will unfold throughout this book: place, identity, Whiteness, change, culture, and oppression. It articulates democratic modes of interaction and communication: witnessing, counternarrative, dialogue, and public voice. I will be paying close attention to voice—students' voices and voices of writers of color, who employ modes of language that may sound strange to White ears like mine. Attending to voices also means emphasizing that there is much that I do not pick up. When I walk in territory that is not mine, the risk of fetishizing, essentializing, and making mistakes is enormous.

This is part of why the going here is slow and tentative. In writing about cultures to which I am an outsider, I must reflect, question, listen for what I am missing, and check my rush to act, to conclude, to pronounce. The kind of social action that *Ceremony* depicts is not cause-and-effect, actor-and-subject, accomplishment-oriented action. In *Ceremony*, change in the world comes out of human beings changing, through reflection, struggle, risk taking, and love. This is a helpful model for young people, in the midst of change and highly interested in changes in the world around them.

Theories of counternarrative help to articulate group identity. In recent decades, critical educators have developed descriptions of counternarrative as a framework for social justice that is particularly important for young people developing racial awareness. Counternarrative, or "counterstorytelling" (Solorzano & Bernal, 2001), is a practice of telling stories that are not usually told, coming from the experiences of people pushed to the margins of society. Simultaneously, counternarrative offers a means of analyzing and challenging the dominant story perpetuated and unconsciously embraced in majority culture.[7]

Counternarrative, like ritual, unmasks the authoritative voice of dominant discourse, allowing for human culture to burst forth. There is new life in this destruction of the old. "How do we create an oppositional worldview, a consciousness, an identity, a standpoint that exists not only as that struggle which also opposes dehumanization but as that movement which enables creative, expansive self-actualization?" (hooks, 1990, p. 15). Counternarrative extends beyond the conventions of mental activity that dominate education.

In my telling of social action through the frame of *Ceremony*, I draw on the understanding of collective work articulated in civil rights struggles that Guinier and Torres (2003) describe in their book *The Miner's Canary*. Civil rights struggles too can be seen as counternarratives: Collective consciousness contrasts sharply with the value for individual achievement propagated by our education system, following the demands of our capitalist economy.

Ceremony tells a story of Native Americans' experiences of colonization and cultural genocide, a heritage that has formed the ground we stand on in America and that is uncomfortable, painful, and confusing for people in this country of all backgrounds. White people, Native peoples, Latinos, African Americans, Asians—we are all affected by the American legacy of conquest, slavery, and disenfranchisement, and we owe it to our children to face this legacy.

In telling the story of one social action project, I focus not on the event itself but on the learning processes leading into and out of it. I am not concerned with describing a success or analyzing a failure—these polarities are reductive and give rise to more barriers than growth. Rather, I am interested in exploring *change*, at an individual level and a group level.

I am referring as much to my own changing as that of my students. My students and I are in a school where we have time to experience and space to think—experimental space. To be precise, *we* are experimenting; we are not being experimented *on*. Unlike most of the public schools in our city of Chicago, in independent schools we have the privilege of walking on stable ground. Learning takes place in a context of respect for human beings' developmental processes and value for continuity and connection. In keeping with the spirit of this book as a documentation of experimentation, I tell this story to explain how I came to understand democratic dispositions, which I have introduced as *questioning power*, *dialogic hunger*, and *self-reflection*. Subsequent chapters will develop these themes further.

ENVIRONMENTAL JUSTICE AND THE LITERATURE CLASSROOM

The only cure
I know
is a good ceremony,
that's what she said.

Like a ceremony, social action enacts values and expresses a human worldview that stands in opposition to generic societal norms. A ceremony helps to align individual human lives with a larger, deeper human and natural community. The "free" songs of Bernice Johnson Reagon, of the band Sweet Honey in the Rock, have this quality of ceremony. With songs like "We Are the Ones We Have Been Waiting For," quoting June Jordan's hymn to the women who stood in collective leadership against apartheid in South Africa, they resist authoritarian power with the movement of body and soul.

Spirituals and protest movement songs connect the person singing with a reality that counters the reality of self-centeredness, and they strengthen this counterreality:

The singing is running this sound through your body. . . . You cannot sing a song, and not change your condition. . . . This part of your being, the part of your being that is "tampered with" when you run this sound through your body is a part of you that our culture thinks should be developed and cultivated . . . that you should be familiar with, that you should be able to get to as often as possible, and that if you go through your life and don't meet up with this part of yourself, the culture has failed you. (Reagon, 1991)

Reagon is talking about words, rhythms, feelings, that connect the person to her body and to human collectivity. Her singing is ceremonial; it activates her and others in ways that cannot be apprehended with regular words. Like art, ceremonies "place something in play"; they draw people "into the play of something much larger than what is evident to subjective consciousness" (Gadamer, 1987, p. 57). Whereas routine language and action can be mechanistic and impersonal, ceremonies activate aesthetic energies that deepen experience.

Ceremonies assist with passages and transitions, in part through subverting the expected reality. Transitoriness, and the shift ceremonies enact, naturally resonate with adolescents. *Ceremony* offers a metaphor for adolescence; like most myths, it tells the story of the hazardous journey young people take from childhood to adulthood in a way that respects the dignity of the traveler.

I came into high school teaching driven by a desire to accompany young people through the passage of adolescence. Not to help them or shape them, but to be *alongside*, keeping them company, reflecting the meaning of who they were and where they were in their lives. I have always felt moved to be in the presence of people on a journey; as a teacher, I am able to be with people whose whole lives are a journey.

Ceremonies express the importance of these passages. Ceremonies take place along spatial lines where borders are unusually heavily marked. Without consciousness around borders and movement across borders, young people drift—or are forced—into separations that deplete them individually and collectively. In his exploration of schools as liminal spaces, Vincent Anfara (1999) focuses on schooling as sites of transition, where the separations and "betwixt and between" that usually go ignored can be constructively studied: "Schools are among the few institutions remaining in modern society that provide the opportunity to 'safely' test, and push the boundaries and borders that are established by society" (p. 1). Adolescence is a liminal state; it cannot be contained, understood, or guided in purely cognitive terms, but requires images and supports that the domain of ritual—along with its cousin, art—provides.

Individual rites of passage are connected with transformation of society. In *The Ritual Process*, anthropologist Victor Turner writes, "If liminality is regarded as a time and place of withdrawal from normal modes of social action, it can be seen as potentially a period of scrutinization of the central values and axioms of the culture in which it occurs" (Turner, 1977/1995, p. 167). Focusing on the borders associated with rites of passage allows for critical analysis of the contradictions, tensions, and possibilities for change in society.

The relationship between borders and rituals also involves fields of cultural and ethnic identity, immigration, and segregation. Borders are complex and ambivalent: They signal oppressive processes of marginalization *and* the counternarrative that can emerge from outside of dominant culture:

> Marginality [is] much more than a site of deprivation; in fact . . . it is also the site of radical possibility, a space of resistance . . . a central location for the production of a counter-hegemonic discourse that is not found just in words but in habits of being and the way one lives . . . it nourishes one's capacity to resist. It offers to one the possibility of a radical perspective from which to see and create, to imagine alternatives, new worlds. (hooks, 1990, pp. 149–150)

Margins and borders frame both inequality and possibilities for change. As hooks explains, the margins offer a foothold for challenging a racist reality. Attenting to border spaces can also encourage cultural and historical awareness on the part of White people. In the absence of integration, consciousness around border-crossing can contribute to healthy racial identity development: "White identity exists in the margins. We are like a people caught between two lands. There is the old country of oppression and racism from which we are attempting to emigrate, and the new country of hope, transformation, and healing, that we are only beginning to explore and inhabit" (Howard, 1999, pp. 115–116). On the borders, we are able to see the past and the future more clearly; we are able to break away from programmed racist behaviors and create new stories of who we can be, as groups and as a country.

Ceremonies and Schooling

It is impossible to discuss adolescence and ceremonies without bearing in mind the cultural assault that the American education system has sustained against Native American peoples. In a holdover of colonialist mentality, the U.S. government has, throughout the course of its history, attacked Native American cultures in the belief that it was bringing enlightenment to primitive peoples. Native American children were taken from their families and communities and all markings of their Native culture—language, customs, and dress—were taken away.[8] In this context, the rituals, songs, and beliefs conveyed in Native American literature are not just representations of the culture, but ceremonies of resistance to oppression.

Laguna Pueblo scholar Paula Gunn Allen (1992) describes the literature of many Native American writers, including Silko, as a form of ceremony that sustains tribal culture. She writes,

> The tribes seek—through song, ceremony, legend, sacred stories (myths), and tales—to embody, articulate, and share reality, to bring the isolated, private self into harmony and balance with this reality, to verbalize the sense of the majesty and reverent mystery of all things, and to actualize, in language, those truths that give to humanity its greatest significance and dignity. . . . The artistry of the tribes is married to the essence of language itself, for through language one can share one's singular being with that of the community and know within oneself the communal knowledge of the tribe. (p. 55)

In aligning with the language, stories, and songs of Native American tribal cultures, literary works like the novel *Ceremony* connect the individual to the community—in a country where such connection is heavily threatened.

Connection to group identity is, of course, also important for people who are not from Native American tribes, especially when this group is vulnerable. Religious scholar Carol Flinders's book, *At the Root of This Longing*, describes coming-of-age rituals for young girls in cultures across the world and across time. She focuses particularly on rituals that not only protect the girl entering into womanhood but that express reverence for the *power* that the young woman is connected to in her time of transition. Flinders describes the Navajo ceremony of Kindala, for instance, in which the girl who has just started menstruation cooks, fasts, and runs for her tribe, and all these ritual acts are received as blessings that bring power to the whole tribe. Though the main character of *Ceremony* is a young man from the Laguna Pueblo tribe and the rites of passage he undergoes are different, the novel conveys the sacredness of the state of transition and the rituals that accompany the individual moving through this dangerous state.

The power that surrounds a rite of passage is concentrated in the child, but the whole tribe has midwived this power, not only through its participation in the ritual during the ceremony itself but through the ongoing sustenance of ritual life. Flinders (1999) notes that not only girls need protection but

> a girl who is just becoming a woman is . . . particularly defenseless precisely because she is turned inward, absorbed in a momentous transition. And a society's willingness to recognize this and guarantee her safety is a good index of *everybody's* safety: a society that's wise enough to draw a protective circle around her will do the same for everyone who is vulnerable. (p. 222)

Close to life energy and inviting of society's protective impulses, young people make society better in their very existence. The strength of their calls for peace, for an end to racism and poverty, is compounded by the fact that society loves its children. It extends out its "circle of protection" from them.

In many cultures, rituals surrounding young people remind the community of their connection with one another and with the earth. Paula Gunn Allen sees literature like Silko's *Ceremony* as a genre of ritual action that calls forth response of tribal peoples, to protect and carry forward their cultural legacies. The legacy of conquest and racism underlying the novel also call forth response from readers who are not part of Native tribes.

The Fence

Ceremony is set in the space of contradiction—a space that adolescents are strongly aware of. The book explores what happens to people when they are forced to suspend their human values (as soldiers, killing the enemies) and tricked into ignoring their exclusion from national values (the impact of racial prejudice on the values held by diverse ethnic communities). Therefore, when I taught the novel, I sought to encourage exploration of how collective values connect with individual lives.

I thought that social action could offer young people ritual supports that would help them experience a passage into stronger connection with the earth. I drew on the insight from Jewish culture and other cultures that a service project helps the child make the transition from recipient of others' care to an active citizen who cares for others.

So, the first year I taught the book, I asked students to conduct ecological service learning, in a project I called "Fragile World," inspired by the words of the novel's medicine man, Old Ku'oosh: "But you know, grandson, this world is fragile" (Silko, 1986, p. 35). The assignment sent students out to work on natural habitat restoration projects in the Chicago area, to align with *Ceremony*'s focus on people's relationship with the earth. While students were glad to have the opportunity to get outside and get dirty to do their English homework, I was dissatisfied with the project's insularity. The habitat restoration work wasn't prodding us to ask the hard questions that the novel raised about cultural, environmental, and political violence. I decided that for the next year, I would figure out a way to move beyond what in our context had become a romanticized relationship of individual and earth and to delve into the *social* aspects of environmental awareness.

When I taught the book the following year, I wondered how to put into practice something of the spirit of interconnectivity of *Ceremony* as I guided another group of students through a difficult narrative woven of a language with ceremonial reverberations. The novel is a mystery, centered on a dramatic scene in the Philippine jungle during World War II. A platoon of American soldiers, among them the main character, Tayo, shoots down a group of Japanese prisoners of war. During the shooting in the Philippines, Tayo sees the body of his beloved uncle, whom he had left back on the Laguna Pueblo reservation in New Mexico, in the uniform of one of the Japanese soldiers. He returns home after the war to find that his uncle had died. Over the course of the novel, the reader must wrestle with the shooting scene: Was Tayo just hallucinating, or was his uncle Josiah somehow truly there, and was Tayo somehow responsible for his death? If he was hallucinating, why this particular hallucination? Why does it keep returning to haunt him?

In the novel, Tayo's memory of participating in the killing of his uncle is killing *him*, and he undertakes a journey to investigate the death. Tayo's sickness manifests in an agonizing isolation—he is separated from the land, from other people, and from himself. Upon reading about Tayo cutting through a fence separating the reservation from a cattle rancher's land, one of my students wrote,

> the fence could be seen as representing disunity and his cutting and opening a hole for the cattle could help to unify him. It can also be seen as helping unify himself with his people because he sees the fence not only as a barrier for cattle but one to keep Indians and Mexicans out as well.

In *Ceremony*, the fence expresses both internal disconnection and external relationships of cultural oppression. As Silko emphasizes in the novel, the American schooling system functioned as the most powerful of these fences, as it separated Native Americans from their own language and their people's knowledge.[9]

As I read students' comments on the image of the fence, I wondered how they themselves felt fenced in or out, and how they navigated the relationships between external constraints and internal ones. I was curious to see what kind of resources for this navigation the ceremonies embedded in *Ceremony* might offer.

The Witness

Ceremony's narrative lays atop a Laguna Pueblo legend, so part of the reader's experience involves charting out the connections between the legend and the novel's plot. The legend tells a story of change and healing that resonates for adolescents making their way through questions of identity and loyalty:

> Arrowboy got up after she left.
> He followed her into the hills
> up where the caves were.
> The others were waiting.
> They held the hoop
> and danced around the fire
> four times.
> The witchman stepped through the hoop
> he called out that he would be a wolf.
> His head and upper body became hairy like a wolf
> but his lower body was still human.

"Something is wrong," he said.
"Ck'o'yo' magic won't work
if someone is watching us."

The hoop dance legend corresponds to Tayo going up to the hills to carry out the final part of the ceremony. Other young men getting drunk (mindlessness feeds destructive Ck'o'yo' magic) are enacting a ceremony of murder at the uranium mine, the womb of destruction. Every ritual of healing and connection has a corresponding ritual of death and separation (P. G. Allen, 1992). The legend traces the steps of the hoop dance, designed for transition to wholeness but distorted by the destroyers to *separate* humans from one another and from themselves. In the book's plot, Tayo has to witness his friend being destroyed without entering into the ceremony of destruction himself.

The key of the legend, though, is that *the witness defuses the power of the destroyers*: "Ck'o'yo' magic won't work/if someone is watching us." By remaining aware, the witness resists the seduction of witchery and stops the momentum of violence. When Tayo watches the destroyers—without turning away and without getting caught up in the violence himself—he turns the vortex of hatred back on itself. He completes the ritual without knowing what it was or what would happen: "He had only to complete this night, to keep the story out of the reach of the destroyers for a few more hours, and their witchery would turn, upon itself, upon them" (Silko, 1986, p. 229).

By enduring his agonizing vigil, Tayo holds the story safe: "The witchery had almost ended the story according to its plan; Tayo had almost jammed the screwdriver into Emo's skull the way the witchery had wanted," and Tayo not only keeps himself alive, he brings life back to the earth: "In the west and in the south too, the clouds with heavy round bellies had gathered for the dawn" (Silko, 1986, p. 235). In the legend that unfolds throughout the novel and in the intersecting world of Tayo's story, the rain will come and human life will continue.

The hardest part of Tayo's ceremony is the act of *witnessing* on which the story hinges. This scene is very foreign to White readers (like myself), expecting to see Tayo jump out and save the day in accordance with the American Superman mythology. That Tayo's healing ritual is one of witnessing and not perpetuating the violence means that the reader, who witnesses with Tayo, is able to participate in both the agony and in the despair of his best friend's death. If Tayo had jumped out, the ritual would be destroyed for him and his people—and for us, however distantly, participating too.

The activity of witnessing has a tremendous charge in the Native American context, in which so much has been lost. Learning active witnessing, seeing and not turning away, knowing one does not have the answers, and questioning the impetus to jump into action, might be some ways for White Americans to show respect for Native American culture and history. The ceremony of witnessing goes beyond instrumentalism, or cause-and-effect logic. It involves engagement, a process of *internal* change, not change *of* someone or something else. In Chapter 4, I describe this change process in terms of *activation*, in contrast to *action*.

Tayo's intuitive sense of ceremony helps him to register the patterns that convey the connectedness of all life:

> He cried the relief he felt at finally seeing the pattern, the way all the stories fit together—the old stories, the war stories, their stories—to become the story that was still being told. He was not crazy; he had never been crazy. He had only seen and heard the world as it always was: no boundaries, only transitions through all distances and time. (Silko, 1986, p. 229)

As a result of his process, Tayo comes to feel the stories of his heritage activating his own unfolding life story, in a web of tension between destruction and life. The stories help Tayo know that he is not alone and that he has an inner reserve of power enabling him to fight for life, his own and the earth's.

The novel culminates in Tayo's ceremony of nonviolence, which will help him heal from the sickness of war, and will, in accordance with Pueblo belief and ritual, help to heal the whole world. Tayo's nonviolent act takes place in an old uranium mine, and it is this setting that reveals that the key to the novel's mystery is *ecological* in nature, rather than psychological, physical, or sociopolitical:

> Human beings were one clan again, united by the fate the destroyers planned for all of them, for all living things; united by a circle of death that devoured people in cities twelve thousand miles away, victims who had never known these mesas, who had never seen the delicate colors of the rocks which boiled up their slaughter. . . . The gray stone was streaked with powdery yellow uranium, bright and alive as pollen; veins of sooty black formed lines with the yellow, making mountain ranges and rivers across the stone. But they had taken these beautiful rocks from deep within the earth and they had laid them in a monstrous design, realizing destruction on a scale only they could have dreamed. (Silko, 1986, p. 229)

Silko illustrates the universe of connections through the destructive trail of yellow uranium that leads from the Laguna Pueblo reservation to Japan. This sandpainting stretched across the ocean shows that just as the two peoples across the world from each other are connected by the suffering and death carried by the uranium, they are also connected by the force of nonviolence and love.

Environmental Violence from Reservation to Chicago

In my American Literature class, I wanted students to apprehend the power of the ceremony Silko constructs in her novel by participating in its message collectively. How? While I puzzled this over, I came across Denise Levertov's (2001) poem "What It Could Be," and was particularly struck by these lines:

> Uranium, with which we know
> only how to destroy,
>
> lies always under the most sacred lands—
>
> Australia, Africa, America,
> wherever it's found is found an oppressed
> ancient people who knew
> long before white people found it and named it
> that there under their feet . . .
> lay a great power. (p. 23)

Both Silko and Levertov touch lightly on the healing power of connection. They maintain a respectful space for the individual reader to undergo her own ceremonial response to the invisible threads of relationship that make up life. Levertov, like Silko, counters the heavy-handed activity that uses and abuses the earth, with the human power of respect for living things:

> providing witness,
> occasion,
> ritual
> for the continuing act of
> *non*violence, of passionate
> reverence, active love. (p. 24)

The witness is not passive: The witness brings to the urgency of the present moment stories of past generations and commitment to future generations. *Environmental justice* actualizes this witnessing. Both Silko and Levertov confront the reader with the heavy weight of racial, cultural, and environmental violence that shapes the world we live in and demands a response.

Environmental injustice (also called environmental racism) refers to the widespread practice of locating industry, dumps, and other polluters in minority and low-income areas, where residents' concerns and voices are ignored or repressed. While higher-income White communities might see pollution as unfortunate by-products of industry and commerce, in many areas of the country it is communities of color who are left to handle pollution's by-products, illness and death. These communities experience pollution as violent racism. As Michael Schill and Regina Austin (1991) note, "The 'eco' in eco-justice stands as much for 'economic' as for 'ecological.'

For many communities of color, it is too late for NIMBY ['Not In My Back Yard']. They already have a dump, an incinerator, a smelter, a petrochemical plant, or a military base in their neighborhood" (p. 78).

When I learned that Chicago was one of the most environmentally racist cities in the nation, I wondered if the study of environmental justice might offer a framework for diving into some of the tensions around race and class that I was drawn to learn and teach about but did not know how to approach. Schill and Austin (1991) explain that the environmental justice movement

> capitalizes on the social and cultural differences of people of color as it cautiously builds alliances with whites and persons of the middle class. It is both fiercely environmental and conscious of the need for economic development in economically disenfranchised communities. Most distinctive of all, this movement has been extremely outspoken in challenging the integrity and bona fides of mainstream establishment environmental organizations. (p. 71)

Studying environmental justice enabled my students and me to analyze how class, race, and power played out in Chicago, and learn concrete ways individuals and groups could move beyond the individualist ecology framework of "reduce, reuse, recycle," to work for *social change*. Tangible stories about environmental injustice were a form of place-based education that helped us move from abstract philosophical discussions about social conditions to political analysis of our context. Talking about specific situations and people close to home heightened our curiosity about others, interest in exposing hidden power structures, and self-reflection.

Learning about environmental justice prompted students to scrutinize the liberal values that dominated our school. They started to notice contradictions and tensions between Democratic politics and democratic responsibility. This helped them to develop more rigorousness and precision in their thinking.

We recognized our own community in environmental sociologist Dorceta Taylor's characterization of liberal White people. Taylor challenges those who make donations to mainstream environmental organizations and love nature as an idyllic escape to see their complicity in the consumption, exploitation, and waste that poisons the air, water, and soil in low-income communities. For communities of color under the assault of pollution environmental health is not communing with nature; it is survival:

> There are a number of reasons why people of color might not share such feelings. Their prospects for transcendental communion with nature are restricted. Parks and recreational areas have been closed to them because of discrimination, inaccessibility, cost, their lack of specialized skills or equipment, and residence requirements for admission. They must find their recreation close to home. Harm to the environment caused by industrial development is not

really their responsibility because they have relatively little economic power or control over the exploitation of natural resources. Since rich white people messed it up, rich white people ought to clean it up. In any event, emphasis on the environment in the abstract diverts attention and resources from the pressing, concrete problems that people of color—especially those with little or no income—confront every day. (Schill & Austin, 1991, p. 72)

Such perspectives challenged the students and me to reflect on our own local context and think about the relationships between our social and ecological environments.

I contacted the Little Village Environmental Justice Organization (LVEJO) in Chicago to see what else I could find out. At this moment everything changed. My hunt for interesting curricular connections became a consuming, many-year study of the relationships between political power and education. Since it began here, in Little Village, I offer the story not as a model but as a case study of the questions and dynamics that arise from the question "How can education prepare students to contribute to democratic society?"

A Journey of Witness Begins with the "Toxic Tour"

I had lived in Chicago for 3 years and had never been to the Little Village neighborhood. The further south I drove from my school's North Side neighborhood by the lake, the more bumpy my ride. The streets were full of holes, the viaducts I drove under were crumbly and leaky, the buildings crowded the streets. No one was White. I drove down 26th Street, lined with tempting taco shops and families out shopping. I later learned that La Villita's 26th Street is second only to Michigan Avenue downtown in terms of tax revenue for the city of Chicago.

I drove to 2816 S. Millard Avenue and walked up and down the block a couple of times before I found the office—it was in the basement of a brick two-flat in a residential neighborhood. Inside, I met Kim Wasserman, a young, vibrant Latina woman with luscious black curls and an enormous smile. She introduced me to her dad, who was as small and unassuming as his daughter was larger-than-life, and we sat at a big metal fold-out table that I would find myself at countless times in the coming years. Howard looked out at me with dark blue eyes under bushy eyebrows and a beard.

"Your neighborhood is pushing its heavy industries into our neighborhood. What might happen if you and your students started asking some questions about why this is, how it happens, what the impact is on the city?" With these words, LVEJO leader Howard Ehrman told me the story of environmental justice in Chicago. Chicago's electricity, he told me, was generated from the coal power plant down the street that was poisoning the neighborhood; the trash from throughout the city was also processed in this neighborhood. Even the feel-good recycling industry was tainted by the poison of environmental injustice: A plastics recycling plant in Lincoln Park was being moved to Little Village because of neighborhood complaints. The city changed the zoning laws to protect the health of Lincoln Park residents—at the expense of Little Village residents' health. "Will it impact the media, will the politicians listen, if Chicago's young people are asking these questions?"

Howard posed his questions in an inviting way—he was offering some framing questions that students might be intrigued by. He neither reproached nor assigned responsibility. He started from a standpoint that went something like this: "This is our city's shared problem; you have the potential and opportunity to investigate it." He *did not* say, "We want you to change this"—and this was important too. It would become a central part of my work to remind myself and my students of our limits, to make sure that we were paying close attention to what the people who welcomed us into their neighborhoods were asking us to think about and do, and not projecting our analyses and solutions at them. Like the elders in *Ceremony* who guide Tayo's quest for healing, Howard was guiding me and my students in the process of *witnessing*, an activity that can be ritual, art, and political act.

A few weeks later, Kim led my class on a "toxic tour":[10] We walked out the map of the industrial area, where residents had recently built a park, in accordance with the city's original promise for that site. In spite of the fact that only one park served this community of 100,000 people, and that that one park was gang controlled, the city destroyed the park the community had built. It had enclosed the area in barbed wire while waiting for the new owners. A plastics recycling company would be moving into Little Village after city rezoning processes forced it out of Lincoln Park, our school's neighborhood. Kim explained to us that the zoning laws had been designed with a distinct slant: It is illegal to build new residences across the street from industry —thus industry must make way for gentrification. However, it is not illegal to locate industry across the street from existing houses—thus the residents least capable of escaping toxic fumes are burdened with the worst of them.

Unequal protection was institutionalized in the city's legal code. We learned from Kim that people in Little Village were exposed to a number of highly polluting industries, and that the city had for years been promising more schools, libraries, and parks but delivering only more and more industry, which in large part did not even employ people from the community.

After my class had visited the waste processing plant, coal power plant, and steel drum factory side-by-side with residences all within a three-block radius within Little Village and had read articles about environmental injustice, the students wanted to go beyond learning about the issues to respond publicly. They wanted to push the city to shut down the polluting power plants. I was an English teacher who had not yet heard of "participatory action research," but in trying to support the students' engagement, I set up structures that I later learned the terms for. Students used class time to make phone calls, write letters, track down information, and develop informational materials. The environmental science class, including some of the same students, worked in tandem with us. The environmental science teachers stewarding the project with me, Morgan Rich and Alvin Bisarya, asked the students, "Who do you want to read these materials? Who should know what you know?"

It was important to us to visit Little Village with an interest in the people, culture, and stories in the community, not only the issues. A couple of students suggested that we develop a project in partnership with the high school in Little Village, where they had friends. Alvin and Morgan and I, with our colleagues Mateo Katz and Charles Kuner from Farragut, led a number of cross-school visits. In the course of their conversations, the students from both schools collectively decided they wanted to plan and carry out an Earth Day protest, to urge Chicago city council members to force the energy company to clean up the polluting power plants.

The students' public statement on the event conveys what it looked like and meant to them as organizers:

> On Earth Day . . . students and activists from across Chicago organized and simultaneously held two rallies and human-chain protests. Hundreds of people linked arms on city streets to demonstrate our connectedness as one humanity—forever interlinked across communities, age, race, gender, culture and class, dependent upon one another's respect for the environment for each of our survival.
>
> Our goal is for Midwest Generation to stop burning coal and to switch to a cleaner fuel source, to stop needlessly killing and sickening people. We will continue our activism until this goal is reached.
>
> Our goals, however, go beyond changing the way Midwest Generation runs its business. We want to see a profound change in how each of us views our role and behavior as world citizens. We strive to educate one another about the multiple ways we can decrease our own exhaustion of these resources and how we can facilitate this change in others as well.
>
> In the face of divisiveness and hostility at a local and international level, we seek to bring out the connections between communities and people. These are the connections that can triumph over chaos and lead to a clearer awareness of our city and our world.

FROM SERVICE LEARNING TO DEMOCRATIC EDUCATION

The great force of history comes from the fact that we carry it within us, are unconsciously controlled by it in many ways, and history is literally present in all that we do.

—James Baldwin

While the environmental justice project engaged students as active participants in society, it also revealed to students the profound *limits* of the project. The language of unity that the students forged was silent on the dynamic of power and privilege that was the subject of the students' political analysis and action. The White Parker students did not have a working vocabulary or framework by which to understand their own power and privilege. As a teacher interested in supporting young people's civic education, I needed to learn about racial identity development.

One obvious marker of inequality that framed our context was that Parker students could walk in and out of the neighborhood and the campaign, while Farragut students and their families remained vulnerable to the pollution and corresponding political disenfranchisement—and the profound discouragement evoked by the contrast between our communities. The campaign's momentum slowed with the end of the school year, although students and teachers from both Parker and Farragut continued to meet, plan, and take action for years after the protest project. A decade later, the movement they took part in led to the closing of the coal power plants. For all those years, however, the coal power plants and the city politics that sanctioned the pollution continued to operate. Engaging in realistic discourse about the possibilities for and obstacles to social change was a critical part of the learning process.

Without ongoing exploration of what it means to work for social change, students can remain stuck in a clichéd expectation of "making a difference." Good intentions aren't enough: The impulse to help, to try to fix problems we see around us, can do more harm than good both to oneself and to others. If we work hard for change and see no results, we can become frustrated and resentful, reluctant to get burned again by sinking good intentions and energy into possibly fruitless projects. I think of this dynamic as *efficacy entitlement*.

The harm that the desire to "make a difference" can do to others is even more drastic, when we unconsciously advance our cultural assumptions and privileges on others—making a goodwill offering feel like an assault on another's dignity.[11] Cross-race, cross-class service or action that takes place without firm mooring in awareness of racial identity and power analysis can be damaging. As Gary Howard (1999) explains White identity development, an early stage takes the form of "a desire to 'help' people from other racial groups rather than to systematically change the dynamics of dominance" (p. 92). To develop beyond this stage, White people must examine how they benefit from racist systems. They must open their eyes to unacknowledged habits of believing in "White moral superiority," which the impulse to "help" may convey. A later stage in White identity development is marked by "movement away from paternalistic efforts to help other groups and toward an internalized desire to change oneself and one's fellow Whites in a positive way" (1999, p. 93). These "stages" provide a framework for self-reflection, but they are not linear, nor ever finally mastered. Just speaking for myself, the "helping" impulse continues to dominate my automatic responses. My racial awareness is intermittent at best even though I have been thinking, speaking, and writing about race, and especially about my struggles with my White privilege, for many years.

Over the course of the school year, my class spent as much time processing as we did planning and acting. The processing slowed us down in the project we had taken on as well as in the planned course curriculum. My students' privilege made them accustomed to seeing results for their labor, and some were furious that their letters to the mayor and phone calls to aldermen and other civic leaders were not having the effect they sought. Midyear, I had asked students to jot down their feelings about the progress of the project. Several comments went along these lines: "it looks like a pointless cause. I don't see how our class can truly make a difference when our elected leaders do not respond or want to take action." Together, we analyzed the assumptions behind this kind of reaction. Would students have the same sense of pointlessness if they lived in Little Village, if they or their loved ones were suffering from asthma as a result of the pollution there?[12] Why would it be pointless to write letters to elected officials, but not to write a paper, solve math equations, write a lab report—how do they evaluate what work they do is important and what is not? Did their resistance correspond to a growing and disturbing awareness that the civic institutions they believed to be fair in fact were not?

The students perceived another limitation to our project: the segregation that divided the neighborhoods, the schools, and the students from one another, which they did not understand and did not know how to approach. Students from privileged backgrounds who are isolated in their schools and neighborhoods are being trained for the entitlement they are meant to maintain throughout their lives. As Sharon Sutton (1996) asks in her study of place and power in educational inequality, "If places are texts that instruct children about a way of life, what types of landscapes might enable them to take leave of their assigned ranks and roles in the hierarchies of the dominant culture?" (p. 197). Their out-of-school learning was leading my students to see how economic interests and people with social power shaped the plan of the city with designated insiders and outsiders, winners and losers. How could my students live on this map without participating in undemocratic systems? This problem—which had surfaced in other social action projects I had led, though I was not able to articulate it yet—became a central focus for us, as I will discuss further in coming chapters.

Putting *place* at the center of our learning raises questions about our racial, class, and cultural identities as well as our political context. It helps us to see the political processes we are complicit in whether we want to be or not. A focus on place is necessary to democratic education: Challenges to unjust systems of control must be grounded in study of local sources of knowledge and power, which are messy and contingent in comparison to the glossy pages of textbooks and brochures.

However, the experience of local knowledge and power changes people, long-term. When students and teachers "witness and develop forms of empathetic connection with other human beings," David Gruenewald (2003a, p. 8) writes of place-based learning, they "deepen empathetic connections and expand the possibilities for learning outward." Being in places of struggle for the community, around people who are committed to social justice at a local level, encourages the growth of lifelong social responsibility (Berman, 1997).[13] This is education for sustainable democracy.

Inquiry happens on the verge. That's why it feels dangerous. Foregrounding borders, and studying how people cross borders of race, culture, and class, offers an experiential way to illuminate political questions for students.

***

The "Connect Chicago" project challenged my assumptions and expectations in ways that I continue to wrestle with now, many years and countless social action projects later. The service-learning framework that connected our literary study of *Ceremony* with ecological stewardship could no longer hold up when my students sought to be allies with peers from another neighborhood. If Parker students viewed this as a service project, we could not even try to forge a relationship with Farragut students on an equal footing, and the connections that the project sought to strengthen would be damaged. It was already hard enough to encourage relationships among students who never would have encountered one another otherwise.

The project led my colleague and me to change our language from "service-learning" to "civic education." Because our school includes a large number of privileged families, students might assume that when they go to other neighborhoods and meet with other students, they are "helping others," performing community service. This is a conceptual model that accords with the stance many privileged people are accustomed to occupying in the world; it expresses a meritocratic view of success and a benevolent self-image. Our challenge is to provide students with experiences that help them develop an understanding of democratic life as complex, interdependent, and challenging.[14] Civic education means that students and teachers are confronting together the biggest obstacle before us in making change, which is not political or material but *internal*. Democracy requires that we learn to recognize how power acts on, around, and through us, personally, in terms of race, class, culture, gender, and sexual orientation.

Social action alongside our internal work means aiming more toward partnerships and coalitions instead of service or advocacy projects. Internal shifts must occur in order for people of privilege to engage with people of different ethnic or class backgrounds as interesting, complex, equal human beings, not as victims or as projects. Working *with*, not *for*, others, means that allies *must change their own location*. In the next chapters I will study further dimensions of partnership building, especially in relation to leadership, learning, and change.

Our environmental justice project led us to realize that our school needed to develop the following:

- Relationships between schools and between schools and community organizations
- Institutional support for ongoing partnerships (in contrast to "one-off" events)
- Professional community and cross-disciplinary work within the school
- Expanded attention to social awareness in learning, supporting students' relationships both within the school and in the wider community
- Working understanding of race and class and power in coalitions: self-awareness and ability to listen to the other

Throughout the book I will delve into implications of this learning.

Power-with: A Framework for Awareness and Solidarity

Democratic growth depends on the existence of relationships of equality and respect that cross class and race lines—but this does not mean democracy-as-melting-pot. Border-crossing relationships must prioritize the rights of different cultural groups to create and sustain community space focused on their own values.

In my research on cross-race and cross-class coalitions, one of the most generative models I have encountered is the analysis offered by Guinier and Torres (2003) in *The Miner's Canary*. It offers the guidelines for what I call "playing with power" that I draw on throughout this book. Already in the title of the book the reader begins to learn a new paradigm. The metaphor of the miner's canary offers a more nuanced lens by which to see inequality than the fixed terms of oppressed and oppressor. It posits a reality in which low-income, historically disadvantaged populations are like "the miner's canary" for people who enjoy more privilege. Calamity hits the disadvantaged people first, but everybody else will be hit by the calamity a little further down the line. Thus, it is in everybody's interest to ensure that the people who are most vulnerable receive the most protection.

This happens through conscious recognition and creative transformation of inherited power structures, or "meta-narratives of power-over." Adapting the influential theory of power presented in Michel Foucault's work, Guinier and Torres (2003) offer stories of democratic power, "power-with." Cross-race, cross-class coalitions of people learn to break through the power systems that have shaped their lives, through confronting injustice in the community they live in and the institutions they are part of. Many of these stories are current-generation civil rights issues. For example, the authors tell the story of a Kmart unionization effort in Greensboro, North Carolina, that required building a coalition between African American and White workers who had not previously associated. I will summarize the story of this coalition, which illuminates the meaning of "power-with."

The Pulpit Forum is a key player in this story. Founded in the 1960s to involve Black churches in the Civil Rights Movement, its leaders knew how to go about coalition building: through shared struggle. This contrasted with the White unions' emphasis on action over relationship: "From the perspective of the Pulpit Forum, the union's approach to the community was 'Help us do what we've already decided to do,' rather than 'Help us think through the issues together'" (Guinier & Torres, 2003, p. 132). An instrumentalist focus on action can blind potential allies to their assumptions of superiority and the damage they cause to coalition work. Guinier and Torres (2003) emphasize that foregrounding race was an essential part of the process of building the "beloved community" across races:

> Rather than seeing power only in the labor unions or the black church . . . Johnson brought together the power of each in order to mobilize the entire community of Greensboro. By moving back and forth between the black workers and the white workers, between the workers and the community, between the church that restored their courage and the courtroom that tested it, they reconfigured traditional power relations and forged new relationships with others in the community as well. (p. 137)

The coalition that successfully campaigned for labor rights formed in movement between spaces that had always been separate. Power-with expresses the heightened awareness that comes with movement across boundaries.

Elements of Guinier and Torres's (2003) stories bear similarities to our cross-school environmental justice coalition. The analysis offered in *The Miner's Canary* helped me to understand the dynamics that had emerged around racial identity, cultural privilege, and political processes—and to imagine possibilities for doing things differently. The authors address alliances between groups that have unequal access to power, and they urge developing "power-with" practices that contrast with the unhealthy power dynamics found in both formal and informal organizations where power is assumed, unquestioned, or unacknowledged:

> Collective action that is cross-racial and sustainable depends on three key ingredients: 1) a reconceptualization of the meta-narratives of power-over, 2) a commitment to sharing power in ways that are generative, that build from familiar settings, and that emphasize human agency within an organized community, and 3) a willingness to engage with internally embedded hierarchies of race and class privilege. (Guinier & Torres, 2003, p. 137)

Guinier and Torres are talking about understanding the world, interaction across different levels of power, and self-reflection. The deconstruction–reconstruction of metanarratives of power is, they show, a process that is renewing and energizing for everyone. Unlike power-over, *power-with* "is generative, it involves sharing something or becoming something, not just giving or demanding or consuming. It expands in its exercise. It finds a way to call on people to connect with something larger than themselves" (Guinier & Torres, 2003, p. 141). By taking risks that expose and threaten some of their privilege—again and again—allies move past guilt and into solidarity. Power-with offers a constructive approach to relationships between groups facing unequal degrees of power.

This model also reframes the idea of success, heightening attention to the relationship between process and outcome:

> Power-with is the psychological and social power gained through collective resistance and struggle and through the creation of an alternative set of narratives. It is relational and interactive. It requires participation. . . . Participation affords power even aside from direct results . . . it offers a chance for claiming dignity even at the moment that it is at risk of being denied. (Guinier & Torres, 2003, p. 141)

When students exclaimed of our cross-neighborhood, cross-culture partnership with Farragut, "*This isn't supposed to happen*," they were aware that they were in the process of creating "an alternative set of narratives" that enabled them to take part in "collective resistance" despite the inequality that the partnership exposed. The power-with model affirms the power of the relationship, and the power analysis it engages takes place within the framework of this affirmation. This is important for all the participants to be able to enter into. Democratic education hammers out spaces of equality in an environment of inequality.

Guinier and Torres (2003) offer a description of collective ritual that reframes the idea of success. The image of building a sandcastle provides a new perspective on the relationship between process and outcome:

> Imagine that the participants understand the project's transient state, but the very fluidity of the project attracts many different people with a range of skills who experiment with alternative architectural forms. Their goal is not to participate in a sandcastle competition but to learn how to work together under stressful circumstances to keep the sandcastle standing as long as possible. The mere fact that the inevitable tide will eventually wash away the effort does not destroy the learning and satisfaction that are generated by this collective and creative activity. The community spirit built in this process will withstand the tide. (p. 141)

The intense commitment among participants of a community project becomes in itself a source of power. The community spirit changes individuals' understanding of themselves and helps them develop as leaders. The participants' own willingness to sacrifice convinces others to participate. Community work disrupts individualist habits of thought; it builds counternarratives that help people over time to confront internally embedded hierarchies and engage productively with conflict. An understanding of group identity is at the core of this counternarrative: "In order to understand the multiple levels at which race and power intersect, it is necessary to move from the primacy of individual status to a focus on group interactions and their relationship to power" (Guinier & Torres, 2003, p. 12).

***

As I finished the year of my first environmental justice project, I had a whole new set of questions. I also realized that I was in a school where I could experiment with these questions. I saw that all my questions centered on how we cross borders.

How do we . . .

- balance youth voice and power with humility?
- explore privilege and power within ourselves and the various circles of our community?
- work with other schools and develop relationships that recognize and deal with inequality without being wholly defined by it?
- join education practices and structures with the assets and challenges of community organizations?
- foster cross-race, cross-neighborhood leadership—that lasts?
- as adults, help students develop in awareness and support taking a stand, without imposing our own values on them?
- develop authentic ways for people who are not directly affected by a problem to take part in addressing it, without imposing their cultural values, power, or biases?
- talk about the oppression others experience, in their company?
- teach collective consciousness in an individualistic environment?
- encourage people to sustain struggle when they are not immediately affected and there are many very good reasons for leaving?

The following chapters will engage these questions, with reference to stories of Parker and other contexts.

Chapter 2

Leadership in Love and Struggle

Learning to Be Allies

If you have come to help me, you are wasting your time. But if you have come because your liberation is bound up with mine, come, let us walk together.

—Aboriginal council led by Lila Watson

Whether one is a leader fighting against one's own or others' oppression, the qualities of respect and humility are essential . . . this defies rather than continues oppressive structures.

—Francis W. Parker student leader

Our cross-town environmental justice project aimed to make connections, between literature and life, between different races and neighborhoods, between disparate areas of learning—after all, the students of Farragut and Parker had named their joint campaign "Connect Chicago." Yet the more connections we made, the more conflict surfaced. This complicated processes of community building; it also illuminated dynamics of community relationships that most of the students who lived in the Lincoln Park neighborhood of our school had not previously been aware of. As I discussed in Chapter 1, the political conflict that drove our campaign brought to the surface tensions around race, privilege, and power.

Such tensions are felt in different ways by people of differing levels of power, whether that be a student in relation to a teacher or a White person in relation to a Black person, so it is important to pay close attention to them. This is particularly necessary when White people seek to be in alliance with people of color. For, although democratic alliances activate the energy of participants and highlight public activity, they still take form among human beings who have been conditioned over the course of lives and generations by power systems that generate injustice.

Addressing this conditioning is a key concern of democratic leadership. Power systems chug away; a vast economic and cultural infrastructure supports them—as does widespread inattention to their workings. The more direct the confrontation with power and the more unequal the inherited power relations within the alliance, the more likely it is that the democratic action will include internal conflict among the very people who are standing together against injustice. If these groups do not recognize and cannot deal with the tensions caused by the workings of systems of oppression, democratic energy can turn bad, can feed the defensiveness, self-righteousness, and miscommunication that the democratic action sought to counter (Guinier & Torres, 2003).

"It's not easy," says Old Betonie in *Ceremony*, "It has never been easy" (Silko, 1986, p. 254). Studying the stories of social struggle over time and across the world helps people recognize that confusion and struggle are part of democratic growth. We need to develop "conflict literacy" (Gerzon, 2006) to help us learn from and in conflict.

This chapter studies the commitment and love that enable people to work through the struggles that are part of democratic action. I deepen my focus on relationships in and around schools as a crucible for democratic life. The book *The Miner's Canary*, which I introduced in the previous chapter, offers key terms for democratic coalition-building work. The alliances that *The Miner's Canary* describes emerge from people influenced by the Civil Rights Movement. Foundations of contemporary coalitions, documented in civil rights narratives, such as Barbara Ransby's (2005) *Ella Baker and the Black Freedom Movement* and John Lewis's (1998) *Walking with the Wind*, represent a corpus of social knowledge that educators can apply to their work with students, with colleagues, and in the community. Reading diverse narratives of the Civil Rights Movement brings home the understanding that different, conflicting, context-heavy versions are essential for a working and usable history of the movement.

In this chapter, I dwell particularly on the story of Highlander Folk School that Myles Horton tells in his book *The Long Haul* (Horton et al., 1997). I articulate the educational legacy of Highlander in terms of practices of *relational learning, soaking up stories,* and *questioning hierarchical power,* and I apply these practices to classroom contexts. This legacy calls upon teachers to examine their acceptance of authority expressed in routine dismissial of informal, personally grounded and socially relevant education. I discuss the pedagogy of oral history as a way to translate the ongoing cycles of stories and social change at Highlander into the context of schools. I argue that, as a mode of learning that crosses disciplines and enlarges the field of social knowledge, and as an exchange that builds trust, self-reflection, and solidarity, oral history strengthens democratic life.

I begin with a couple of stories about problems that cross-school connections expose. They illustrate the dangers of focusing on social issues without critiques like Mateo's "Rules of the Matrix" and other tools for growing self-awareness, questions about power, and appreciation for difference.

"Community Service?"

The quality of owning freezes you forever in "I," and cuts you off forever from the "we."

—John Steinbeck, *The Grapes of Wrath*

"What is wrong with gentrification?" my student Jerry asked. "Isn't it a good thing for a neighborhood to get cleaned up?" My American Literature class was reading *The Grapes of Wrath*, and our exploration of displacement in Chicago had led us to consider urban gentrification. Our school is in a neighborhood that was gentrified generations ago, and it is green and lovely, but markedly White. Maria, a Latina student in my class, raised her hand and described a neighborhood a couple of miles away from ours, where people she knew were having to leave because wealthier people were moving in and property costs were sharply rising. She mentioned a class in the alternative school there, whose students, acutely aware of the economic forces that might well drive them and their school out of the community, were studying gentrification. Maria suggested that we take a field trip and learn from them. So we did.

I wanted my students to develop their civic leadership capacities by learning from their peers across town and seeing other young people in the role of researchers and experts. I hoped that the alternative school students' presentation would model critical awareness for my students. I wondered if our cross-neighborhood discussion of gentrification could evolve into a democratic dialogue about power, privilege, and education. Could the meeting of multiple perspectives enable students to see their own experiences in relationship to the social processes they are part of? Could students from different backgrounds, divided by inequality, develop as leaders through dialogue with one another?[1]

"While not abandoning their own perspective," Iris Marian Young writes, "through listening across difference...participants gain a wider picture of the social processes in which their own partial experience is embedded" (Young, 1996, p. 128). Could their exchange lead students in both groups to expand their frame of reference—basing their social map not on stereotypes or news stories, but conversations with other young people?

I was interested in the kind of frame Henry Giroux (2005) provides in his theory of "border pedagogy," which

> suggests more than simply opening diverse cultural histories and spaces to students. It also means understanding how fragile identity is as it moves into borderlands crisscrossed within a variety of languages, experiences, and voices . . . these pedagogical borderlands where Blacks, Whites, Latinos, and others meet

demonstrate the importance of a multicentric perspective that allows students to recognize and analyze how difference within and between various groups can expand the potential of human life and democratic possibilities. (p. 34)

I had seen students widen their range of vision through reading, discussion, and social action—would "border-crossing" experiences help them to integrate democratic dispositions into their lives beyond school? Would more exposure to people who experienced marginalization make my students more competent in allyship and leadership?

A few weeks later, the students in my English class were sitting in the English class at the alternative high school. About one-third of my group of 16 students were from Asian American, African American, and Latino backgrounds; the rest were White. The alternative high school class of about 12 students was predominantly Latino, with a few White and a few African American students. The alternative high school students presented their participatory action research project on gentrification with photos, interviews, research, and analysis. I was impressed by the group's project and grateful for their generosity in sharing their work with us. I turned to my students, expecting them to share my enthusiasm.

I was surprised to see my students who were normally vibrantly engaged wholly unresponsive—no questions, no comments. They looked bored. One of the presenting students finally broke into the uncomfortable silence and asked my students why they had come. No one answered. At random, I called on one my students, sitting at the other end of the table from me, to respond. "Community service?" my Asian American student ventured. The kids from the other school burst out laughing and teased, "What do you want to do, clean up our school or something?" "Want me to find you a mop?!"

As my students hurried onto the bus to head back to our school, I asked them, "What was going on in there? Why were you so silent?!" "We're afraid that the second we open our mouths," they answered, "we'll confirm all their assumptions about us—that we're snobby rich White kids."

Like fairies whose magic only works in particular places, my students had deflated. The abilities that so impressed me in my students—to discuss ideas intelligently, listen with empathy, discern unexpected ways of looking at things—were frozen in this West Side neighborhood. I worried about the hurt my students' frozenness may have caused to their peers in the other school. My students' worries about how they would be perceived not only made the possibility of future connection between our schools a lot less likely, but also blocked the students themselves from an important learning opportunity. Their fears crowded out the preparations we had done for days before the field trip, talking through the purpose of our visit. I was dismayed that my students' range of interaction turned out to be so limited. Their identities were indeed, to use Giroux's term, more "fragile" in this context than I had expected.

I was also disturbed that the only imaginable conduit for connection between our communities was *community service*, that the idea of learning from and with one another across differences was not available to my students—even when I had explicitly "taught" this objective. Why was "community service" the only thinkable form of connection between communities that were racially and socioeconomically different? What assumptions did we have about what separated us? Could analyzing these assumptions help us to build relationships more intentionally—and more sustainably?

The Danger of the Social Action Excursion

People from different race and class backgrounds may agree on a social justice issue but, whether they are aware of it or not, their identities shape their approach, which may lead to entirely different interpretations and outcomes. Unwatched, systems of power block alliance across differences. In *The Miner's Canary* (2003), Guinier and Torres tell a story of border-crossing social action that is instructive for schools and groups seeking to build democratic relationships, so I retell it here.

The story begins when students from a predominantly White, privileged private Boston school (where Guinier's son Niko was a student)[2] join with students from a low-income school in the Jamaica Plains neighborhood, composed mostly of students of color, to protest the New York City Police Department's racial profiling of Ron Howard, an African American teacher who had taught at both schools. Young people marching from across races and neighborhoods to publicly defend their teacher and call out systemic racism—it does not get more democratic than that!

The way power and privilege entered into the space, however, damaged the democratic potential of this moment. In Chapter 1, I talked about awareness of place, and the movement and placement of bodies and voices within a space, an awareness which tends to be underdeveloped in education structures in the United States. In the case of this student march, unconsciousness around inherited hierarchies of race polluted the democratic space the march was meant to affirm. Patterns of domination are the default in schools; it takes conscious struggle to construct relationships of mutuality, care, and vulnerability (Kreisberg, 1992). The 8th-grade students from the Young Achievers Public School, with their parents and teachers, had planned and prepared for the march. The private school students who showed up in support arrived late to the march and happened to be pushed to the front. Media coverage focused on them, although they were not the leaders of the march.

Nobody meant for the march to look like it was led by the White students, but that's how it turned out. Thus, the White students' act of solidarity unintentionally gave rise to conflict and mistrust. Members of the Young Achievers community "did not trust the private school kids, who departed as quickly as they had arrived, while the predominantly black and brown Young Achievers were left to confront the issue of racial profiling every day on the streets of their city" (Guinier & Torres, 2003, p. 285). It seemed like the private school kids and parents were exercising their choice to come into a neighborhood they might never otherwise go to and then leave for their secure neighborhoods, insulated from the problems that the people in the community had to deal with day in and day out.

How can people of privilege enter oppressed neighborhoods respect-fully? Can they shake the toxic fumes of their privilege? Perhaps it would help for them to think hard about *why* they want to take action:

> The magnitude of the challenge facing the Young Achievers included the need to learn how to confront wrongdoing by those in authority and to speak in their own collective voice, especially when criticized or threatened. For the private school kids the rally served an entirely different purpose. It was a one-time ef-fort to support a beloved teacher. (Guinier & Torres, 2003, p. 289)

An exchange that takes place at the private school in the aftermath of the march illuminates the importance of these diverging motivations. A faculty member of the private school, a woman of color who lived in Jamaica Plains, pointed out that when the private school students walked at the front of the march, they had inappropriately eclipsed the public school students. She was insulted by the attitude the students had brought into the neighborhood action. She felt that the students should have known that their place was *behind* the Young Achievers who were leading the march and surmised that they "were not marching with the Young Achievers com-munity but they were marching alone and for their own glory" (Guinier & Torres, 2003, p. 285). The public school kids who had planned the march, themselves far more vulnerable to the racial profiling that was the reason for the march, were marching against systemic oppression; the private school students were not challenging systemic oppression.

Students and parents took issue with this teacher's reproach. The par-ents were concerned that the negativity the teacher generated might dis-courage their children from participating in social action in the future. A parent who gives voice to this concern writes, "One thing that I am scared of is that the 'hardness' of this learning will diminish my son's willingness to go public with his support of social justice—whether it be in conversa-tions with his peers who don't agree with him or in public demonstrations of activism." This parent, however, recognized that the real issue at hand here was not how her child feels about social activism but her family and community's ongoing unacknowledged complicity in what Guinier and Tor-res (2003) call "embedded hierarchies." In a letter to the other parents, the White mother reflects on her own accountability for what happened. She recognizes that she made a mistake in not seeing what was going on: She had been "thoughtless." She notes, "when you're white, as I am, thoughtlessness has far-reaching implications." She explains how she seeks to learn, together with her son, from the experience:

> My son and I will talk about the chant that the YA students taught us, "We have the power. You have the power. I have the power." What does this mean if you are a person of color? How does it change, even if used in support, if you are a white person? What is support without taking center stage? . . . Why is it critical to our lives to keep acting and learning? (Guinier & Torres, 2003, pp. 287–288)

These questions of location and relationship are the kind of questions, Guinier and Torres (2003) suggest, that would-be allies need to be asking before asking themselves what they can *do*. Such questions help to adjust the individualized experience of "hardness" so that allies can focus on the *shared* hardness of obstacles, internal and external, to changing oppressive systems—rather than getting stuck on uncomfortable or unpleasant symptoms of these systems. Such questions emerge from and express a sense of "linked fate" that allies need to develop, without which they will be "temporary associates" "who can opt to leave at any moment." As much as protesting racial profiling on city streets, confronting hierarchical power systems means addressing unintended and unnoticed workings of privilege day in and day out. Fresh possibilities for collaboration, perspective, and change emerge when people are conscious of undemocratic patterns. They are able to choose how they want to act, with whom they will try to ally themselves, and to escape the trap of unconscious default roles.[3]

This is what Guinier and Torres (2003) call "political race":

> At its core [political race] does not ask what you call yourself but with whom do you link your fate. It is a fundamentally creative political project that begins from the ground up, starting with race and all its complexity, and then builds cross-racial relationships through race and with race to issues of class and gender in order to make democracy real. (p. 10)

Democracy does not exist in itself but in the struggle for it. It is process; it is relationships. Developing "political race" involves sequence and study. For White people especially, the high degree of complexity involved in antiracist behavior requires emotional involvement and self-awareness, as well as intense cognitive work. When we become conscious of the intersections of race, power, and injustice both within and around us, we are able to choose what we want to do about them.

This choice is a catalyst for leadership-in-alliance. Internal and social processes work in tandem in the growth of "political race" that makes possible trust relationships across race. These relationships are not support for leadership; they *are* leadership. Unlike individualist views of leadership in the United States that are tied to meritocratic systems of power, and are thus marked by Whiteness, healthy democratic life requires collective and cooperative leadership: a "charismatic community."[4] As Guinier and Torres and other democratic thinkers make clear, White middle-class people need to stay engaged in a process of deconstructing their inherited assumptions about identity, success, and access if they are going to be able to learn leadership-in-alliance.[5]

"A Drama of Transformation"

Relationship building is not just coming together; it involves active reflection and learning. As we saw in the students' march, to be an ally means not just to show up, but to think and analyze, watch and listen, as I suggested in Chapter 1, to *witness*. "Racial group consciousness becomes a form of cognitive, political, and moral literacy" (Guinier & Torres, 2003, p. 81). Allies need to develop a part of their identity that emerges only through this ongoing process of analysis and action-in-relationship: to develop political race.

> To be respectful allies whose support is not only needed but welcome over time, white progressives may have to learn . . . that through the agency of political race, they need to yoke their fate to those with a long history of struggling for justice, a struggle lived in the exigencies of daily life and not just in the risks taken on a single day of activism. Resistance . . . needs to become a drama of transformation, as the participants struggle to envision more democratic forms of relationships and of power itself. [Allies] need to make concerted and ongoing efforts to build the trust and create the context for solidarity that is necessary for the project to be effective and sustainable. [In taking action,] they need to find communities of color who are mobilizing and to build sustained relationships with those communities to support their local efforts. . . . Unless allies challenge their own embedded privilege, they face the real danger of reproducing the very hierarchies of power they seek to topple. (Guinier & Torres, 2003, p. 290)

Social action must involve action on oneself—*activation*, as I will discuss in Chapter 4. The process of challenging embedded privilege does not end but rather changes, and continues to disturb the developing ally, even as he or she feels the transformation. Conflict is an inevitable part of that process. This is uncomfortable for many people who seek to be in solidarity, but it can be sustaining to have a framework for understanding the bigger picture.

Supports and challenges must be in place for people participating in democratic action, so that when mistakes and changes come up, the actions do not undo themselves. Democratic relationships require that people accept that they have to be wrong sometimes, and take the risk of making mistakes. This represents a commitment that supports a more conscious way of acting together. Too often, would-be White allies opt in or out; if it does not feel good, they will stay out. That's not how commitment works. If potential allies withdraw, bitter and confused, they lose a precious part of themselves to the default setting of the prevailing narrative. Creating and sustaining a counternarrative of alliance-in-struggle is difficult, but liberating.

Crossing Borders

As I considered unexamined power relationships that were damaging the connective tissue between our schools and our neighborhoods, I realized that my students and I needed to learn how to be border-crossers. Physically crossing neighborhood lines had to be accompanied by recognizing boundaries within our minds. We needed to ask questions about what was happening in our community and in other communities and about the relationships between them. We needed to notice places where we found ourselves outside of our comfort zone and support one another in investigating how that comfort zone had been zoned and how it might be expanded. We needed to seek out our blind spots, and heighten our resolve to notice how power and privilege was operating in, on, and through us.

I decided to apply the guidance for democratic education that Walter Parker (2002), like Dewey, based in student–student exchange: "Increase the variety and frequency of interaction among students who are different from one another; orchestrate these contacts to foster deliberation about the problems that inevitably arise from the friction of that interaction; and strive to develop communicative competence, particularly the receptive practice of listening across social perspectives" (p. xxi). Students have a better chance of developing communicative competence when they spend more time with people from different backgrounds. Reflection is a key part of this learning.

Critical literacy means becoming aware of the cultural norms that underlie our language and thinking and analyzing how these norms can separate us from people with different cultural norms—and contribute to systemic oppression—if they go unnoticed (Giroux, 2005). For instance, unrecognized stereotypes projected at students of color and internalized by them widen "achievement gaps" between students of different racial identities (Steele & Aronson, 1995). Border-crossing requires that teachers openly share and examine our own stories and our own contingent knowledge; sharing *this* story is a border-crossing move for me.

When people make changes to become border-crossers, they move past the assigned hierarchical identities of race and class to more readily shape their identities in ways that foster relationship and growth. We get stuck in roles and functions that are set before us but that we do not choose. How disempowering and dulling this routine is! Especially for students, whom adults load with one activity or assignment after another, right at a time in life when young people really need to learn how to make choices well. Educationally guided xperiences of educated border-crossing may help people to desire and to construct what Guinier and Torres (2003) called "political race," the foundation of leadership-in-alliance.

HIGHLANDER FOLK SCHOOL: LEARNING LEADERSHIP-IN-ALLIANCE

The social actions, questions, and curricular connections that made up civic learning at Parker required that we build foundations for leadership-in-alliance. The educational structures available to us emphasized subject matter learning and college readiness, not developing capacities for collaboration across differences—though these capacities are needed in every area of life, from the classroom to the home to the workplace. To develop a wider range of action, work, and learning we created more pathways for "working with." These projects offered us a field where we could, together with our partners in other schools, practice democratic education.

How, within and across an unequal educational system, could we create more democratic environments, attitudes, and activities? Dewey (2008) articulates the problem with precision:

> A democracy is more than a form of government; it is primarily a mode of associated living, of conjoint communicated experience. The extension in space of the number of individuals who participate in an interest so that each has to refer his own action to that of others, and to consider the action of others to give point and direction to his own, is equivalent to the breaking down of those barriers of class, race, and national territory which kept men from perceiving the full import of their activity. These more numerous and more varied points of contact denote a greater diversity of stimuli to which an individual has to respond; they consequently put a premium on variation in his action. They secure a liberation of powers which remain suppressed as long as the incitations to action are partial, as they must be in a group which in its exclusiveness shuts out many interests. (p. 101)

We cannot fully develop when we are isolated by race, class, and culture; the more connections across difference we experience, the greater our range of responsiveness in life. Democratic education, then, is concerned with the relational capacities all people need to develop. How could we increase the number and diversity of "points of contact" people in schools have with one another and with people outside of the school?

For guidance, my colleagues and I looked to the most sustainable democratic organizations we could find, where people deliberately experimented with challenging power, both politically, through cross-race, cross-class coalitions, and internally, through attention to what Guinier and Torres (2003) call "embedded hierarchies" that play out in relationships of people within and around the organization. As I mentioned in the Introduction, the 120-year-old Hull-House (still going strong in Chicago albeit in a different iteration) offered a rich history for our study. Another important model was Highlander Folk Center, which began in the 1930s and today continues its legacy of incubating social movements. In what follows, I discuss the development of leadership-in-alliance through a focus on Highlander.

Highlander was modeled after the Danish Folk Schools that Myles Horton visited in 1931. In describing the Folk School as a "School of Life," Bishop Grundtvig proposed that "the people would find their identity not within themselves but in their relationship with others" (Ball & Larsson, 1989). From the informal, life-based, artistically vibrant folk schools, Horton concluded, "The job is to organize a school just well enough to get teachers and students together *and see that it gets no better organized*" (Horton et al., 1997, p. 51). Like the Folk Schools of Scandinavia, at Highlander people spent as much time singing and dancing as they did on political education. Throughout the generations of Highlander's life, and throughout the social movements it has fostered, it has retained an organic character, its processes never hardening into fixed methodologies.

Horton's educational philosophy is that democratic life arises from a belief in the power within and between people, which no formal systems can contain or sustain:

> The universe is one: nature and mind and spirit and the heavens and time and the future are all part of the big ball of life. Instead of thinking that you put pieces together that will add up to a whole, I think you have to start with the premise that they're already together and you try to keep from destroying life by segmenting it, overorganizing it and dehumanizing it. (Horton et. al, 1997, p. 130)

On the one hand, Guinier and Torres (2003) note that the conflict that surfaces in racial justice work was there all along; on the other hand, Horton says that the unity of all things has been there all along. Both perspectives offer a phenomenological understanding of education that encourages democratic experimentation: "It was essential that people learned to make decisions on the basis of analyzing and trusting their own experiences, and learning from that what was good and what was bad" (Horton et al., 1997, p. 57).

One famous example of this process is Rosa Parks's role in sparking the bus boycott that helped to launch the Civil Rights Movement. Like many other participants in the Civil Rights Movement, Parks was trained at Highlander and came onto the bus in Montgomery on December 1, 1955, prepared to take action against the racist system. Furthermore, Parks, along with countless other African American activists, had been part of civil rights education and organizing in Montgomery for years.

Disregarding this context of the bus boycott, the conventional version of the story casts Rosa Parks as a lone heroine, omitting the collective action by which the bus boycott was prepared and carried out. This version of the story rejects democratic power, as Meira Levinson (2012) notes:

> Instead of a story about a mass-organizing movement—a narrative of empowerment and agency among ordinary people who in a single weekend printed 52,000 leaflets (enough, and then some, for every member of Montgomery's

black community) and distributed them to churches while organizing phone trees and Monday morning car pools so that no one would have to walk to work—we meet the singular figure of Mrs. Parks. Together with King, she sets out on her civil rights walkabout, only to return to lead a passive and faceless people in their struggle for racial equity. (p. 161)[6]

Highlander fostered leadership-in-alliance by holding space for people's reflection and dialogue on their life experiences and encouraging ongoing experiments in collectively led social change.

Challenging the Geography of Segregation

Toward the beginning of *The Long Haul*, his story of Highlander Folk School, Myles Horton tells a story of organizing an interracial YMCA banquet at an Atlanta restaurant in 1950. The mixed-race group came in through the back door and sat down at the tables. The waiters walked into the room and took a look around—and refused to serve them. Then, Horton asked the restaurant staff what they were going to do with the food for 120 people they had prepared. Faced with the practical reality of instantly losing thousands of dollars, the restaurant backed down and served the interracial group. Horton did not make a moral argument; he set up the situation in accordance with his objectives and put the restaurant in the position of having to scramble to practice business as usual. Horton explains, "I just reversed the process that was going on in churches, universities, and schools, and over 120 people learned that they could change things if they wanted to" (Horton et al., 1997, p. 18).

These are the kinds of stories of social change that Horton loves to tell. They are not stories of triumphant marching and fiery speeches but of quietly making change by making good use of the back door—which often takes the banal form of manners and money: the pragmatic, not idealistic, domain. Ideals and ideas can be unreliable; Horton preferred the solid ground of response in the here and now.

Horton is also talking about allowing for a particular kind of chemistry to take place within a person, rather than setting out a program for development. "If you want to change people's ideas," Horton says, "you shouldn't try to convince them intellectually. What you need to do is get them into a situation where they'll have to act on ideas, not argue about them" (Horton et al., 1997, p. 16). At Highlander, people learned together how to respond to challenges and opportunities in the immediate moment by exercising presence strategically: This was the kind of action that led to real change.

Such change converts internal processes into collective energy. Highlander stirred up resistance, reflected in stories like Maxine Waller's: "Myles taught me to say, 'Hell no. I don't like the world the way it is and I'm going to change it.' I hope I can get a lot of people to spend a lot of sleepless nights. I haven't slept well myself" (Ayers, Hunt, & Quinn, 1998, p. 154). Collective work grows not out of mental or moral reasoning but out of a felt sense of urgency, which needs to be shared, uncomfortable as it is. As Guinier and Torres (2003) described it, "shared fates." As we saw in Chapter 1, social action is transformative when, like a ritual, it connects with intuition, feeling, and the body and is not limited to a person's reasoning and will.

Internal and external processes intersect to lead to social change, as Bernard Lafayette's reflections on Highlander suggest: "We had become convicts: convicted and jailed by the courts, and convicted by our principles. Our convictions drove us, and they were inescapable" (Ayers et al., 1998, p. 155). The double meaning of *convict* expresses the power of commitment to justice that holds a person faster than any jail cell. Paradoxically, this conviction is liberatory: Collective commitments help people to shape their identities outside the boundaries prescribed for them by an unequal society (Greene, 1988).

As a space where people learn from one another about collective commitments, Highlander represents a crucible of leadership-in-alliance that has fostered the most successful social movements of the last century. At Highlander, people learn to "tell new public stories," to use Marshall Ganz's phrase for the activity that builds "charismatic community." These public stories are counternarrative, enabling people in social movements to "focus less on allocating goods than on redefining them—not only on winning the game, but also changing the rules" (Ganz, 2010, p. 509).

Unlearning

At Highlander, people learned through ongoing observation, exploration, and self-reflection. Horton describes how people with educational and cultural privilege learn to be part of social movements, seasoned guidance for cross-race, cross-class alliance building today. Early Highlander leaders were middle-class White people who did not live with the same vulnerabilities as the people who were coming to Highlander for workshops. They did not ignore or underestimate these differences. In order to create the space for the catalyzing work of convergence to happen, people of privilege had to go through an ongoing process of "unlearning." Horton (Horton et al., 1997) explains:

> The biggest stumbling block was that all of us at Highlander had academic backgrounds. We thought that the way we had learned and what we had learned could somehow be tailored to the needs of poor people, the working people of Appalachia. . . . We ended up doing what most people do when they come to a place like Appalachia: we saw problems that we thought we had the answers to, rather than seeing the problems and the answers that the people had themselves. . . . We had to learn a new language . . . we spoke

many foreign languages . . . but the one language we lacked was the one the people spoke. Since we didn't have the right language, we had to learn to observe people: to watch the way they related to each other, how they took care of their kids, and to be sensitive to their reactions to their experience. (pp. 68–69)

Not having the answers enabled Highlander leaders to expand their capacities as witnesses. This was not a passive witnessing; Horton's stories make it clear that witnessing is both sustainable and sustaining.

Over and over again Horton says *we have to keep learning*. He presents a dynamic spirit of humility, and makes very productive use of ignorance. He simultaneously widens the space of equality and models critical questioning. "What, you want us to eat separately? I don't understand." "I'm not allowed to hand out flyers? I don't understand." By ignoring the expectations of the status quo, Horton playfully topples its authority. At Highlander, the intertwining of song, dance, and social action helped to loosen the constraints of intellectual language and habits of thinking.

Unlearning requires self-reflection, which Horton calls "knowing yourself." Horton recognizes his tendency to identify with people, and he has to remind himself:

> Look, Horton, get as close to people as you can, have as much interest as you can, but don't get things mixed up. You're white, and black people can't say they are color-blind. Whites and white-controlled institutions always remind them they're black, so you've got to recognize color. (Horton et al., 1997, p. 195)

The honesty of self-reflection is generative. Far from being a cause of guilt or antagonism, "knowing yourself" creates more space for connection.

Horton emphasizes that collective consciousness is liberating for everyone, privileged as well as oppressed. He writes,

> I think that we may all be mixed up psychologically but I don't think that we are going to solve our personal problems just by searching our souls or getting a professional therapist to help us work out our internal, individual problems. I think these problems get resolved much faster in action, preferably in some kind of social movement . . . you don't have to work out your problems alone, one by one. When people get involved in a movement, they must take sides, and in the struggle, individual problems become less important or disappear altogether. (Horton et al., 1997, pp. 93–95)

Horton is describing a paradigm shift from the isolation of individualism to the restorative power of collective work. Through political commitment— "taking sides"—people have a chance to loosen the constriction of inherited social (class, culture, race) roles, and consciously choose their group. Again, as Guinier and Torres (2003) argue, "political race" helps people confront the realities of the roles they have been assigned, and develop ways to move beyond those roles. This change upends the default narrative of helpless separation.

Highlander's focus on building space where integration could and must happen laid the groundwork for the Civil Rights Movement. People who went to Highlander experienced integration and generated ideas and strategies for making it happen back home. They found that racial integration generated more ripples of integration within and around them—they became more whole.

As a devoted grandchild of the Civil Rights Movement, I believed that aligning with Highlander practices could help to address the educational challenges of segregated schools and oppressed communities. I wanted to see how the Highlander way could be translated into school spaces and school days. Did one have to go far to have these kinds of experiences? How far? Could people create spaces between neighborhoods in Chicago, between schools, where people come together, and recognize one another's and their own humanity, and spread humanizing energy? Were there spaces in other cities that had been carved out specifically to allow people to come together from across neighborhoods, ethnicities, and cultures? Where the focus was not to develop a particular method or skill but to value and learn from one another's stories?

Highlander resists any kind of systematization, but the democratic educational practices it evolved over generations of ally formation include *relational learning*, *soaking up stories*, and *questioning hierarchical power*.

This book's articulation of democratic dispositions is rooted in large part in Highlander's model. The competencies that Highlander folk developed are eminently applicable to humanizing education. Such as:

- Capacity for power-with relationships
- Ability to analyze and creatively transform power
- Heightened self-reflectiveness
- Attentiveness to and interest in race, class, and culture in everyday interaction
- Humility
- Creativity

The rest of this chapter will show explorations of such informal education principles, which bear directly on work, learning, and life beyond schools.

Creating In-Between Space

As I researched schools across the country, I saw that schools that seek to build more equity within the school—and in society—by "taking care of" this requirement through one-off days, assemblies, or months did not see significant growth as a community that thrived in its multicultural life. They did nothing to shake up the "embedded hierarchies" of the school culture. Designated programs were more successful in holding the attention of the community on matters of race, class, and justice, but only moderately so. I saw that the more democratic practices are developed collaboratively and integrated into all areas of the school, the better they work.

However, it seemed to me that too often programs and lessons focused on *direct teaching* of multicultural awareness and social justice were not working very well. Lack of student engagement had toxic effects. I saw students from privileged backgrounds get defensive and shut off, and students from low-income backgrounds, or students who were gay or lesbian, get isolated. Schools were "addressing" social justice and diversity, knowing it needed to be done, but the methods were routinely hit-or-miss.[7] I saw that while the changes, opportunities, and complexity of our world require that we educate students for multicultural fluency and for social justice leadership, educational practices had not been developed enough to reliably do more good than harm.[8]

Isolation—and consequent lack of democratic skills—weakens students' intellectual capacities. When schools focus uncritically on individualistic and meritocratic systems of learning, they hinder the development of critical thinking (Giroux, 1988). As Maxine Greene (1988) writes, "There must be a coming together of those who choose themselves as affected and involved. There must be an opening of a space between them, what Hannah Arendt called an 'in-between'" (p. 17). For Arendt (and, following her, Greene), freedom was to be found not in private rights—physical needs and desires—but in the medium of public relationships (Arendt, 1958). Deliberate cross-school, cross-cultural gatherings provide opportunities for creating "in-between" space, allowing for the growth of new social capacities in individuals—leadership-in-alliance—as well as a stronger public life for everyone.

Highlander's model of leadership stands in contrast to the individualist orientation that prevails in leadership literature, expressed in formulas and methodologies, templates for goal setting, and personality analysis. Highlander is a place made of stories of people building the unpredictable, relational, in-between space of democratic leadership. It affirms the contingency that adolescents, like many other groups, experience, not the climb with the next stage in view, but celebrating the present moment that life in the "in-between" makes possible.[9]

In contrast to individualist models of community service, philanthropy, and leadership, the collectively based activity of community organizing creates domestic change.[10] The Highlander model helps people to develop organizing skills, beginning with a movement from an individual orientation to a collective one of "power-with." This is leadership that practices humility and recognizes dependence on others: It expresses *dialogic hunger.*

Highlander shows what it could look like for schools to provide stewardship for human connection and growth. Visiting different schools and studying popular education models helped me see that practice in border-crossing can take place within regular school structures, in any school, with any teachers and students, as long as growing in-between space includes the development of "political race." For, as I learned from experience, border-crossing isn't just a matter of going someplace: People need to carefully build in-between spaces. Applying the lessons from *The Long Haul* and *The Miner's Canary* help us to ground relationships in awareness and analysis of our own contexts. And, as all the singing and dancing at Highlander suggests, the arts help us to build out from there.

RELATIONAL LEARNING:
CROSS-CULTURAL EXCHANGE AS COUNTERNARRATIVE

> The thing I think that moves me so is the sudden sight of the Pacific and his men looking at each other. And I think that the men who are members of the crew who live with orders and regulation and a kind of naval bureaucracy, and they see that, and they look at each other with a wild surmise, I think how wonderful, I want my students sometimes to look at each other with a wild surmise. That's what moves me.
>
> —Maxine Greene

On a Martin Luther King Day holiday some years ago, I saw a drumming and dance performance by S.O.U.L. Creations, an after-school community group of African American, Latino, and White kids. I thought, wow, *that's* what this city should look like! I was amazed by the energy and *soul* of this interracial group, and I realized that the arts provide common ground for young people to come together across race, culture, and neighborhood boundaries within and between schools as well as out of school space.

Community arts educators know that when young people have access to organic processes of social learning, where they grow in an environment of rich, invigorating, and thought-provoking experiences, they develop clear vision and powerful voices. Creating space for border-crossing connections communicates to young people the value of relationship building and the faith older generations place in them. These experiences also provide fertile ground for self-reflection. As S.O.U.L. Creations founder Dr.

Gilo Kwesi Logan said to my students, "Traveling the world, I have come to see that many people want to change the world, but I often ask myself, how many of us are willing to change ourselves?"

There is much for people in schools to learn from our community arts colleagues. Community arts create border-crossing play that fosters connections between people from different backgrounds. Such experience, more than cognitive processes, leads people to develop a hunger for racial and cultural difference in their lives, and attention to difference heightens creativity and political intelligence. By participating in diverse social relationships, people develop more self-awareness and versatility (Ayers, Kumashiro, Meiners, Quinn, & Stovall, 2010). Meaningful cross-cultural relationships influence young people's future choices about jobs, housing, education, and policy. They develop a *collective orientation*, which becomes a base for public life. While young people need to learn to think for themselves, they also need to understand that there is much they cannot know, do, and *be* without others.

Social learning is not, however, easy. At Parker, we based part of our Civic Engagement program in social learning, inspired by models of cross-race, cross-neighborhood collaborations of organizations like S.OU.L. Creations, and often assisted by such arts-based groups.[11] When students look at the inequality that creates such different lives and options for them and their peers across town, discomfort and pain arise. Tim, a Parker 10th-grade student, comments after his first visit with the school his group partnered with:

> When we met with the other students it was difficult at first to intertwine with them. Everyone felt uncomfortable with each other. I think that it was only uncomfortable because we live in different areas of Chicago and there are huge differences between them. I remember one kid told me that his neighborhood used to be full of White people but then a few Black families moved in and the White people migrated north. This really made me feel bad because people hurt him and his family not by discrimination but by avoiding them.[12]

This student is grappling with the history of injustice in the present moment, in the space of an encounter with a peer living with the legacy of systemic forces of segregation. He is starting to see how a heritage of racist economic policy and White privilege has divided him from his peers throughout the city.[13] Our histories live not only within us but between us; systems of power that have separated people over time in the form of slavery, segregation, prejudice, and racist laws continue to reverberate in and around us.

Contact with new perspectives, voices, and experiences, mediated through the arts, helps people to recognize and confront old patterns of injustice. Later in the year, another Parker 10th-grader describes the energy that differences between the students provides to the group as they make music together:

> An interesting moment that happened during our group's composition process was when I noticed the incredible creative synchronicity and group chemistry formed after a couple minutes of work. [Among the] things I learned about how society interacts is that bringing groups together, whether they are from different communities or not, makes collaboration a fusion process. Collaboration for a common cause is much easier than I had expected, if only people could change their focus and attention to things that matter around them, within their local area, and areas adjacent.

Patrick was struck by the fact that the difference between the students of different races could itself be a powerful point of connection, what he calls "synchronicity." People who do not know one another can struggle in their first encounters, yet when youth from different neighborhoods come together to examine and challenge barriers of segregation, they are often amazed to find how quickly they connect.

While some students talk about such experiences as "life-changing" and "healing," it is not all feel-good. These border-crossings can be awkward and even agonizing. Students are often uncomfortably aware of their own assumptions—especially their assumptions about one another's assumptions!

Teacher leaders want to make sure they take this opportunity of ongoing partnership and relationship building for students to talk with one another about race and identity across differences. Many teachers feel that it is their responsibility to expose young people to more faces and voices, to give them the chance to build a wide range of relationships. One effect of this exposure is that students who have been steeped in "dominant-group hegemony" start to question it—an activity which is fundamental to multicultural literacy. Democratic society requires that students learn to engage "in a process of attaining knowledge in which they are required to critically analyze conflicting paradigms and explanations and the values and assumptions of different knowledge systems, forms, and categories" (Banks, 1990, p. 126). Young people have been handed a segregated and unjust world. When teachers involve students in more intentional ways of doing things and relating to one another, they are helping them to develop counternarratives that expose and undo injustice.

Democratic Dialogue?

Counternarratives and dialogues are provisional and experimental. Because they challenge prescribed social patterns, they are full of questions, doubt, analysis. Democratic dialogue actually begins with the question of whether democratic dialogue across differences is actually possible. As Nicolas Burbules writes:

> Dialogue in the sense of an egalitarian, reciprocal, respectful model of interchange may be unrealistic to expect in many situations in a society divided by prejudices and imbalances of power—and attempting to do so places certain vulnerable individuals and groups disproportionately at risk. (Boler, 2006, p. xvi)

Dialogue cannot be democratic if it serves people from dominant culture but increases the vulnerability of people of color, low-income people, and gay and lesbian people. Though dominant culture often disregards the context that permeates people's words, acts, and presence, people who are marginalized do not have the privilege of dismissing context. Creating the conditions for context-specific exchange is an act of purposeful resistance.

This means asking uncomfortable questions. "Who is dialogue for," as Burbules asks, "and what is it supposed to be about: Is it a means of solidarity-building within homogenous groups of the subjugated? Is it a way of sharing personal (or group) perspectives and experiences with others not like you—or does this promote a kind of voyeurism that abrogates personal responsibility?" (Boler, 2006, p. xxx). Keeping alive questions about power and privilege does not shut down dialogue, but it ensures that the dialogue will take participants into new places within themselves as well as in the city.

Miguel and Francisco Guajardo (2013) offer a framework for the personal and political work of democratic dialogue that emphasizes context, voice, and place. Plática is a practice of culturally grounded conversation that emerges from Mexican culture, and has in recent years entered university as well as K–12 and community education contexts in the U.S. "When engaged in plática," the Guajardos write, "we learned you have to pay attention to the story, to the form of the story, to the environment surrounding the story; you have to pay attention to the question, to the form of the question, and to context" (p. 160). Plática supports learning that begins with one's own experience, in connection with others, and grows outward from there; it engages both critical analysis and cultural affirmation.

Students have mixed responses to the structures for border-crossing that their teachers set up as part of nuturing their leadership capacities. One cross-school partnership, for instance, exposes ambivalence when the students from a predominantly White, wealthy neighborhood and students from a predominantly African American low-income neighborhood discuss the question "Why haven't we met?" David, an African American student, needles his teacher about her insistent focus on racial awareness—then goes on to describe how he needled his White partner about his *lack* of racial awareness! He wrote in a reflection:

1. I have always enjoyed going to Francis Parker because I get to talk to other teens like me. Race isn't important to me and I felt like it was dwelled on too heavily. I mean, I know that because I'm Black and that they're White we will be different, but there are far more important and relevant things to talk about than to keep drilling on about the same topic. I'm just saying that basically it got on my nerves and I didn't want to talk about it. I wasn't uncomfortable about talking about it because I've had your class and we've talked about it countless times. However, I did learn new things about why they thought we haven't met even though all agreed with my first idea, that we all just live too far away from each other, also that transportation is difficult to and fro.

2. We started to talk about if you saw me on the street would you be afraid of me, and I feel like because they knew me that they couldn't answer the question honestly. Like, there was this time that my partner had used the term *colored people* and I guess that he meant Blacks, Latinos, etc. as a whole but I got offended and I talked to him about it. Although he said that he didn't know the correct term to use because it keeps changing and that different people take offense to different things. I wonder do they feel upset when we just refer to them as White people? Food for thought, I guess.

3. There wasn't much that we didn't talk about. We talked about what each of us saw in our communities, how people float to their own race, how stereotypes upset us all, how the police are racist on both sides, and how we felt. I believe we could have gone deeper into the conversation but Sam is a stickler with time. Andrew and I tried our best to keep him from any clock, but he had a phone. We talked about how African Americans and Latinos feel comfortable with one another and why. I made a joke and I still don't know if I went too far or not. I had said that Latinos are like our spicy other brother from another mother while White people are like a stepbrother that mama left in the closet that we really didn't want but we have anyway. Andrew and Sam laughed, but Andrew made a comment that made me think that I might have offended him. He said "Wow! That makes me feel better about being White!" I laughed and he laughed, but I still feel a little worried. This paper could go on for a while so I'll just end it with that.

The dialogue among David, Sam, and Andrew focused on edges: Geographic borders and the boundaries of racial identity become clearer the more these boundaries overlap in the course of their conversation. All the young men in this scene find themselves in risky territory, and they are aware of one another's protective mechanisms (looking at the clock, downplaying the significance of race) even as they seek out the safety of common ground.

Conversations about race across race catapult participants into charged metacognitive space, where they are attending closely to their responses, limits, and strategies, in real time. Metacognitive learning spurs realization of how much more one has to learn, and it ends not in conclusions but in questions and intensified thinking. Education for democratic leadership hinges on processes of heightening self-awareness through dialogue with others.

Many leadership and service programs emphasize the importance of developing a sense of social responsibility and civic efficacy through taking meaningful social action. These are important outcomes, but to be sustainable, they must be paired with supports for metacognitive growth. Effective civic education requires that educators and students resist the separation of academic learning from critical awareness of race, class, and gender.[14]

Democratic society implicitly relies on schools to cultivate a vibrant civic identity in young people. However, the academic discourse that predominates in schools cannot accommodate this learning. Where are the supports for the relational intelligence that people need if they are going to understand—and act on—economic inequality, racial identity development, and democratic transformation?

Oral Histories as Counternarratives

Regardless of their class or race, many students in segregated schools (whether predominantly White, Latino, or African American) experience their isolation as disempowering and dismissive. Democratic education addresses this isolation, by addressing how people understand self and other, and what it means to be part of a wider community. It cultivates appreciation for difference, and promotes awareness of interdependence.

However, relationships, and especially relationships that are impacted by historic patterns of inequality, cannot be engaged solely through the rational processes that schools and other institutions focus on to the exclusion of physical and social-emotional processes (Ochoa, Benavides Lopez, & Solorzano, 2013). The language and logic of schooling, like other institutions in American society, have been shaped by generations of mostly White, privileged men who understand their frame of reference as neutral and objective (and so, as the only legitimate frame of reference). To quote Audre Lorde's famous challenge, "The master's tools will never dismantle the master's house." When educational frames stand unquestioned, they perpetuate racial inequality (Ladson-Billings, 2009). Arts encourage people to challenge inherited logic by constructing respectful languages of human response.

Arts-based experiences provide situations that people cannot think or doubt or argue their way out of. Having a "third thing"—social arts—to focus on together helps students from different backgrounds to connect.

Social arts can take the form of physical projects like mosaics or theatre, or communication or advocacy projects in the form of political analysis workshops or campaigns for equitable school funding. A focus on the sharing of narratives—processes that allow people to make sense of their own lives—makes oral histories a particularly important social art.

Oral histories offer a means of integrating into school structures and curriculum the kind of mutual exchange that transformed people who came to Highlander. As Rick and Bill Ayers write, through oral history pedagogies,

> Students can approach the world as artists, filled with creativity and inventiveness, generative mistakes and sparkling epiphanies. Teachers can learn to take an attentive and supportive backseat, after sufficient preparation, and watch democratic education emerge from projects that the student themselves have learned to own. Through these projects, the stories that have been hidden, suppressed, and ignored begin to take center stage, and the real dimensions of one's community and its struggles burst forth and grab the mic. (Mayotte, 2013, p. 7)

The oral history process creates a structure that supports listening, and that proceeds from a foundation of honoring others' stories. Just as importantly, the oral history process involves *exchange*: Students engaged in oral history making are also telling their own stories, which enables them to reflect, open up, connect.

In sharing stories, people experience a form of authentic exchange that interrupts the habits and hurry that allow alienation to fester. "Stories are the oldest, most primordial meeting ground in human existence, their allure will often provide the most effective means of overcoming otherness, of forming a new collectivity based on the shared story" (Delgado, 2011, p. 239). Stories provide a meeting ground that allows people to hear one another across lines of difference, privilege, and injustice, and to develop solidarity. The absence of shared stories perpetuates a racist status quo: "Racial and class-based isolation prevents the hearing of diverse stories and counterstories. It diminishes the conversation through which we create reality, construct our communal lives" (Delgado, 2011, p. 239). By exchanging stories, people can overcome ethnocentrism, broaden their awareness, and heighten empathy. "Political race," which Guinier and Torres (2003) put at the heart of cross-race, cross-class social justice coalitions, can develop in the practice of this social art.

For example, in a recent oral history exchange, a Parker 10th-grader reflects on her experience sharing a personal story about her grandmother with a student she was just meeting from a partner school. That the students, a White girl and an African American boy, sat under the painting of Flora J. Cooke, the first principal of Francis W. Parker School and a leading progressive educator of the 20th century, is suggestive. Cooke is literally an icon of Francis W. Parker School, and Gloria's story hints at a conflation of her grandmother and Cooke—two matriarchs of meaning in her life:

> I was paired with a boy named Brian whom I had seen before, but never talked to. He was incredibly kind and respectful, but I didn't know this until later. When we first met, Brian wasn't too friendly. He wasn't unfriendly, but he just didn't talk much. It made me upset that I would have to share my very personal and close-to-my-heart story with him, because I thought that he wouldn't be interested. We went to the library, and we sat under the painting of Cooke. After I showed him my oral history, he looked at me and said, "Your grandma must have been a really, really amazing woman, huh?" My oral history was about my grandmother who died in February. She was my mom's mom, and we were very close. After we finished we talked more, and actually became friends.
>
> When we went back to the room, the art teacher led us in a project based on the AIDS Quilt. We were to make a square with a silhouette in the middle and a border design. They would be sewn together to make a quilt about nonviolence, antibullying and standing up to gang violence and drugs. Brian decided that he wanted the outside border of our piece to be the female symbol with a bomb on top. Based off my grandmother. He said not only was she "the bomb" but it can also show that everyone is powerful, and that no one should feel as if they can't stand up for themselves.

The interweaving of students' stories widens the circles of their lives. Gloria's conversation with Brian shifted a personal, private experience of loss into a shared event. The quilt that the students from different neighborhoods create together is a physical manifestation of what they have been weaving in the in-between space of their partnership. Brian's affirmation of Gloria's love for her grandmother expresses the relational learning of this scene; it adds a new range of values to her life and understanding. These values are epitomized in Brian's feminist gesture, emphasizing the power of connection over the fragmentation of violence and segregation.

SOAKING UP STORIES: ORAL HISTORY FOR DEMOCRATIC LEARNING

> My father was a fireman for thirty years, and on his days off he worked at a music shop delivering televisions and furniture. One day, with his partner, Elmer Cantor, who was a black man, they were delivering a television set in River Forest, and when they got to the door, the woman asked Elmer to take off his shoes,

but didn't ask my father to do that. My father said, "Elmer, this television's going back on the truck. She ain't getting it." I always remember that.

—John Donahue, interviewed by Studs Terkel

Oral histories as curriculum change the usual patterns of education. Instead of adults imposing on them what the adult world has deemed educational, students, with their own questions, are coming to adults and asking them to share their experiences and stories. Young people are framing and leading the exchange, not adults. The words and ideas of oral histories have a subjective weight for the students collecting, organizing, and sharing them—unlike textbooks, tests, and other forms of "objective knowledge," which come at them from the outside and from above. "Oral history projects empower students with an inclusive and participatory vision of the world" (Mayotte, 2013, p. 4). Oral histories foster curiosity and empathy: They evoke *dialogic hunger*.

Oral histories express the respect for real and regular human beings that is at the core of democratic education. They help to illuminate the context that surrounds relationships and power dynamics, inaccessible to and unnoticed by traditional curriculum. Unlike the impersonalism of written text, the voice conveys context and creates relationships (Ong, 1991). Respect for the voice holds space for the ongoing change of democratic life, the back-and-forth motion of interaction that dislodges fixed identities and ideologies. "Our art of listening," Alessandro Portelli (1997) writes, "is based on the awareness that we gain something of importance from virtually every person we meet" (p. 58). Oral histories, Portelli notes, "insist on the relationship of the individual and the public . . . they are usually stories of 'standing up to the big man'" (p. 7). As we saw in the exchange of students from different neighborhoods recounted above, oral histories register differences between people while fostering connection. Subverting prevailing hierarchies of knowledge, they build collective wisdom.

When Francis W. Parker School Civic Engagement leaders decided to plant our program in oral history work (I will discuss this collectively designed curriculum further in the next chapter), we were impelled in large part by our reverence for fellow Chicagoan and preeminent oral historian Studs Terkel. His collection of interviews of social justice activists offers a model for students learning to be oral historians. Additionally, Terkel's stories of Chicago leaders help students to see the marvelous concatenation of accident and willpower and mistakes and humanity that underlie the social justice history of our time. "There are nascent stirrings in the neighborhood and in the field, articulated by noncelebrated people who bespeak the dreams of their fellows. It may be catching. Unfortunately, it is not covered on the six o'clock news" (Terkel, 1983, p. xxv). By teaching the art of oral history, teachers illuminate pathways into the community where elders and allies educate young people by sharing their own lived accounts of historical processes. Perhaps more important, the stories of community experts often trigger questions about the legitimacy of the education students are receiving *outside of* the community's voices, struggles, and love. When teachers hold up voices of wisdom in the community and teach students to listen to them, they are communicating the limits of textbook information and urging students to question the authority of "the experts."

As oral historians, students learn how people make meaning of their stories. This meaning emerges largely in dialogue—the storyteller often comes to deeper awareness of the meaning of his or her story in the course of the questions and listening of the oral historian. Knowledge that emerges from context, shaped by the bodies, gestures, and experiences of speaker and listener, is counternarrative. By grounding itself in life experience, questions, and challenges, oral history breaks down the hierarchy that usually structures learning relationships. This dialogic learning takes place not in the isolated space normally associated with thinking and learning, but in connection, in the moment. It makes for a fuller *present*, both in time and in space. From these stories, students are able to construct maps and histories of their city that show consistent patterns—and suggest future possibilities.

QUESTIONING HIERARCHICAL POWER: ADULT ALLIES AND YOUTH LEADERS

> Words are nothing because you can lie or hide something behind them, like your boss does, and it's going to be difficult to get any guarantee that what someone is saying is the truth. . . . It's better to rely on instincts, emotions, feelings and good experiences with friendly people because they don't have the words to cheat.
>
> —Christina Nichol, *Waiting for the Electricity*

Teachers are oral historians par excellence. They listen to the stories of young people and often are transformed by them. "The degree to which adults partner with youth to draw on their ways of being, doing and sense making, determines the degree to which youth of various ethnic, socioeconomic, linguistic and other backgrounds feel alienated or welcomed" (Funders' Collaborative on Youth Organizing/Movement Strategy Center, 2012, p. 10). This activity, which I will discuss in the next chapter as "listening acts," is a critical foundation in the development of adult allies.

Xian Barrett is a teacher on the South Side of Chicago who has taught me most about what it means to be an adult ally. As a teacher activist, he takes his lead from young people, and from this place of loyal commitment, he fights at their side. For instance, listening to the stories of his students prompted him to publicly fight over-testing in Chicago Public Schools, which led eventually to his firing. He writes in a 2013 blog post,

> I think of my own students like Araceli Medrano who snuck into the principal's conference room to scrawl on the data board a powerful message, "Reading scores aren't everything. Reevaluate the rules you have imposed for next year because students and teachers agree the atmosphere is suppressive; we have all lost our spirits. Do not take offense; take action. Listen to those you work for," and then signed it in her own name with her graduation year.

Xian takes to heart his student's demand that educators "listen to those you work for." When he was fired as a consequence of his education activism, he wrote to supporters, "I thank you for your anger at my unjust firing, but I would ask you to reserve the same rage for the educations ruined by arrests on school grounds, over-testing and under-resourcing" (Barrett, 2013). Xian listens, he acts, and his students act with him. He and his students replace a vertical structure of schooling with a horizontal structure of learning, walking, and fighting side-by-side.

This teacher soaks up his students' stories; they become part of his identity and his work. He uses his platform as a teacher, as a movement leader, and as an internationally known writer and speaker to *broadcast students' voices*. This is the other side of oral history.

Adult allies cross the border between children and adults. They do this primarily through questioning power: drawing attention to the implications of these borders. They point out double standards and hypocrisy on the part of the adult world, including themselves. In this way, they model the work of both questioning power and self-reflection. Adult allies emphasize stories of mentors, but with a special emphasis on how these mentors challenged the rules. Shared struggle, handed down from generation to generation like a cherished heirloom, bridges difference and electrifies the present moment:

> Stories hold in their narrative layers, the sedimented knowledge accumulated by our progenitors. To hear a tale told and retold in one's childhood, and to recount that tale in turn when one has earned the right to do so (now inflected by the patterns of one's own experience and the rhythms of one's own voice) is to actively preserve the coherence of one's culture. (Abram, 1997, p. 181)

Not only do adult allies communicate to young people value for their older mentors; *they include young people among their mentors*. This is not patronizing recognition of young people's achievements or the cliché declaration that, "I learn more from my students than they learn from me"; it is being *changed* by a young person's words, acts, and life.

***

Connections, continuity, the long haul, sustainability—the porous structures that enable young people to soak up the stories of love and struggle—are excluded from schooling because schools are temporary at base and fragmented all the way through. Not just in terms of time and subject matter, learning over the course of the school day is, for too many students, separated from life and learning. Even more important at a human level, learning is structured so as to divide young people from other young people geographically *and* temporally. The political strength natural to learning processes, to youth, to change, too often dies stillborn, because students and teachers have to start over every year, every unit.

However, this is due to the individualist and "outcomes-based" bias built into education practices. In some democratic schools, teachers begin the year with the history of what has been, what previous years of students have done, and set the students the challenge of building on their predecessors' work. That's where the sustain is. And that's where the teachers are the bridges between generations, between past and future, clarifying and encouraging and sustaining the interests of the young as over against the interests of the old, which are what now governs education. Teachers can be godparents to a continuum of democratic youth leadership, but these capacities atrophy in a standards-based educational regime.

Democratic education involves adults questioning themselves, questioning authority, banding together with students in wondering, wandering, speaking up—not necessarily being on equal ground but foregrounding what difference it makes that they're not. And strategizing together playfully, conspiratorially, on how to exploit the differences. The next chapter will explore how teachers do that, in the company of one another and their students.

CHAPTER 3

Unruly Teachers

Collective Reflective Resistance

> Knowledge emerges only through invention and re-invention, through the restless, impatient, continuing, hopeful inquiry human beings pursue in the world, with the world, and with each other.
>
> —Paulo Freire

The Children's Crusade

> Don't worry about your children; they are going to be alright. Don't hold them back if they want to go to jail, for they are not only doing a job for themselves, but for all of America and for all of mankind.
>
> —Martin Luther King, Jr.

When Martin Luther King reassured the parents of Birmingham's African American children, he sounded a lot more confident than he had been a month before, when he first realized that the children were preparing to occupy the Birmingham jails. In April 1963, Dr. King had just emerged from solitary confinement, where he wrote his famous tract on civil disobedience, "Letter from a Birmingham Jail."

In that letter, he wrote,

> I am in Birmingham because injustice is here. . . . I cannot sit idly by in Atlanta and not be concerned about what happens in Birmingham. Injustice anywhere is a threat to justice everywhere. We are caught in an inescapable network of mutuality, tied in a single garment of destiny. Whatever affects one directly, affects all indirectly. (King, 1963)

The White religious community of the South rejected King's call for solidarity, so King asked the Black people of Birmingham to join him in jail. They were reluctant. However, the Black children of Birmingham were ready to march. King's initial response to the children was "No!" Like their parents, he did not want to see them get hurt. They marched anyway. "Dr. King was severely criticized for allowing the children to be involved, but the children insisted themselves," said the Rev. Virgil Wood, a longtime King associate. "The children were the self-initiators of their own freedom" (Teaching Tolerance, 2004).[1]

The young people defied their parents as well as the laws. When 12-year-old Freeman Hrabowski announced that he wanted to march, his parents told him, "Absolutely not." "Then," Hrabowski continues, "I did something you just didn't do back then. I asked them why they would take me to hear this man [King] talk about marching for better education, but tell me I couldn't do it. . . . My dad said, 'Boy, go to your room'" (Stewart, 2013). Hrabowski puts his finger on the quintessential contradiction that the young generation perceives in its elders: the split between political conviction and actual fulfillment of this conviction. Young people call on us to walk our talk, and we chronically fail to do so.

The Children's Crusade is a story of young people leading the adults in social change. Other examples of such actions in history and current reality abound—yet the stories are usually neither told in schools nor considered in education policy and practices. How is it that examples of young people embodying ideal citizenship are not *at the core* of education?

The omission of stories of youth leadership limits multicultural literacy and critical understanding of racial injustice. Stories of school walkouts, for instance, are essential to understanding power dynamics in schools—and how action to change these dynamics affects the wider society as well (Guajardo & Guajardo, 2004).[2] As Michelle Alexander, author of *The New Jim Crow*, said to Parker student filmmakers,

> You look back in history, and you see that so many of the major movements were driven by young folks, who weren't willing to believe the myths any more, who weren't willing to accept the status quo, who were willing to take great risks, and speak the truth LOUDLY, and we need that today. (Friend & Mullen, 2012)

Alexander points out that adult society binds young people not only in schools and in prisons but also in "myths" that perpetuate an unjust status quo—and that young people have the power to counter these myths.

This chapter will focus on adults who are learning by paying close attention to young people as leaders—not just as youth leaders, but leaders of social change for *everyone*. Central to this view is the recognition that young people are complete human beings, in themselves, as they are. This stance contrasts with a common assumption in education: Young people are deficient and need to be fixed.

My study of adult learning in this chapter will intensify the focus on *conflict* that previous chapters engaged. Here, I explore issues of political bias and power struggles, which bubble on the edges of education discourse but permeate all aspects of schooling—including teachers' very existence as teachers. "Too many teachers have stopped asking, 'Is this good for our kids,' because they fear that questioning authority puts their jobs at risk" (Weiner,

2012, p. 11). In an educational climate that imposes heavy stress on teachers and students, "Urban teachers must know how to create breathing space in an environment that is intellectually suffocating because of scarce resources and curricular mandates" (Weiner, 1993, p. 122). As Lois Weiner emphasizes, stifling conflict—and other manifestations of human beings intelligently engaging difference—depletes teachers both personally and professionally.

Teachers who reject the prevailing dictates about education to honor the vision and voices of children are practicing resistance. I propose that the ongoing democratic education of teachers takes the same form that I have been describing in student learning: self-reflection, questioning power, and dialogic hunger. The children marching, and the teachers marching for their children,[3] come out of a context of thinking, questioning, and dialogue. To emphasize the inextricability of politics from education, instead of describing scenes of activism and advocacy, I focus here on contexts of intellectual and pedagogical engagement.

Taking learning seriously means overturning the dominant narrative of authoritative knowledge, adult superiority, and meritocratic hierarchies, so that teachers are not only enabling students to be border-crossers, but themselves learning through border-crossing:

> By being able to listen critically to the voices of their students, teachers also become border-crossers through their ability both to make different narratives available to themselves and to legitimate difference as a basic condition for understanding the limits of one's own knowledge. . . . Such a position reconstructs teachers as intellectuals whose own narratives must be situated and examined as discourses that are open, partial, and subject to ongoing debate and revision. (Giroux, 2005, pp. 34–35)

The more attentively teachers focus on the importance of respect for the lives of human beings—their students, one another, their own working–breathing–thinking selves—the more powerfully they can resist authoritative schooling structures that discount the importance of differences between human beings.[4] This chapter, then, will discuss pedagogy that recognizes the presence of conflict and connection and works with them as elements of the common life.

Counternarratives of Conflict and Continuity

I begin this chapter's version of "teaching and learning on the verge" with my own story of politicization as a high school student catching hold of a crack of subversion that widened as I paid more attention to it. Then, I tell stories of two different groups of educators as they explore the boundaries between their institutional identities and their philosophical values, especially when these come in conflict. The first story is set among the 11th-grade Civic Engagement leadership team at Francis W. Parker School.

They are considering the relevance of Henry David Thoreau's (1849/1966) classic essay, "On Civil Disobedience," to questions about political bias in teaching and learning. The conflict that I focus on in the second story has to do with teachers learning to be adult allies to their students, experimenting with resistance to dehumanizing mandates and rules. The context of this story is a cross-neighborhood, cross-context group of teachers from different schools, museums, and community organizations engaged in reflection on practice.

These scenes spotlight institutional power—forces of coercion, based in government, school, or other spaces, that usually go unrecognized. I focus on moments that feature power conflicts, in the belief that studying conflict heightens awareness. Ignoring the realities of power threatens democracy—yet educators often avoid conflict and remain silent in the face of injustice (MacDonald & Shirley, 2009). Middle-class norms and moral systems pressure many educators to acquiesce to authority and suppress their own intelligence.

When conflict remains unacknowledged, important sources of personal and social power get lost. June Jordan (1985) urges us not to underestimate the democratic power of unmasking authority:

> If we lived in a democratic state our language would have to hurtle, fly, curse, and sing, in all the common American names, all the undeniable and representative participating voices of everybody here. We would not tolerate the language of the powerful and, thereby, lose all respect for words, per se. We would make our language conform to the truth of our many selves and we would make our language lead us into the equality of power that a democratic state must represent. (pp. 30–31)

The particularity of individual voices counters institutional controls, challenging systemic power with the songs and curses of local power.

"Local" means more than *place*; it takes body in the interaction and relationships that happen in a place. When education is local, it can feel and look like a beehive. As we saw in Chapter 2, students spring out from the school and collect information, perspectives, and stories that they bring back and process, together. The school-hive has solid structures to support this processing and to ensure that each student's experiences are integrated into the hive. The processing that happens within the school-hive sustains the ongoing growth of the hive: learning and working and being together. The honey of wisdom sustains the life of the hive. A vibrant learning community cannot grow from a papery diet of information, expectations, and agendas imposed indiscriminately from the outside.

Young people going out from the school and learning in the community are also engaged in the important work of pollination. What is more generative for democratic life than the spreading of resources, perspectives, and relationships that comes from young people talking to one another across neighborhood, race, and culture lines? They can do this when teachers and students are supported in education that is slanted toward the local.

CIVIL DISOBEDIENCE CLASS:
A PEDAGOGY OF HEARING MANY VOICES

> If (the law) is of such a nature that it requires you to be the agent of injustice to another, then, I say, break the law.
>
> —Henry David Thoreau

1984: Liberation Theology Meets Catholic School

When I was a senior in a Catholic girls' school in California, my English teacher taught Shakespeare through comic books and hung out with the girls curling their hair and putting on makeup in the back of the class. The one expectation she had of us was that we give speeches. I do not remember mine, but I do remember one classmate's speeches. Anita was smart and kind; students and teachers alike adored her. One of her speeches was about the importance of wearing seatbelts. She was impassioned—perhaps that's why the speech stuck with me; I could not imagine getting so worked up about such a dull topic. But she was a little more nervous about her next subject, which was more controversial and complex.

Anita's second speech was a defense of U.S. policy in Central America. She pointed to the ravages Daniel Ortega's communist government had wreaked on the economy of Nicaragua and explained the dangers of communism spreading in Central America. As I listened to her, I wondered how someone as thoughtful as Anita could ignore the atrocities being committed by U.S.-armed soldiers in Central America, and could believe that our government was in the right.

Later, in Religion class, a small man with clear, bright brown eyes came in and talked to us about his region in El Salvador, where soldiers, armed and trained by the United States, were massacring whole villages: men, women, and children. Villagers dug tunnel systems to hide—but how long could they hold out? Father José Alas told us about Oxfam's underground rabbits and honey campaign: The rabbits were a nutritious, transportable source of food the villagers could rely on; the honey was to give the babies, so they would not cry and alert the soldiers to their presence.

Rabbits and honey and underground. This trio of images—subversive, quiet, practical—was to become an icon of social justice for me. I asked our guest speaker about the relationship between the rabbits and the honey and the liberation theology that I had heard people talking about on the news. Instead of explaining, Father José invited me to come to the next talk he was giving, at a local church. I went, and after that, I just followed Father José around the diocese as he gave his speeches. I saw that he was going far beyond raising money for rabbits and honey—those were the gateway stories and actions. He was trying to get well-intentioned (read: *complacent*) Catholics to challenge their government's policies and actions. I came to realize that liberation theology in suburban America meant educating people to criticize the societal structures that condoned oppression, especially the church and the government.

Archbishop Romero had recently been assassinated, and enormous numbers of clergy in addition to students, workers, and others continued to be killed. However, in the suburban Catholic schools and churches I sat in, Father José—seen by many as a renegade priest—was the only person talking about it. Father José was trying to get Catholics to see that their faith required that they take part in struggle, take risks, take sides. "The denunciation of injustice implies the rejection of the use of Christianity to legitimize the established order" (Gutierrez, 1973, p. 115).

I saw my Catholic school expel a student for getting pregnant and remain silent about the deaths of thousands of innocent people in Central America. Pope John Paul II's 1979 statement on liberation theology appeared to be the only word that mattered in our churches: "*This conception of Christ as a political figure, a revolutionary, as the subversive of Nazareth, does not tally with the Church's teachings*" (I. 4). We were taught that the Pope was infallible, but a liberation theologian was making the rounds of the diocese countering the Pope's pronouncement. I got a feeling that the nuns in charge of the school were glad the Religion teachers were bringing in speakers like Father José, even if they did not encourage discussion about them.

As a student, I was confused about these contradictions, which nobody spoke to. As a teacher, I am still confused about political contradictions that pervade educational life: encouraging students to "own" their education while controlling almost every moment of their waking lives with classes, homework, and other required activities; teaching the importance of civic engagement while myself skipping out on important community events; and so forth. I do not think I am freer from hypocrisy than my own high school teachers and administrators were, but it is important to me that I am in a place where people speak up about contradictions and wrestle openly with them.

I offer some scenes from a social justice curriculum unit at Francis W. Parker School in Chicago as an example of colleagues experimenting with acts of resistance. The teachers' exploration of the boundaries between politics and education registers in students' dialogue about public relationships.

2011: Civil Disobedience Meets Private Progressive School

What is the relationship between individual interest and collective benefit in democratic life? Who is the collective? Who decides what is in the interests of the collective? With what authority? As an institution that guides people in studying these questions, the school lives in the democratic space of tension between independence and community.

For our 11th-grade interdisciplinary team of seven U.S. History and American Literature teachers who coplan civic engagement curriculum, activities, and coordination with other areas of the school, these questions are omnipresent. They have implications that are both practical (do we always have to assign the same readings in order to align our shared objectives?) and political (does democratic mean offering "two sides" to every position we expose the students to?).

The Francis W. Parker School, founded in the Progressive Era, is rooted in what its first principal, Flora J. Cooke (1912), called "the social motive." In this philosophy, committed action takes precedence over intellectual accomplishment: "The establishment [of the social motive] as an impulse in school makes of work there a real and worthy thing, converts school activities into earnest living, creates and trains for mature society the sine qua non of its existence—people of social conscience and social power" (p. 11). In "real and worthy" work, young people help their society to develop in social responsibility.

In its founding, Parker was charged with carrying out political and social values: "*The needs of society should determine the work of the school*" (Parker, 1937/2001, p. xix). There is here a question of selection—who chooses which "needs" are to be addressed, and how? Is "the work" intellectual, a matter of analysis and understanding, or is it engagement, social action? Are "the needs of society" social, do they demand disruption of an unequal status quo? Or are they economic, corresponding to mechanisms for training students for careers or employment—according to their station, decided by the income level of their parents? At Parker, the teachers both independently and collectively choose how they will approach the relationship between education and society. Different teachers decide differently, and we argue about it. This difference is valued. We share a conviction that teachers' judgment is a professional right, and that a depoliticized teaching force weakens education. Correspondingly, students are trusted to be able to make up their own minds about their values and actions: They are not treated as fragile or docile beings who will be corrupted by a teacher's opinions.

Indeed, our civic engagement is based on the opposite premise: Social action helps people come to understand an issue more precisely and holistically than studying about it on computer screens. We encourage students to take sides and challenge them to reach beyond the "neutral" stance that feels more comfortable. Students in my immigration justice group, for instance, learned more about immigration issues by attending a rally supporting undocumented students' dreams of higher education than by reading "objectively written" articles back in the classroom.[5]

On Teachers and Students Taking a Stand

Our interdisciplinary program works intensively with controversy, starting with the annual Henry David Thoreau Civil Disobedience Lecture. Students read Thoreau's essay "On the Duty of Civil Disobedience," which he wrote to defend his stand against the Mexican-American War, specifically his refusal to pay war taxes that would go toward the spread of slavery. This refusal landed him in jail, where the famous (though probably apocryphal) interchange took place between the war tax resister and his friend Ralph Waldo Emerson: Emerson asked Thoreau what he was doing here in jail, and Thoreau answered "Waldo, the question is, *why are you out there?*" In "On Civil Disobedience" Thoreau (1849/2008) writes, "*Under a government which imprisons any unjustly, the true place for a just man is also a prison . . . the only house in a slave State in which a free man can abide with honor*" (p. 21). Thoreau expresses a perspective that courses through American literature and history and that young people can identify with: Rebellion is righteous!

Considering Thoreau's stance against his democratically elected government and against the views of the majority of his fellow Americans is fundamental to a civic education curriculum. However, the implications of the issues it raises about public identity and private values go far beyond the walls of the classroom.

Although Thoreau's 2-day incarceration was, in my opinion, too short to prove his moral stand, his writing helped to frame the work of civil disobedience for generations to come. "*Let your life be a counter-friction to stop the machine,*" (p. 19) he wrote, anticipating workers' protests that accompanied the industrial era decades later. Civil disobedience over the years has been defined by Thoreau's seminal words: "*A minority is powerless while it conforms to the majority; it is not even a minority then; but it is irresistible when it clogs by its whole weight*" (p. 22). The Civil Rights Movement a hundred years later actualized the power of Thoreau's words in a way that he never did in his own life.

As the 11th-graders mull over Thoreau's challenge to actualize citizenship through civil disobedience, they are also studying antebellum social reformers like disability rights activist Dorothea Dix and women's rights activist Elizabeth Cady Stanton and are meeting contemporary social reformers in the fields of housing, immigration, and other areas. Later, they will engage in social action themselves, but at this point in the year (November), the students are thinking hard about the work of reformers in bringing about social change: If activists do not see any progress on an issue in their lifetime, what keeps them going? Is social justice more often than not a fool's errand? For the culmination of our social reformers unit, we invite an activist to speak to the juniors—someone whose work resisting "unjust laws" is in the spirit of Thoreau.

Our annual Henry David Thoreau Civil Disobedience speakers have included war tax resisters (Kathy Kelly, who is at press time once more in prison) and resisters of a more violent sort (former Weather Underground member Bill Ayers). They are controversial, provocative, disturbing figures. While their stories are compelling, their realistic cautions to the students contrast strongly with their own actions: They urge students *not* to commit civil disobedience. However, civil disobedience can render a person larger than life, and our activists' reputations speak louder than their words.

Sometimes we get calls from parents asking questions like, "Where's the other side? If you're going to invite a war resister to speak, you should also invite a speaker who supports war."

Our response is this: *We are on the side of hearing many voices.* Democratic education means to us the inclusion of as many voices as possible—*and privileging voices that are numerous and under-represented.* We do not see this as taking sides so much as *taking a stand.* This program, shaped by *A People's History of the United States* and *The Grapes of Wrath*—and most of all by engaging with Chicago's community organizers, civil authorities, and workers—we foreground *voices.* Students study how systems of power are expressed in who has voice and who does not in American society. Questions of voice are important to students, who are keenly aware of the limits of *their* voices—and curious about how they might break through these limits.

Our civic engagement team engages in dialogue in the tradition of Progressive philosopher George Counts (1934), who spoke of education as "the struggle for survival that is ever going on among institutions, ideas, and values; it cannot remain neutral in any final and complete sense. Partiality is the very essence of education, as it is of life itself" (p. 534). We expect students to question their own and others' "neutrality." When people in schools avoid taking a stand, they are agreeing that their voices should not be heard in the world. Civic engagement prepares students to take a stand and involves curricular supports for students to decide what they will take a stand for. This is not to say that any and all stands students—or, for that matter, teachers—might take are valid.

Our team of teachers coteaches a social justice program within which we aim to welcome the views and involvement of all students regardless of political position. This is not easy. We are constantly walking the line, asking, "If a student is antigay, what's the place for him in our class? Anti-immigrant?" And, beyond the classroom, "If politicians and media channels are deliberately *miseducating* people to perpetuate the military industrial complex, is it my job as an educator to *counter* this miseducation for the people in my charge?" In civic engagement (and throughout our school), we constantly raise these questions; we discuss them with one another and with our students—and we reaffirm the importance of standing by our commitment to democratic education. As a member of our team said in one of our many conversations about political bias, "We [teachers] must be able to speak about who we are politically." Workshops with Diana Hess on teaching controversy helped us to navigate the field of "open" and "settled" questions with one another and with our students. "Democratic education," Hess and McAvoy (2015) write, "requires teachers to create a political classroom in which young people develop the skills, knowledge, and dispositions that allow them to collectively make decisions about how we ought to live together" (p. 11). This means deliberating together in an ongoing way about how to foster political engagement and mutual respect: In some school contexts, students are more able to engage when teachers "withhold" their political views; in others, they engage more when teachers "disclose."

At the same time, teachers are conscious that they hold power over students and students are keenly aware of their vulnerability in relation to this power. In his study of dialogue in the classroom, Jim Garrison (2006) writes,

> Those who assume they can create safe spaces to sustain dialogues across difference in technocratic institutions must ignore the terrible asymmetries and inequalities of power perpetuated by technocratic rationality and its technologies. . . . Often, instead of attempting to create safe spaces in their classroom, it would be better if teachers sought to grow in relationship with their students by rendering themselves vulnerable and at risk without necessarily requiring their students to do the same. (pp. 93–94)

In posing questions they don't know the answers to, teachers are vulnerable with students. Regulating political bias may not matter as much as working together to be upfront with students about questions about bias. The teachers of our civic engagment are aware that we cannot eliminate bias—and we do not think we should. We agree that the danger in bias is when we do not recognize it, or when we pretend it is not there.

When we share our concerns about bias with our students, we open ourselves up, as people, to debate and disagreement. This invitation to dialogue is, we believe, a requirement for teaching that respects both the student and the teacher.

Civic Education Through Oral Histories

Ultimately civic action is not a question of choosing sides or about political convictions. It means cultivating direct response to the present moment, in its complexity, beauty, and horror. It is an expression of freedom.

In this understanding, civic action does not stand apart from other subjects and ways of learning. It applies to artistic, intellectual, and social realms. Civic engagement is a mode of *being present* that crosses disciplinary boundaries. As I discussed in the previous chapter, oral histories facilitate boundary-crossing. There, I looked at oral histories from the perspective of students, with an emphasis on the responsiveness they engender. Here, I expand my discussion of oral histories with a focus on pedagogic frameworks. From the perspective of our teaching team, oral histories are important touchstones of democratic education: When our students have access to a range of voices and experiences that they can explore deeply, they think more and better.

This is because oral histories "amplify unheard voices" (Mayotte, 2013) and spark questions about the social and cultural forces that are shaping these stories. As teachers, we are choosing voices that will be heard. We are curators of culture. Teachers stand on the borders—between cultures, between child and adult worlds, and between fields of knowledge. This role requires that we hear many, many voices, have many experiences, and develop much experience in discerning what is important. We figure that out together. Gaining access to as many voices as possible strengthens students' cognitive development as well as teachers'. We teach oral history in part to challenge the hierarchies of knowledge—we are saying to students: The information you need about the world is here in your community, not only in our books. Your means of learning are the real-time use of your own voice and ears, not only reading the materials and practicing the skills that *we* declare to be important.

When teachers insist that students learn for themselves, when they encourage students in independent thinking, they are pushing against strong social controls. According to the educational model that has prevailed in America for well over 100 years, teachers are supposed to receive knowledge and methods that they pass on to students. New technologies, more information, and new opportunities have not fundamentally changed the passivity and obedience that underlies the education system, though here and there a school, a class, a student will rise up brilliantly. "We can't transform American society," Meira Levinson (2012) points out, "simply by transforming opportunities for one kid at a time. . . . schools need to teach young people knowledge and skills to upend and reshape power relationships, directly, through public, political, and civic action, not just private self-improvement" (p. 13). Education for social change begins with a shift from individualized notions of achievement, to learning that asks about and promotes the public good.

Civic education requires technologies of relational intelligence. Oral histories are a vehicle for educational relationships that lead both to clarity of mind and to questions, generating more complex, free, daring thinking. Similarly to the ritual act of *witnessing* discussed in Chapter 1 and consonant with my emphasis on the *play* of civic life, people doing oral histories create by rearranging the prevailing order.

Conflict, Commitment, Continuity

In February, our team of teachers meets with all the juniors to introduce the oral history project. We start off with one of our teacher leaders' stories of civil disobedience. I interview my colleague Andy Kaplan, who talks about his involvement in Students for a Democratic Society during the 1960s, an experience which led him into a life of activism. His story offers an example of an oral history as it unfolds. It also invites the students to consider how the political affiliations of their teachers might impact the learning experiences we design.

After this introduction, students conduct their own oral history projects. As they learn about social justice over the course of the year from Chicago activists on a wide variety of issues, the students become attuned to the personal and social ripples of the conflicts involved in public work. The impact of hearing the activists is more methodological than ideological: Students may or may not agree with their positions, but they learn from activists how to look out for and point out hypocrisies in laws and practices of people in power. This honesty helps young people to name and analyze a gap they already perceive between what they are told to do and be—and what people in power do and are.

Oral histories give young people close and meditated access to difficult dilemmas about power and justice that the adult world is grappling with. As examples to illustrate oral history pedagogy, I chose interviews conducted by students in the Civic Engagement group called Students for a Sensible Drug Policy (SSDP). One interview features a passionate advocate for drug law reform and one features a politically powerful—and equally passionate—defender of drug laws. The SSDP group, led by history teacher Jeanne Barr, has spent the year examining, debating, and advocating on the controversy. The students encountered different perspectives on the War on Drugs throughout the year and ended up deciding to advocate for medical marijuana legislation. The oral history project gave students the opportunity to deepen their inquiry into one of the perspectives they encountered that intrigued them personally.

The focus on the War on Drugs highlights the importance of multiple voices in understanding an issue. As with the larger issue of incarceration, many people accept the War on Drugs as a necessary societal protection; they do not ask who drives it, for what purpose, and whether or not it is working. Stopping to listen to the voices of people who are deeply connected to the War on Drugs—people who have been incarcerated for drug possession, people who design drug policy, or people who seek to change drug policy—takes listeners outside the zone of passive acceptance often expected of the public in relation to public policy.

Hearing different activists' perspectives on an issue helps students see conflict more from the inside than from the outside, with the attendant nuances, textures, and stories of this deeper perspective. In the process of conducting oral histories with activists, young people learn about dealing with conflict from people who in important ways make conflict their life's work, who wrestle consciously and creatively with conflict. When students have the chance to witness and reflect on this process, it helps them to recognize their own capacities for dealing with conflict productively in their own lives, to develop what Mark Gerzon (2006) calls "conflict literacy."

The differing perspectives students get from collecting, sharing, and discussing their oral histories take them beyond political rhetoric and positioning.[6] Oral history pedagogy centers on helping students gain access to a wide range of perspectives, especially perspectives that they do not usually encounter. Such multiplicity helps students to slow down judgment, to realize that things are far more contingent than they appear, and to begin to discern the interests and stakes of different players in different positions.

Students' comments convey this process of listening to and considering multiple voices. Two young women in the SSDP group have chosen to interview Dan Linn, an activist in drug law reform in Illinois. After conducting the interview, the students edit it to a 5-minute clip and post it on a wiki site for their peers to listen to. They also post a "question for listeners to consider while listening": "What do justice and injustice mean to you?"

The clip begins with Linn's definition of justice and injustice, which leads him to talk about his development as an activist. He focuses squarely on the repellent hypocrisy that his activism sought to challenge:

> When I was a student in college, I really saw how the War on Drugs, especially the prohibition of cannabis, was hypocrisy, founded and rooted in racism. It became like a patriotic duty to try to change these laws. I found myself questioning how proud I was to be an American, you know, learning what we did to the Native Americans, learning what we did with slavery, and stuff like that, and then to see this law that I really disagreed with, I saw it as an injustice that needed to be changed, so then it . . . sparked this political activism in me.

Linn grounds his opposition to the drug war in patriotism. His way of dealing with the horror of America's racist history was to fight the War on Drugs that criminalizes whole classes of people. Drug laws lead to mass incarceration, segregation, and divestment from communities—a mechanism of systemic racism that Michelle Alexander (2010) names "The New Jim Crow."

As part of the oral history assignment, students listen to several of their peers' oral histories, and post comments. They will later discuss the interviews and comments in class. The aim of this complex processing structure is to provide maximal circulation of the voices the students have chosen to feature, which they have distilled in accordance with their interests. Here are two excerpts of classmates' responses after listening to Dan Linn's interview:

> I think Dan's explanation that the drug war "is rooted in racism" is very interesting. This then again proves the persistent ways elite classes try to create methods promising their status and power.

> One section of this podcast that I found very compelling was when Dan Linn spoke about the paradox between what politicians believe and how they vote. He said many of the politicians will say to a patient that they believe that patient should have the right to use marijuana medicinally because they should have a right to control their pain. However, those politicians then will refuse to vote for medicinal marijuana legalization because it will affect their next election, or will make people in society potentially look at them differently. This is an extremely frustrating fact, and really demonstrates how politics work in this country.

The students listening to this oral history are clearly particularly interested in the hypocrisy of what Linn calls unjust drug laws. The first comment expresses the student's understanding of the racial profiling built into drug laws, with harsher and more frequent sentencing for people of color than for White drug users. The student sees the legal code reinforcing the privilege of "elite classes" and driving mass incarceration. The second student also focuses on the problem of self-interest over the common good—in this case, the legislators who will not pass medical marijuana legislation for political reasons.

Meanwhile, two other students have interviewed Peter Bensinger, who used to direct the U.S. Drug Enforcement Administration, and before that, the Illinois prison system. Like the students who interviewed Dan Linn, these students are interested in questions of bias and consistency. The students frame the clip they chose and posted with this "question listeners should be considering while listening": "What are the biases of teenagers versus adults, and liberals versus conservatives, when considering drug enforcement policy?"

Like Linn, Bensinger bases his position on medical marijuana in a systemic analysis. However, where Linn was analyzing historical patterns, Bensinger's analysis addresses social conditions on the ground. Arguing against medical marijuana legislation, he points to the availability of guns and the sparsity of education and employment supports that are connected with damaging marijuana use. He says,

> I don't think we want to get into the business of having incompetent people in Springfield, that is, our legislators, decide on what's medicine. . . . in terms of curbing drug use, we need to take automatic weapons off the streets. I would ban handguns . . . we need to have more economic opportunity for those with less education.

Students comment on Bensinger's interview:

> What an interesting and enlightening guy! I loved how instead of attacking the consequences of using marijuana, he focused on his personal solution towards eliminating the increase in usage of the drug. One thing I believe he emphasized was how crimes and drug use often are parallel to one another, and can be solved by putting more funding into our educational system.

> He . . . focuses on the people that it has harmed so gravely, to a point of no return as long as marijuana exists: victims from lower socioeconomic classes in public school systems around the nation. As he implores the necessity of lengthening the school day, both in curricular and extracurricular aspects, to help give potential students who could get swept into drug usage, dealing, and eventually dropping out of high school, he depicts an interesting contrast to the rhetoric of SSDP's cause. Where

SSDP campaigns for the legalization of medicinal marijuana to help the patient, Mr. Bensinger deplores medicinal marijuana out of the harm it does to the vulnerable student.

Both of these students were impressed by Bensinger's emphasis on the social context surrounding drug use. The second student explicitly challenges the paritality that he sees in SSDP's work, pointing to the "rhetoric of SSDP's cause." He highlights a different center of value that he posits as equally valid to SSDP's concern for patients in need of medical marijuana: He appreciates Bensinger's concern for "the vulnerable student."

Listening Acts

We teachers do not care so much which side of the issue the students end up on. We care that they are thinking about the issue, listening to other people and to one another. We believe that this information-rich society is dialogue-poor. By setting up multiple structures for dialogue that honor students' capacities for listening and discerning, we seek to habituate them to dialogue, lead them to seek it out and create it in the course of their lives. "When students engage in this kind of talk," Hess and McAvoy (2015) write, "it encourages them to move from the self-interested thinking of 'What is best for me?' to the deliberative question, 'Which option seems best for society as a whole, given varied views and perspectives?'" (p. 6). I call such civic activity "listening acts." They help people to widen their circle of concern as well as action, helping with the crucial shift from "me" to "we" (Hess & McAvoy, 2015).

In contrast to textbook-and-test learning, the oral history process is a form of experiential learning that mobilizes multidimensional thinking. Multiple layers of filtering take place, as the students listen to their narrator, then to one another's posted oral history, and to one another's comments online and in class. The emphasis on multiple perspectives affirms young people's need to make up their own minds rather than passively absorbing received knowledge (or opinions) from their teachers. These listening acts may or may not change their opinion on the issue, but they do make it more likely that students will prioritize thinking something through—ask questions, reflect, discuss—before drawing a conclusion. This is democratic thinking: "It is our commitment to communicate about and across our multiple perspectives that is the essence of democracy and the glue that holds a democratic society together" (Darling-Hammond, 1997, p. 48). Democratic society requires that people have the capacity to search out, insist on, and learn from, multiplicity. This is where oral history helps to form "the public."

Again, the pedagogy of oral histories expresses our bias as teachers. *We are on the side of hearing many voices, especially the ones that usually go unheard.* Our teaching emphasizes not just seeing different sides to an issue but hearing multiple voices, with the human bodies, inflections, cultures, accents in these voices. Underlying the collecting of activists' stories is a democratic bias: The people who are most affected by policies need to be part of shaping those policies.

ARTS OF TEACHING AND LEARNING DISSENT: CROSS-SCHOOL EDUCATORS IN PUBLIC SPACES

To resist a constricted educational vision and the devaluing of humanness, I offer humanness itself, I offer humanness as widely distributed capacity, as active making, as value, as resource, as scale, as process, and as responsibility. Drawing on my long history as an observer of children, I anchor this view of humanness in children and ourselves, as makers: as drawers, story tellers, painters, sculptors, builders, engineers, teachers, writers . . . as makers and remakers of a human world.

—Patricia Carini

In the previous section I touched on civil disobedience as a direct response to injustice. I want to consider other forms of resistance also, that, like civil disobedience, place demands on the resister as well as on the power she or he resists, and that proffer a different view of how the world could be. In this section I look at cross-neighborhood connections between teachers as a vehicle for resistance that is expressed in the politics of *who* gathers *where,* and *for what purpose.* This question involves confronting segregation, privilege, and mechanisms of power that affect the life work of education no matter what a teacher's or a student's political leanings. To focus on the "what" of education without equal consideration to the "who," "where," "why," and "with whom" is to miss the conditions needed for democratic life.

Education is social; it grows in and through relationships. Thus, collaboration should be the basis of teaching. Teachers should not be in their classrooms, separated from one another and from the rest of the world, responsible for the 20 or 30 or more human stories in the room that each holds infinite complexity *and* for delivering content assigned by noneducators—who are in places disconnected from the school, its neighborhood, and the lives of the people there.[7]

If they are not encouraged in resistance, in the conscious construction of counternarrative, teachers may perpetuate schooling routines that isolate their students as well as themselves. As Ingersoll (2003) observes, "Given the combination of a highly altruistic workforce, a highly isolating work environment, and high demands, it is not surprising that one of the most pervasive aspects of the culture of teaching is an ethos of individual responsibility and accountability" (p. 170). This ethos, which reigns unquestioned in most schools, is culturally marked: It aligns with values more commonly taught and believed in middle-class, White, educated households, and it is associated with success. A focus on individual success without equal attention to collective growth weakens schools—and the contributions our schools make to democratic life.[8]

The issue of teacher isolation cuts close to the bone in Chicago, a heavily segregated city that has been called "Two Chicagos," in reference to separate realities inhabited by middle-to-upper-class people who are predominantly White, and by lower-income families of color, many of which are African American and Latino. The boundaries between these worlds are difficult to cross. Thus, teachers and students who seek to come together across neighborhood, culture, and race boundaries must fight to carve out time and space for meaningful connections between them. When we do, we widen the boundaries of our classrooms and strengthen our intellectual muscles. We expand the space of democratic education.

"Poets of Our Own Lives"

In addition to the boundaries of location, our schools are subject to boundaries of inherited roles and canons that can hinder rather than help learning. In her account of curriculum based in community issues and needs, Carol Rodgers (2006) describes experiential learning as a living—and life-giving—creature: "The curriculum wanders over into life, eats big chunks of it, and comes back into the classroom permanently enriched" (p. 1273). But in many schools, she observes, "Students' experiences as learners lay scattered . . . like so many bits of colorful cloth that too often were never sorted, organized, analyzed, or put together into any explicit pedagogical design" (p. 1280). How do we practice democratic education that honors people's actual lives, from within hierarchically structured schools and disciplines that are not connected?

These disconnects are also debilitating for teachers when, instead of learning to grow as public intellectuals, they are trained to be "operators" of compartmentalized knowledge. Compartmentalization by discipline and grade level mirrors a more basic cognitive disconnect. Teachers get little support for the metacognitive work of questioning, reflecting, and discussing. Often, teachers are expected to assimilate methods rather than to do the intellectual work of examining their own experiences in and perspectives on education.

The educators who helped to shape progressive education over the past century put the teacher's intellectual and political work at the heart of democratic life. For example, 100 years ago, Chicago teacher and union leader Margaret Haley held up teachers as leaders in democratic society. She wrote that the "special contribution to society" of public school teachers is "their own power to think, the moral courage to follow their convictions, and the training of citizens to think and to express thought in free and intelligent action" (Hoffman, 1991, p. 293). Haley saw teachers as the protectors of democracy and rallied them to resist corporate influences on civic and educational integrity:

> Two ideals are struggling for supremacy in American life today: one the in-
> dustrial ideal, dominating through the supremacy of commercialism, which
> subordinates the worker to the product and the machine; the other, the ideal
> of democracy, the ideal of the educators, which places humanity above all
> machines, and demands that all activity shall be the expression of life. If this
> ideal of the educators cannot be carried over into the industrial field, then the
> ideal of industrialism will be carried over into the school. (Hoffman, 1991, p.
> 294)

The intellectual, social-emotional, and spiritual work of teaching focuses
on honoring human life. Defending human dignity in a profit-driven world
requires ongoing, determined, fierce battle. Teachers' unions today face
a similar challenge from market-based education policy. In her study of
teachers' unions as a force for social justice in America, Lois Weiner (2012)
observes,

> Minimally educated workers need only minimally educated teachers. Oversight
> of lowered expectations for educational outcomes can be achieved through the
> use of standardized testing. Therefore, a well-educated (and well-paid) teach-
> ing force, it is argued by elites establishing educational policy, is a waste of
> scarce public money. (p. 6)

Aligning education with the values and methods of free-market systems
makes children into products and tools in global competition. These assumptions, like the industrialists' control of education that Haley denounced
in 1904, undermine democratic education. Education practices rooted in
community values and the individual human lives in the school cannot be
sustained without the corresponding growth of the public that stretches out
beyond the school.

While undemocratic structures must be dismantled, my focus here is
on democratic practices people in schools can use even in undemocratic
environments. Reflective practices enable teachers and students to deepen
learning by grounding themselves in the present. This humanizing, democ-
ratizing process counters forces of impersonal, profit-driven education.

Democratic education is closely concerned with how we look at the
actual work of learning. The *teacher's* active learning stance is at the heart
of processes like Descriptive Inquiry.[9] Developed by educators around the
Prospect School and Prospect Institute in Vermont, this pedagogy cultivates
the art of description to help educators gain deeper knowledge of student
work, students' lives, and human relationships. This is creative intellectual
work, as Traugh et al. (1986) write, "a mode of expression and as an aesthetic way of knowing" (p. 3). By cooperatively applying artistic seeing
practices to the work of students and teachers, participants change their
own perception. Descriptive Inquiry processes are rooted in and expand
respect for people's work, whether the work be a 4-year-old's drawing of

a house or a hip-hop literacy exercise developed by a teacher. The shared activity of respectful engagement makes Descriptive Inquiry an important resource for democratic education.

Teachers engaged in inquiry challenge authorities of knowledge; in doing so, they change learning relationships. Reflective practice is focused on process, not product; this frees learning from functional, behavioral, and imaginative constraints propagated through tests and worksheets. Attending to the work of children and adults affirms the dignity of the work, the perceiver, and the human capacity for working and appreciating.

Reflective practice is resistant because it honors people's learning, work, and living as subjects in themselves, rather than as workers for external authorities:

> To affirm a view of our human possibility by calling attention to the widely distributed capacity of ourselves as makers and doers, in which works are understood as the self's medium, is an enactable educational, social, and political stance. For me that view of the self and the enactment of it offers a solid center and compelling aim for education: to be the poets of our own lives. (Carini, 2001, p. 52)

The experience of freedom conveyed in the notion of "poets of our own lives"[10] is more than intellectual engagement; it is social, emotional, and spiritual. A snippet of educators' reflections-on-reflection in the course of a conversation I heard at the Institute for Descriptive Inquiry gives a taste of this life poetry.

It is a quiet afternoon in August, and the educators gathered in the room from all over the country have spent the last couple of weeks at the Institute reading philosophy and poetry and novels together and discussing how they will approach challenges in their classrooms and communities and in education policy. Institute convener Cecelia Traugh is talking about "inquiry as resistance to standard ways of knowing things." Teacher Andy Doan adds, "Description breaks through habitual perception . . . the order that surrounds the seeing. What does it mean to be compliant with a system that privileges you? Compliance with an unjust order destroys one's humanness." Principal Olga Winbush comments, "We need to learn to resist the systems so we're not casting the kids into fixed places in the system. This work makes us look at ourselves so we don't practice oppression on any children." "Joy," Andy says, "is always in the encounter . . . the disruption and challenge joy offers to education. . . . 'I'm not singing because I'm happy, I'm happy because I'm singing.'" Collective reflective practice, the educators agree, enables them to "play cat-and-mouse with the standards." "It is the *play*," Cecelia says, "in the intellectual that makes it intellectual, not just content."

Throughout the country informal groups of teachers practice Descriptive Inquiry philosophy and practice (including a sister organization, North Dakota Study Group, which is the focus of Chapter 6), growing as public intellectuals in their home contexts. In Chicago, one of these groups, which I co-lead, is called the Teachers' Inquiry Project. This story is about teachers from schools throughout Chicago, who participated in a Teachers' Inquiry Project seminar. By reaching beyond boundaries of discipline, institution, and geography, these educators engaged in resistance to education that compartmentalizes, fragments, and dehumanizes.

"Teach-Ins in Public Spaces"

Three teachers meet in a crowded deli on a cold Martin Luther King Day in Chicago. We shake off the snow and settle in to plan for an experimental professional development session. Adam hangs a big sign on the table that says, "Teach-Ins in Public Spaces."

This is the third or fourth time this year my fellow Teachers' Inquiry Project leaders Joan Bradbury, Tina Nolan, and I have met Adam Heenan somewhere downtown under the umbrella of this sign. "Teach-Ins in Public Spaces" always adds a charge to the proceedings—the sign punctuates meetings with civic significance, draws in curious strangers, sharpens conversation. Adam's simple but grand theatrical gesture defies the unwritten rules and limits of public spaces; it reminds people downtown that though people in schools may be cordoned off from view, what happens in schools is inseparable from public life.

Adam is asking questions about his teaching of Civics: How do you measure civic engagement? When do students develop the language of civic agency for themselves? If leadership for social change is supported by a capacity for resistance, where does that connect with students' academic skills?

Adam is a young teacher leader who wants his students to gain awareness of their world and learn to organize for social change. In his work with students and with colleagues, he teaches dissent. He comes to social actions fighting for youth rights—and, as a member of the activist teachers' group CORE (Caucus of Rank and File Educators), Adam is involved in leading such actions too. In his classroom, part of a large Chicago public high school of mainly African American and Latino students, Adam, along with hundreds of other Chicago teachers, incorporates a dynamic "Action Civics" curriculum cooperatively developed by teachers with the support of an organization called Mikva Challenge.

Adam considers ongoing reflection to be vital to his professional growth and to the growth of the profession, and he has asked our group of teachers and community and museum educators to help him think through the connections between academic and civic learning.

Thus, the work of today's meeting is to design Adam's upcoming Review of Practice. In a couple of weeks we will meet in our larger group of educators; we will home in on concerns and commitments that drive

Adam's teaching, connecting them to the specifics of student work, achievement, and understanding. We want to explore the meaning of our work across educational contexts, to multiply the perspectives available to us. Through collective reflection on our own practice, we engage our professional responsibility as thinkers, learners, and innovators.

Review of Practice is one of a number of Descriptive Inquiry processes developed by educators at Prospect Institute (in recent years, renamed The Institute for Descriptive Inquiry) to engage teachers in phenomenological inquiry into learning. The Review of Practice is an opportunity for a teacher to describe and reflect on the goals, development, and challenges of his or her work in precise and artful ways. The teacher's own questions, considered in a circle of colleagues, are the core of this professional development practice.[11]

As we sit in the deli, the three of us decide that Adam's Review of Practice should connect with his final evaluation process for class since it is the end of the semester. In this planning session for our upcoming meeting of educators, we try to organize the time and materials carefully. We know we will have less than 2 hours for this Review of Practice, and we want to make sure that participants will be able to understand enough of the context to offer useful feedback during the session.

When our group of 12 school, museum, and community educators gathers a couple of weeks later for our monthly meeting, it is in one of our schools. Our meetings rotate between the school, museum, and community centers that the participants come from. Coming together at these different sites in the city, we are continually carrying out the charge implicit in Adam's sign: We affirm that our collective education work is part of what creates and sustains our "public spaces."

Common Language for a Common Life

The assembled educators begin the meeting with a close reading of Dewey's (1934/2008) article "The Need for a Philosophy of Education." In it, Dewey describes the intellectual work of teaching for democratic life—which includes naming and resisting the corporate forces that see human beings in terms of production instead of growth and change. Our close reading sends us into pressing questions about teaching and identity. How much of learning comes from what is within the student, and how much comes from outside—from experiences, ideas, and agendas that teachers, parents, and policymakers impose on the child? What processes help the teacher to partner with the student in balancing innate powers and interests with new stimuli and future needs? How can teachers direct learning toward improved common life, not only toward individual success?

This group has a stake in articulating the terms and practices of this common life. As educators from widely different contexts (different schools, museums, and community organizations), we gather to emphasize the inter-dependence of school and community. Without such deliberate conjoint intellectual work, entropic forces proliferate: testing that does not correspond to actual learning, domination of textbook curriculum, and other conditions imposed on teachers by noneducators. If they do not take a stand, educators allow policies and politics to ignore—and thus, critically weaken—our public space, our public creativity.

Continuing our reading, we discuss the metaphors Dewey (1934/2008) uses to describe teaching. He compares the teacher to a metalworker and a gardener, who "must observe and pay attention to the properties of his material." Dewey says that it is not enough to allow for the "natural development" of these properties; the teacher must project growth beyond the present capacities of the student. The art of teaching, Dewey asserts, is a meticulous balance of attending to how students already are, and creating an empowering vision for what they can become. We delve into a host of questions about this—How do you recognize these abilities? How can you tell which abilities are really important to who each individual student is? How do you imagine a future for a student without projecting, imposing, injecting your own values? These questions help us to imagine practices that counter mechanized approaches to schooling with respect for students' human integrity.

These are also questions about assessment. Every time our group meets, we focus on assessment—even though it is never explicitly on the agenda, and half of the people in our group are not classroom teachers who grade. We are constantly developing ways of creating and using assessments that expand and deepen learning.

However, considering assessment apart from a philosophy of education is like considering schools apart from society: catastrophically limiting. Assessment is not only a matter of teacher and student work; it is embedded in the very purpose of education. Our reading of Dewey leads us to question how we develop our students' capacities to assess: Are students able to carry out the cycle of assessment of, and action in, the society they are part of? For democracy depends on a citizenship that can do so.

In the essay we are reading, Dewey (1934/2008) calls for schools to teach for the common good, confronting and transforming the violence of racism, militarism, and materialism: "Perhaps the greatest need for a philosophy of education today is [to make] clear in idea and effective in practice the social character of its end and that the criterion of value in school practices is social" (p. 202). Schools need to lead the way in creating democratic society, and to do so they have to be able to foster social learning. This means both the capacity for learning in and from interaction and a sense of being part of something bigger than oneself, which drives civic learning and action.

Curators of Our Own Work

The group of educators transitions from reading Dewey to Adam's Review of Practice focused on his class, which he introduces as "Not Your Grandma's Civics Class." He briefly sketches out the demographics of his school: It is a large public school on the South Side of Chicago; the students are mostly from Hispanic and African American families in low-income neighborhoods. As in most public schools in Chicago, the students are accustomed to a schooling system driven by numbers: enrollment, test scores, dollars. In his class, Adam seeks to counter the passivity and isolation propagated by the system he and his students are part of.

In tandem with the Mikva Challenge Democracy in Action curriculum, Adam's class focuses on the Five Cs of Civic Action: Collaboration, Communication, Critical thinking, Civic attitudes, and Creative problem solving.[12] For their semester final, students had to assess their own and one another's mastery of these skills. Adam had come to our Teachers' Inquiry Project meeting straight from this final exam period, during which he had filmed his students' presentations to one another. As we watch his students' oral defense of their Civics Portfolios, Adam asks us to consider these questions: Are students becoming more powerful, thoughtful citizens? Where do you see this? Are students able to clearly define the attributes of civic action for themselves? Are the students taking ownership of the content and processes of the class? How does my feedback contribute to the process of learning?

This final exam structure, Adam explains, was itself a case study in civic action, with all the conflicts, surprises, and shifting that come when groups of people try to make decisions that have real consequences for everybody. When Adam had told the students that their grade would be based on their own assessment of their work, some rebelled: "We worked hard for our grade; other students shouldn't be able to argue for a good grade without having done the work." Adam invited these students to write a resolution rejecting his assessment plan. They wrote it; the class voted it down. Adam then urged the frustrated students to revise their resolution in such a way that it would include other beneficiaries. When they did so, their resolution passed. The revised resolution mandated that the student had to "demonstrate growth" in order to argue for a higher grade than what was recorded in Mr. Heenan's grade book.

Some students used this process itself (i.e., drafting and arguing the resolution before their peers) as evidence of mastery of civic skills in their portfolio. Others, taking seriously Adam's invitation to include material from their out-of-school life, included in their portfolio items like advocating for themselves or a family member in medical, academic, or legal proceedings. By framing the actions of their day-to-day life as substantive work—in public space—that improves their own and others' lives and by providing terms to assess the power of this work, Adam heightens students' expectations of learning and of themselves. "Students, throughout their actualization as public intellectuals, see themselves as knowledgeable and thus solidify their academic identities" (Cammarota & Romero, 2014, p. 128). The civic assessment process makes visible the public nature of classroom space; it strengthens students' recognition of the many public spaces in their lives and affirms their own dynamic activity within those spaces.

Our group of educators watches the video of students' presentations and the interviews Adam subsequently conducted with students on the presentation process. He had asked them, "Did your judges earn the right to decide on your grade?"

We wonder how often students in our schools get asked this kind of question. We take note of the growth of metalevel awareness that the students demonstrated as they articulated their struggles and breakthroughs as learners. "They know how they got to where they are," one teacher comments. There is a clear relationship between the presentation process and the students' practice of civic skills: "They were making choices all along," a teacher observes. "They even had the choice not to do it." A question arose: "It's so clear that students (or anyone) gets stronger at civic action through practice. What would it look like if students had been practicing this for years? What does 'mastery' of civic engagement look like?"

One teacher comments,

If the student is allowed to connect the classroom concepts to other areas of their life, the educational material suddenly becomes useful, applicable, worthy of my effort. . . . It also challenges the student to open their perspective to incorporate lateral thinking in making connections between concepts they probably have kept separate in their understanding. I like this idea as it involves the creativity of both the teacher and the student. Both work together to enhance the learning process and it becomes more vibrant.

The feedback we hear most from the students on film is "This makes us think." The students are curators of their own work, of their own lives. The curatorial-educational work stretches across the roles of teacher and learner. Adam has set up this activity in such a way as to shift learning relationships from the vertical ordering that usually happens in schools toward the more horizontal space of an exhibit or studio—the teacher is also a curator, inviting the students to look, consider, and share their expertise. Tonight, by bringing their portfolios (which the students themselves are curators of) to other teachers, not to evaluate but to reflect on collaboratively, Adam signaled to the students his high regard for their work.

Instead of following the conventions of teaching and assessing textbook content knowledge, Adam teaches students to organize the materials of their own lives and to articulate the meaning of their work for the wider community they are part of. Young people's capacities to think not only for themselves but *about* themselves, as learners, citizens, and human beings, enable them to be more conscious architects of their own lives.

The respect for student and teacher that courses through collective reflective processes contrasts markedly with mandated professional development that neglects the conditions, dispositions, and knowledge of people in schools.

After the Descriptive Review process, Adam reflects,

> What we have is a crisis of identity as Americans, and young people who before relied on school to figure out how adults in society act in, manipulate, and create the world around them, being taught by adults who have less and less freedom to communicate those ideas, principles, and dispositions, against the narrative of "school is necessary to go to college to get a job to make money." Financial wealth is the end goal of schooling, now.
>
> Reflective practice asks the question, "For what am I teaching?", getting us to ponder the motives behind a given lesson shared with students. Reflection is not standardized; it is free-flowing, and creative in its generative state. It is where we can compare the "goals of the teacher," with the products of students in a place of safety, not judgment, so that we can be open to the idea of changing how we teach.
>
> This stature is quite obviously problematic for groups of non-educators who want to tell us how we should teach. It counters their goals of selling us the next great teaching strategy. As a reflective teacher, I need no more strategies. I just need experience in the classroom, resourceful colleagues, and room to ponder my teaching and learning. This is resistance.

Collective reflective inquiry is not a fuzzy feel-good experience. Inquiry is rooted in political, intellectual, human commitment. This work meets serious opposition, from within and from without the profession. For instance, policymakers seeking a quick fix will not prioritize reflection; neither will most overworked and overstressed educators contemplating yet another professional development session. As Pat Carini (2001) notes, reflection counters efficiency and a simplistic view of self-interest with a narrative of humanness:

> In the face of such complex impulses, passions, and needs, the tendency is to look away; for me to occupy myself with my own affairs (and you with yours), to blinder our eyes to what isn't immediate to our own interests. . . . But it isn't affordable to do that. To fail to keep the fullness of person, of humanness, consciously and actively in view has consequences. What isn't looked at ceases to be seen. What isn't seen is easily dismissed. What is dismissed from discourse and public reference can be altogether overlooked and silenced: It doesn't matter anyhow. What has no importance, what sinks from view, can be trampled and discarded. (p. 102)

We know that learning is in connections, but students' and teachers' experiences in schools are too often marked by *disconnects*. Contradictions between the aims of education and the realities of what is happening, competition and distrust rather than collaboration and solidarity, and destabilized schools and neighborhoods all harm individuals and communities and block learning. It is urgent that educators develop ways to address these contradictions.

The next stage in the life of our group is to move from the connective possibilities of civic learning and teaching, to moments of debilitating disconnect—and to imagine together how to change them.

Allies Creating Public Space

How can we illuminate and transform conflicts in our education work through creative collaborative processes? This is the focus of the next meeting of our Teachers' Inquiry Project group. We choose to gather at the Museum of Contemporary Art. This meeting will be a Theatre of the Oppressed experience, facilitated by theatre artist Jasmin Cardenas. We invite the seminar participants to this session with the note, "At a time when many voices are being silenced and excluded, at local and national levels, focusing on very real experiences of struggle enables us to share in the liberatory process of collectively building critical understanding and creative response."

Theatre of the Oppressed works with and through conflict and develops people's capacities as allies. Theatre of the Oppressed—which I will touch on here, then will continue to explore in Chapter 4—is a set of processes that enable people to look together at problems, conflicts, and tensions that they experience in group life (whether that be in families, in the workplace, or other settings). Together, participants (called spect-actors: in this democratic forum, everyone witnesses and everyone participates) construct new approaches that foster more democratic and more liberating relationships. The boundary-crossing exercises involved in Theatre of the Oppressed enable people to experiment with more human ways of being, interacting, and learning, in the face of constrictions imposed by institutional powers.

Though our Teachers' Inquiry Project sessions continue to focus on specific participants' experiences, the group is now more explicitly addressing power. We will look at the forces that are dismantling public space and listen for the voices that should be giving shape to the common life.

For this session, all the participants share a story from their experience; the educators will work together on one of them. The group chooses the story Amanda has shared with the group. Amanda is a community educator; she works with students at a group home. Her voice shakes as she tells the story of a 5th-grade student she worked with. Over time, she watched the student come into her own as a writer, exploring her unique voice and writing vibrant poetry. Amanda was shocked to find that when the student submitted her poetry in her portfolio, her English teacher, far from recognizing the student's growth, failed her, because the student had not posted her portfolio online. When Amanda saw the student afterwards, the student was sullen and withdrawn, called her work "worthless," and tore it up. Amanda went to the teacher to advocate for the student and was rebuffed. The grade stood, the student was disheartened, and Amanda felt helpless.

The pain that Amanda showed in telling this story was not just tears of empathy: She, as teachers everywhere do, had absorbed something precious in the child she was working with, something deeper than a subject–object relationship between teacher and student.

But like many teachers in Chicago, Amanda's capacity to be an ally —an important source of energy and power for her and for her students— is under assault. Racked by individual students' struggles and by the oppression heaped upon their students by violence, segregation, and stupid school policies, many teachers experience "secondary post-traumatic stress disorder." This is particularly acute when the teachers who are encountering overwhelming problems in students' lives are isolated.

Tonight the group uses a process called Forum Theatre (one of several forms of Theatre of the Oppressed) to investigate the struggles Amanda's story exposed. We replay the scene, and different participants take a part in it to see how the story might play out differently. One tries to sweet-talk the teacher; one threatens her. No change. As we re-enact the scene again and again, we realize that the main challenge is to bring more people into the scene, to identify allies. The more numerous, and the more varied, the allies, the better the outcome. The more public the scene becomes and the greater the number of people who feel connected to the situation in some way, the less hold the oppressive situation has over Amanda and the student she was advocating for.

Seeing this scene play out, the educators are struck anew by the isolation that cripples our work—and by the transformative possibilities of widening educational space. Where are the allies? Do museums, news media, and parents from the other side of town see and act on their responsibility for public education?

The Theatre of the Oppressed work with Amanda's story brings up questions that intersect with those raised in the Descriptive Review of practice with Adam. The educators are asking questions about the boundaries of assessment and accountability. The group agrees that individual assessment can only be reliable and useful when it is part of a broad social context that includes measures for institutional and community supports. And "supports" are not just physical: Supports involve *advocacy*. Adam pushed his high school students to advocate for themselves. Amanda's 5th-grade student needed more advocates. The story Amanda told, centering around one teacher's assessment of one child, turns out to be only a small part of the story. The bigger story here hinges on why the child's advocates, in the form of an activated public, were not there.

Crossing borders of neighborhood and education context is not just interesting and novel for these educators. Through collective reflection, educators create models of education for the common life, what Carol Rodgers (2006) referred to as "places of quiet revolution." Here, young people are supported by webs of partnerships, adult allies, and advocates who know them. We are outlining the public spaces where students learn to contribute to these webs themselves, and where they can hold our public officials accountable for their part in nurturing the common life.

Our experience of collective reflective resistance is practice. Grounded in our shared commitment to reflection that honors educators as learners, we resist professional development that is oriented only toward immediate application in classroom strategies. Our shared experiences activate new perspectives, words, and energy that have ongoing life.

The next day Amanda writes, "The process last night was quite powerful and empowering, especially to see alternative outcomes in which people were collectively fighting for this student." Filtering the individual teacher's work through a multiply refracting lens of colleagues' reflections deepens professional growth. Educators can address more dimensions of students' lives when they are in creative dialogue across contexts and fields of expertise. Educators' thinking makes space for students' thinking; their collaboration lays the groundwork for students to be able to collaborate, both within the classroom and beyond it.

***

People in schools need to be in dialogue with people in other fields: Curtailing education to the boundaries of specific subjects and school walls limits the learning of people both inside and outside of schools. By the same token, the material educators need to be most deeply learning from is their actual work with students, not externally imposed curricular mandates. Through collaborative inquiry, educators are able to honor the work of their students, to come to know them and how best to teach, guide, and learn from each student.[13] By attending to the ways we learn and think as human beings, reflective practice encourages teachers themselves to grow in the face of a dehumanizing educational climate.

Democracy depends upon teachers engaging in creative intellectual play and developing the social capacities of a changing population in changing times. The default stance of objectivity does not model critical thinking so much as avoidance of difficult problems. Teachers' frequent disinclination to take a stand, Sharon Sutton (1996) argues, cements their "low status in this hierarchical society":

> By accepting the position of being unbiased, apolitical technocrats, educators are disempowered from intervening in those ideas that give meaning and

purpose to a society, relegated instead to providing the state with a literate population that speaks a common language and shares a middle-class ethic of delayed gratification . . . they are technocrats who serve a political system, not philosophers or humanists who shape that system. (p. 220)

In a "technocratic society," the intellectual work of education is not frivolous or elitist; it is resistant, and educators need to use their eyes and their voices and their minds to take a stand for teachers as intellectual leaders. Replacing teacher learning with shiny new methods that disregard the intelligence of the people in schools has denigrated the profession and weakened urban schools. One of the main ways teachers are disempowered is by being siloed by discipline, segregated by educational access, and discouraged from tapping their own sources of knowledge.[14] Collective reflective resistance challenges fragmentation in schooling as well as the barriers of ideology, race, and class that deplete the common life—leading to sustainable education for dignity and democratic empowerment.

CHAPTER 4

Public Play

On Hull-House, Theatre of the Oppressed, and Other Democratic Spaces

> We should be clear about the fact that the Aesthetic Process is not the Work of Art. Its importance and its value reside in its stimulation and development of perceptive and creative capacities which may be atrophied in the subject—in developing the capacity, however small it may be, that every subject has for metaphorising reality.
>
> —Augusto Boal

THE PLAY OF DEMOCRATIC LIFE

Although transformative social movements thrive and grow when they include song, theatrics, and games, democratic education has largely missed the vital force of play. Hull-House epitomizes the play of democratic life. Theatre games, along with singing and other folk arts, enabled Chicago's Hull-House to create space for people to come together across ethnic and class lines, to have fun and to join forces to effect social change. Play and social change went together. This 100-year history provides a framework for exploring the relationship between play and democracy: The legacy of Hull-House demonstrates that local expressions of playing with power can have global impact. In this chapter, I explore questions of public life through theatre. I focus on theatrically mediated cross-neighborhood connections as a means of continuing the progressive heritage, in present-day urban education settings.

Neva Boyd was a colleague of Jane Addams at Hull-House; during the 1910s and 1920s she collected the folk games and songs of the many immigrant groups who came through the settlement house. Her collection of these games honored and celebrated the diverse ethnic heritage of these immigrants—but Boyd's work was not solely archival in purpose. It was *social*, in the most progressive sense of the word—the immigrants would teach one another their traditional games and, through this play, learn appreciation for and solidarity with one another. Beyond Hull-House, Boyd developed these games into what was to become the field of Recreational Studies, writing and teaching extensively on the theory of play.

In play theory, artfully designed group activity enables people to solve problems together—and to challenge patterns of hierarchy within the group. When individuals and groups do not actively engage in this reflective work, democratic development is blocked. Social progress cannot occur when social methods are not part of the corpus of knowledge and skills people are working with. Just as mathematical problems require mathematical approaches, social problems require social approaches: "Social problems," Boyd (1971) writes, "deal with social values in continuous change. The dynamics of social problems does not lend itself to formal logic, nor to statistical treatment, and yet that is precisely what is attempted in general in the current field of social science" (p. 179).[1] She calls for social methods that are experimental and dynamic enough to meet the changing realities of social problems.

In games, cross-neighborhood, cross-culture connections between teachers and between students, like those I have described in previous chapters, tap the resources left to us by our progressive forerunners. Theatre games are a form of social learning that helps people engage the intuition, feeling, and listening that get short shrift in academic curriculum and work contexts. Here the role of leaders is not to control the outcome but to provide space for play where people may develop social curiosity and creativity.

Viola Spolin, who developed improv theatre out of her work with Neva Boyd, emphasizes the intelligent flexibility that play evokes. She notes, "The effort to stay on focus and the uncertainty about outcome diminish prejudices, create mutual support, and generate organic involvement in the playing. All, teacher (sidecoach) and students (players) are tripped into the present moment, alerted to solve the problem" (Spolin, 2000, p. 5). Playing creates a more agile identity and a more fluid set of capacities in individuals and groups.

Independent of the limited moral systems that can get in the way of human connection, play fosters democratic spirit: "Theater games," Spolin (2000) writes, "do not inspire 'proper' moral behavior (good/bad), but rather seek to free each person to feel his or her own true nature, out of which a felt, experienced, actual love of neighbor will appear" (p. xi). Both Boyd and Spolin emphasize play as a means of opening up the interconnection of unconscious, organic, authentic powers in the individual and in the group.

This play is anything but frivolous: It engages its participants in the democratic work that I describe as self-reflection, dialogic hunger, and questioning power. Boyd's (1971) theory of play reads like a manifesto of progressive education:

> The ready-made answer, the obligation to behave in prescribed ways regardless of the relation of such behavior in the total situation as sensed by the individual, is disorganizing to him. It destroys his feelings of unity as an integrating

center, since he must inhibit the impulse to use his intelligence in this or that particular way. A sort of measure of normality in the human being is the ability to keep his mental, emotional, and social balance by assimilating his experiences into a meaningful whole. But how is this possible when the individual is manacled with ready-made answers? (p. 150)

Play helps people to act more freely, to grow their perception and their capacities for making authentic connections. The human integrity Boyd describes, however, does not exist on its own: It is a social construct, and must be wrested from the authority of "prescribed ways."

Thus, Boyd's focus on play is also political: She emphasizes the equalizing power of play. She points out that play shifts power dynamics that extend out from political structures to reach many spheres of life. In play, people practice challenging embedded power and trusting their imaginations. She challenges the assumption that

> the few, who have seemed to have risen to the top, by whatever means, should lead the many and should determine the solution of problems which are in fact the concern of the many. Such are the "little foxes" which, grown large, tend to enslave and attempt to control, even though at times motivated by benevolence. Plainly, this "philosophy" is detrimental to the ideal of democracy and should be guarded against by us in our work and fearlessly condemned by us in the work of others. (Boyd, 1971, p. 179)

It is easy to imagine who in the Chicago political landscape of the early 20th century Boyd had in mind when she eyeballed the "little foxes" now grown fat and oppressive. The powerful wield control as much through their benevolence, by which they impose solutions on communities, as through their profiteering. Democracy requires that people guard against the power systems that work *through* them just as much as those that work *against* them; play helps people face and displace hierarchical power.

Activation and Solidarity

All over the world, theatre games have sprung up as a means of challenging power systems at external, political levels as well as internal, cultural levels. They express the kind of artful defiance that Russian philosopher Mikhail Bakhtin called the "carnival spirit" and that many anthropologists and philosophers recognize in rituals of peoples across the world and across time. The "function of carnival," Bakhtin (1965/2009) writes, is to

> permit the combination of a variety of different elements and their rapprochement, to liberate from the prevailing view of the world, from convention and established truths, from clichés, from all that is humdrum and universally

accepted. This carnival spirit offers the chance to have a new outlook on the world, to realize the relative nature of all that exists, and to enter a completely new order of things. (p. 34)

Theatre games share in the carnival spirit that inserts a pause in the routine, prescriptive order of the world, challenging authoritative versions of truth—what is often referred to as the "master narrative"—and enabling new possibilities to emerge. Bakhtin (1965/2009) presents a political philosophy of laughter as an expression of freedom:

Laughter is essentially not an external but an interior form of truth; it cannot be transformed into seriousness without destroying and distorting the very contents of the truth which it unveils. Laughter liberates not only from external censorship but first of all from the great interior censor. . . . Laughter showed the world anew in its gayest and most sober aspects. Its external privileges are intimately linked with interior forces; they are a recognition of the rights of those forces. (p. 94)

Like Boyd's theory of play, Bakhtin's theory of laughter is democratic: It expresses human energy and power. Hierarchies embedded in people's minds limit their engagement in the world and their relationships with one another; laughter overturns these hierarchies.

Theatre, play, carnival, laughter, ritual—creative resistance to systems of power enables people to circumvent the social and mental controls that underlie rational discourse, social efficiency, and other cornerstones of schooling. Confronting power systems around and within us can be overwhelming, but arts and rituals tap latent intuitive energies and hopeful courage. They are forms of play that enable people to face difficult issues of racism, classism, sexism, and other forms of social violence that control in overt and hidden ways. Theatre of the Oppressed (TO), closely connected with Pedagogy of the Oppressed (taken together, referred to as PTO, Pedagogy and Theatre of the Oppressed), is a set of processes for carrying out such creative resistance at internal, interrelational, and political levels. This chapter will focus on TO experiences that, like the democratic work at Hull-House, strengthen public space, or what Evans and Boyte (1992) call "free spaces," and foster solidarity.

Augusto Boal developed TO to respond to injustice with processes that equalize and humanize. TO is made up of questions, and in Boal's telling, its origins are in a central question of community: *How do people who are not affected by issues enter into them?* This chapter will home in on the ground of inequality. It will study a few TO scenes to explore the possibilities—and the impossibilities—of solidarity, attempts to create common ground among people who come from unequal circumstances.[2] I will describe three different TO experiences in different contexts, each of which suggests that the heart of community is more accessible to play than to rational discourse. TO is not about drama or creativity in terms of individual performance. It is play.

In his book *The Rainbow of Desire*, Boal (1995) describes a scene that took place early in his working life. It shook him up, and left him in a permanently shaking state that was highly generative. Outraged by the poverty and exploitation they saw in their country of Brazil, Boal's acting troupe—made up of sensitive middle-class, educated men—performed plays designed to rouse the peasants to action with lines like "Let us spill our blood for the land!" At one of these plays, a peasant named Virgilio is in the audience. He takes them at their word and proposes that they all grab their guns and go after the landowner, who has been murdering peasants and driving them off the land. Boal has to explain to Virgilio that their guns are fake; the actors are not going to shoot with them. Virgilio challenges them, "So, when you *true artists* speak of the blood that must be spilt, this blood you sing about spilling—it's our blood you mean, isn't it?"

This encounter clues Boal in to his hypocrisy. On the one hand, he knows he must fight injustice nonviolently—he will neither shrug and turn away nor will he pick up real guns. On the other hand, he realizes that it is not enough to oppose injustice, but that his response must be "genuine" in spirit and not only word. He sees that he must learn a balance hinging on very precise work with questions. Response to injustice must emerge from a combination of two operations: attending to the actual situations of people in actual places, and having keen and constant self-awareness.

To illustrate, Boal describes a radical priest who educated him about the local landowner who treats his peasants as slaves. Not only do the peasants work in indentured servitude; the landowner's thugs capture runaways and torture them to death in front of their families. The priest exclaims,

> Why on earth do those lands belong to him? Who gave them to him? Was it Dom Joao III, King of Portugal, when he divided up the Indians' lands among his court friends and gave Hereditary Captainships to his toadies? Not even that. This Matusa bribed the owner of the land registry office, burnt the deeds and made new ones, he arranged for certificates to be forged. Land-grabbing, pure and simple. No one gets thousands of hectares of land round here without stealing them at machine-gun point. (Boal, 2001, p. 197)

In the face of such oppression, the priest responds with liberation theology (though Boal [2001] does not use the term in telling the story): "We have to make the choice between Cain and Abel, Salome and John the Baptist, David and Goliath. We cannot remain neutral, watching the massacre. Living is choosing which side to be on" (p. 201). After this conversation, Boal chooses sides. He embraces Che Guevara's definition of solidarity:

"Solidarity means running the same risks." Boal summarizes: "Let's be clear: [We are] responsible not for what others do, but for what we do in response. Or fail to do" (p. 201).

In his autobiography, Boal (2001) points to an identity crisis for progressive middle-class people seeking to be in solidarity with lower classes:

> The most urgent question that exercised us was: To whom should our theatre be addressed? . . . the dream was to engage in dialogue with "the people" . . . to whom we had never been introduced. . . . We wanted to be at the service of this mysterious and much loved "people." But . . . we were not the people. (p. 175)

As long as they were vague in their desire to help and lacking in self-awareness, the actors' work had more potential for doing harm than doing good in relation to the people they wanted to connect with.[3]

Boal (2001) calls this harm "The Che Syndrome": "Wanting to free slaves by force: I have my truth, I know what's best for them, therefore let us do what I want them to do, now" (pp. 186–187). He writes with tongue in cheek about the approach that led to the encounter with Virgilio:

> It seemed right to us, indeed a matter of great urgency, to exhort the oppressed to struggle against oppression. . . . And we made use of our art to tell Truths, to bring Solutions. We taught the peasants how to fight for their lands—we, who lived in the big cities. We taught the blacks how to combat racial prejudice—we, who were almost all very, very white. We taught women how to struggle against their oppressors. Which oppressors? Why, us, since we were feminists to a man—and virtually all of us were men. Nevertheless, the intention was good.[4]

The exchange with Virgilio effected a critical shift in Boal and his fellow actors, from *action on* (peasants) to *activation* (of themselves). They realized that their concept of liberating, empowering action was ridiculously, dangerously naive and had unintended consequences that were far beyond what they could handle. The theatre work that emerged from this realization embodied their own activation, which creates space for others' activation.

TO moves people beyond solutions, fixes, and charity, opening up possibilities for genuine connection across difference: working with, not working for. Reflections such as the above—biting as they are—create space for self-awareness to play. A living context of questioning, change, and growth prevents self-awareness from getting lodged and bitter.

TO aims to create authentic space for delving into questions of injustice from all the perspectives and interests involved. Targeting roles rather than people, it illuminates and breaks through mechanical responses people get trapped in.

Art and Ritual as Mediating Containers

PTO focuses on the struggle between humanization and dehumanization. If consciousness depends on this struggle at an individual level, at a social level, freedom depends on it. Asking questions, experimentation, and dialogue are the tools for a life in the world that is brilliantly unfinished.

PTO posits the world as far more changeable than it appears, and human beings' work in it is as knowers and creators. "If it is in speaking their word that people, by naming the world, transform it, dialogue imposes itself as the way by which they achieve significance as human beings" (Freire, 2002, p. 89). "Naming the world" takes two principal directions: honoring one's own local world and exposing oppressive power structures that continue to grow by remaining unnamed.

TO offers a space where people can work with differences, conflict, growth, and questions about self and others that feel too dangerous in many other contexts. Theatre is a form of ritual space, a container in which people encounter their borders in an intense but protected way and practice crossing those borders. Victor Turner (2001) explains the process by which theatre changes consciousness:

> Aesthetic drama compels a transformation of the spectators' view of the world by rubbing their senses against enactments of extreme events, much more extreme than they would usually witness. The nesting pattern makes it possible for the spectator to reflect on these events rather than flee from them or intervene in them. That reflection is the liminal time during which the transformation of consciousness takes place. (p. 125)

The three stories centered around TO that I tell here "rub [participants'] senses against enactments of extreme events." Possibilities for "transformation of consciousness" of the participants are evident in their reflection process, and, of course, in my own. By noting pauses, rituals, and questions, I try to make more visible the liminal moments of learning.

In the stories I tell, people of different social classes grapple with the limits that class separations impose on their human connection. The first story involves what I call "the powerful pause" of *self-reflection* that art facilitates. The second story focuses on conflict and on accessing multiple aspects of the self through working with conflict. In this view, conflict is not associated with division but with what I call *dialogic hunger*. The third story illuminates processes of *questioning power*. All scenes unfold under the houselights of real experience: Theatre exercises mediate people's actual interaction, thinking, and lives in democratic ways.

Like any thoughtfully composed interdisciplinary work, the meeting of theatre and art in the public space of the museum has a highly generative potential. Through theatre exercises, viewers can tap into the stories art tells and participate in the art. Such engagement changes the image of museum as highbrow cultural space. I highlight the National Museum of Mexican Art in Chicago as a place that is actively working to break down the barriers between artist and viewer. In so doing, it affirms the local and strengthens the public. In this context, artistic engagement connects with the democratic dispositions that I have been tracing throughout this book: self-reflection, questioning power, and dialogic hunger.

I discuss this museum as a cultural space aware that I, as a non-Mexican, come into it as an outsider; there is a large corpus of cultural, linguistic, and social knowledge that I am ignorant of. Mexican friends and family, much reading, and the museum itself have helped me to grow an appreciation for the opportunity to cross borders and heightened attention to how to do so respectfully, but I still enter into interpretive work here with caution.

Gloria Anzaldúa's *Borderlands* illuminates a vital intersection of museum education, place-based education, and multicultural education—within the human consciousness. Alongside the story of the land-grab at the seams of U.S.-Mexican relations, she describes the clash of realities happening at an internal level as people inquire into their identities:

> The struggle is inner: Chicano, indio, American Indian, mojado, mexicano, immigrant Latino, Anglo in power, working class Anglo, Black, Asian—our psyches resemble the bordertowns and are populated by the same people. The struggle has always been inner, and is played out in outer terrains. Awareness of our situation must come before inner changes, which in turn come before changes in society. Nothing happens in the "real" world unless it first happens in the images in our heads. (1999, p. 87)

We bring things to life with our touch, our word, our gaze, our attention. Foundational myths of many cultures also emphasize that *stories* are in our activated being—curiosity, touching, thinking. Archetypal women from Eve to folktale heroines like Bluebeard's wife and Goldilocks embody the human need to touch, interact with the world around us, even in the face of the Authority (husband, God, good manners) which says, *just look; don't touch!*

Relatedly, as I cross these cultural borders, I try to follow the lead of Augusto Boal (1995, 2002), who crossed borders by dramatizing their importance at personal, human, and collective levels. Many of Boal's stories of TO focus on women. He emphasized the political dimensions of personal life by opening up private oppressions to the healing fresh air of public space. I think that he also gravitates to this emphasis because he is a man, and he is always testing himself to cross boundaries of identity and community in his theatrical work. The TO scene I describe here focuses on borders of gender, bodies, countries, communities, and, most of all, self and other. It emerges from art dedicated to the murdered women of Juarez, Mexico.

DEATH AND THE MAIDENS:
THEATRE OF THE OPPRESSED WITH STUDENTS AT THE NATIONAL
MUSEUM OF MEXICAN ART

In Democracy, knocking is friendly.

—Paulina Escobar, in Ariel Dorfman's *Death and the Maiden*

How do you design a study unit that combines the following objectives?

- Students will come together from deeply divided communities, differing in culture, class, education, and language.
- The students will engage with one another in facing challenging social issues.
- At the end of their work together (several meetings over the course of a year), these students will lead a workshop for other students at the city-wide Social Justice Student Expo.

These were the goals that a cross-school team of teachers—Miguel Guevara and Rick Diaz from Rudy Lozano Leadership Academy and Damian Jones and Ray Llanes from Francis W. Parker School—began with. Big goals, shot through with big questions: What is the common ground between young people who are Latino, many undocumented, growing up in close-knit communities that are also menaced by violence, pollution, and neglect from City Hall, and young people who are mostly White, growing up in safe and well-cushioned homes on the North Side? Is it possible for the activities they engage in together to offset the inequality that surrounds their social positioning? How can the meeting of these very different groups go beyond meet-and-greet, to learn from what matters to both?

To touch on the line from *Death and the Maiden* quoted above: How do we build a world where "knocking is friendly," where strangers reach across borders to connect—and relations between people of different classes and races is not one of distance, service, policing, or economic exploitation? This is a crucial question to answer because when difference evokes fear and oppression, the threshold space between strangers—embodied in the knock at the door—is charged with the threat of violence. In neighborhoods of color in Chicago subject to racial profiling, police brutality, and deportation, death and separation are constant threats, similar to the conditions under Latin American dictatorships that Dorfman alludes to in *Death and the Maiden*.

Art emerging from violence and oppression foregrounds questions of self and other, power and freedom. It reminds educators of the prime existential question that crosses school, culture, and community contexts. Simply put—*how do we teach in the face of death?*

Schools, teacher training, and education policy are drastically unequipped to deal with this question. The education world has allowed for an existential vacuum to expand; this vacuum undermines education. Silence about death communicates to young people that adults neither know how to deal with it nor trust young people to be able to.

Existential questions impose a pause. They are really only naming a pause that is already there. In this section I will be talking about the *powerful pause*. Asking questions about life and death, power and oppression, requires that we pause; it also sustains the pause, embodies it. The pause interrupts routines and cycles of automatic reactions that people get caught up in, enabling people to be more conscious.

The powerful pause is a mysterious thing; no one thing causes it. However, just as multiple modalities help students of multiple intelligences to learn, multiple mediations fertilize the soil in which a pause can grow. Arts offer mediating experiences, pauses that heighten the meaning of the present moment.

The teachers meeting in this partnership respect their students and know that they cannot always shield them from the hard things in life. These teachers are committed to education for real life, and both school administrations are in staunch support of this commitment. The adults in these school communities believe that young people are capable of—and, for their education to be genuine, *need* to be—dealing with death, racism, and human cruelty. The educators are experienced in developing ways of approaching these challenges in their own school and neighborhood contexts.

Efficacy Entitlement

At the same time, each group of students carries the weight of their local contexts to these matters. Threshold spaces highlight differences and call for attention to the role of class, race, and cultural background, which affect the assumptions and experiences people from different groups bring to any situation. On the one hand, Rudy Lozano students, more experienced in dealing with death and struggle, are also more experienced in the gap between effort and outcome: the stock story that hard work results in success often proves to be a lie. This gap can lead to cynicism and indifference. In addition, low-income students of color experience what Meira Levinson (2012) calls "the citizenship gap," exponentially less opportunity and payoff for civic engagement than what more affluent White students, with more social capital, have access to.[5]

In the case of the Parker students, facing the hard matters of life—suffering, violence, death—often evokes a desire to "take action." The impetus to act on empathy comes from a noble place in people, and in many situations acts of empathy are beneficial. However, as Neva Boyd pointed out, social problems must be addressed by means of social approaches. This is a matter of aligning means and ends: Just as a ballet virtuoso would not be the appropriate medium for scoring a touchdown, *individual* acts of empathy are not the appropriate means for solving *social* problems. Action on *social* problems must be rooted in analysis encompassing multiple intersecting and contrasting perspectives. And, to reference Boyd again, developing such understanding is not only an intellectual process. The activities I have been describing throughout this book—oral histories, theatre games, coalition building—are experiments in social learning that draw on capacities of listening, intuition, and reflection, in addressing social problems.

In a society poor in social processes and bloated with efficiency paradigms, social problems are oversimplified, misdiagnosed, and missed. Well-meaning people frequently approach social problems with an expectation of "taking action" and "fixing the problem." This response comes out of hopefulness, idealism, and goodwill—and sometimes has positive outcomes, like increased money for a good community organization. The "fix the problem" response is, however, just as likely to end in disappointment, alienation, and misunderstanding.

People operating from the "fix it" platform are too often critically lacking important data that come into play in contexts that involve people from different backgrounds. They often are not pausing to ask, *What is the impact of who I am in what I am doing? What are possible unintended consequences of my actions?* One of the many uncomfortable moments of self-reflection needed in the delicate in-between space of "helping" across lines of power and privilege has to do with what I think of as *efficacy entitlement*—expecting quick change. The messiness and confusion and difficulty of democratic processes contrasts with the smoothness that people of privilege have come to expect in life. This is often expressed in complaints that they are "wasting their time" if their efforts on behalf of the common good do not bring about immediate results.

Efficacy entitlement has been a function of philanthropic paradigms for generations. Prioritizing quantifiable "outcomes" to ensure that their efforts "pay off," people of privilege may ignore complex social ecologies in other communities. They also may participate in insidious forms of cultural colonialism, paternalistically imposing disciplinary measures on communities they see as troubled (Deloria & Wildcat, 2001).

Efficacy entitlement is blinding; it obstructs the growth of democratic dispositions. However, when people feel safe and affirmed enough to examine it, recognizing one's own efficacy entitlement can be a terrific learning tool. The Parker and Lozano teachers leading this partnership know better than to directly take on these culturally and environmentally shaped dispositions. They seek to create a shared experience in which young people are trusted to engage with questions and problems that lie beyond their familiar circle of experience and response and that can draw forth their capacities: not so much action as *activation*. Activation, as I mentioned when introducing Boal's development of TO, involves the actor's self-transformation in response to the other people around her or him. Whereas the naive notion of "taking action," "making a difference," or "helping" looks for concrete change in the world around one, the change involved in *activation* is grounded in one's study of oneself in one's own context.

Death at the Border

> The practices of the maquiladora industry towards the workers reveal a consume and dispose cycle. This is a system that is maintained by the creation of disposable females, therefore it is no wonder that the authorities and industry use the same discourse concerning the murdered women.
>
> —Julia Monárrez Fragoso

At the beginning of the school year, the Lozano and Parker students and their teachers met and, led by theatre artist Jasmin Cardenas, started learning TO vocabulary. The theatre games Jasmin led resembled icebreaker games but were specifically TO in nature: They were a foundation to build on. TO is not about drama, projection, or hamming it up. TO takes on serious issues in people's lives through play. The students learned TO games like Sculpting and Defender, intermixed with language that played with, explored, and analyzed notions of power.

A month later, on a rainy November day, the two groups of students meet at the National Museum of Mexican Art, for the exhibit *Rastros y Crónicas: Women of Juárez*, featuring art that reflected on the murders of hundreds of women in the Juarez region, right along the border between Mexico and the United States.

The National Museum of Mexican Art introduced the exhibit as a memorial, connecting the *Women of Juarez* to its famous Day of the Dead exhibits. The exhibit description read,

> Since 1993, more than 500 women have been killed in Ciudad Juárez in the northern Mexican state of Chihuahua. For some time now, Mexican and Mexican American artists have been sensitive to the subject of Women of Juarez and have worked on diverse projects to share their perspective on this disturbing situation. The thought provoking pieces throughout the exhibition serve as a chronicle of the struggles of Mexican women and the grievous deaths in Ciudad Juárez. By generating awareness, the artwork supports the cause of the victims' families who search for justice and truth. The artists of Rastros y Crónicas compel the viewer to comprehend and sympathize with what the victims endured and what the living continue to face. In this way, our generation and future generations will not forget or ignore the loss of life in Ciudad Juárez. (October 27, 2009, proyectolatina.org/?cat=113)

The murders in Juarez have been going on for years and have been of so little concern to the Mexican government that they remain unsolved; what little investigation occurred has been in response to the pressure of dedicated activists. Many observers emphasize that the murders are a direct product of U.S.–Mexico economic relations. They argue that North American Free Trade Agreement (NAFTA) policies have heightened poverty in Mexico.

While American attention is predominantly on the illegal immigration that has resulted, there is a larger issue of migration *within* Mexico. Across Mexico, desperate young women have had to leave the protection of their families to go to work in the low-wage factories along the border. There, they are economically exploited and physically vulnerable. The deaths of these women have become an emblem of the collateral damage of U.S. international economic policies (Monárrez Fragoso, 2002; Olivera, 2006).

The economic problem is compounded by prevailing attitudes around the body—both the body of the low-wage worker and the body of the woman, which in Juarez are one and the same. Patriarchal conventions about women's place in the home are fatally outdated in poverty conditions where women are forced to leave the home to survive. Official responses to the murders have focused not on the perpetrators or analyzing the systemic conditions that give rise to "femicide," but on warning and scolding women about stepping "out of line."[6] Furthermore, as Monárrez Fragoso's words in the epigraph above emphasize, the murders are aided and abetted by a capitalist "consume and dispose mentality."

Like any teacher who exposes students to the anguish of the world, whether by showing the film *Death and the Maiden* or reading the novel *The Bluest Eye* (Morrison, 2007), the teachers walk in to this museum experience with trepidation, not confidence. Sexual violence, murder, miscarriage of justice, all against the backdrop of U.S.–Mexican relations and repercussions of NAFTA economic policies: This is *not* safe, sit-in-your-desk-and-read-the-text learning. The teachers do not question that they should be there, but they do come in with big questions about how this experience will land on their students.

The students' presence at this exhibit signals to them that their teachers trust they can handle it. The students are assembled in small cross-school groups, and asked to view the exhibit together. Each group is to choose one scene that deeply affected them, to make a group sculpture of their bodies, and then to present that sculpture to the whole group. The discussion of these sculptures will lead to the next stage of the students' work: to create a small scene based on that sculpture. This scene, and the questions and research and discoveries that emerge from it, will be the basis of a workshop the students will lead for other Chicago students in a few months.

This physical response is a way of taking in the art and acknowledging that such an atrocity is too much for words. Through sculpturing, students stand in empathetic connection with one another and with the artwork. Wordlessly, they express values that counter the isolation, exploitation, and disrespect that allows for femicide.

The students' encounter with femicide is multiply mediated: The museum has commissioned artistic responses, the artists have offered their interpretation of the horror, and the students perceiving this art are filtering it for and with one another first in discussion and then in physical reassemblage. Students' subsequent reflections continue the filtering process. One student, for example, writes,

> My favorite piece was of a girl who was made of glass and faceless. She was sitting on a bench and her head was down. This could have meant a lot of things; one is that she was alone and the glass resembles how fragile a life is and that it can be shattered very easily. I thought this really spoke to me so I brought it up in discussion and we decided to do a skit on it.

This reflection expresses a truth that teachers of writing and art know well: The deeper you go into a specific experience, the more universal its expression becomes. The image the student is depicting could just as well apply to herself, a vulnerable adolescent on a dangerous journey, pausing.

Teachers feel these pauses; they hope to make space for them. There is much here to pause over. We teachers are charged with protecting young people, and teachers whose students suffer and die inhabit an existential morass daily. How do you teach formulas, vocabulary, facts, to young people who have seen family members shot, who have friends in prison, who do not believe they will survive to adulthood? The language and expectations of the classroom too often fail to meet the realities of life.

On the other hand, young people who live in neighborhoods that are not plagued with violence *can* speak this classroom language—but that too fails when we turn to matters as terrible as the femicide in Juarez. Though these studies mean grappling secondhand with death and cruelty, ordinary language and reason do not suffice. Art mediates.

Through art, through play, young people practice grappling with issues of oppression, injustice, and violence. While theatre games help them practice different voices and interventions in different situations, this play is also part of growing *civic muscles*. Young people are developing a sense that situations do not exist in themselves, objectively, but are both part of larger systems and local contexts. Situations provoke, invoke, evoke creative response. As Boal (1985) explains, "The practice of these theatrical forms creates [an] uneasy sense of incompleteness that seeks fulfillment through real action" (p. 142). Theatre and other arts facilitate response that is both more concrete and more active than empathy.

Dialogue, growth, and change emerge from struggling with questions and resisting the urge for immediate resolution. In his book *Theatre for Community, Conflict, and Dialogue*, Michael Rohd (1998) observes, "An activating scene does not show *what to do*. . . . It asks *what can be done*" (pp. 118–119). Art and theatre help to shift the focus from one-time, unidirectional *action*, which is isolated and unsustainable, to *activation*, which is generative and liberating because it stems from personal growth.

Kitty Wants a Corner, AKA a Split World Made Visible

Games can help people to imagine and create public space. They exercise the mental flexibility and cognitive acuity that democratic participation requires. I will discuss one theatre game to demonstrate.

One of the games I like to lead with groups is a Boyd–Spolin classic: Kitty Wants a Corner. In this game, all the players stand in a circle facing one another, with "it" in the middle. "It" is the kitty, trying to find a place for itself. The kitty goes from one person to another in the circle, begging: "Kitty wants a corner." The person approached always says, "Go ask my neighbor," sending the kitty on to the next person in the circle. While the kitty is making its steady pathetic way around the circle, behind the kitty the circle keeps changing. People in the circle are looking at one another, making eye contact with one person, coming to silent agreement, and dashing to exchange spots before the kitty pounces into one of the vacated spaces. When kitty finds a spot, the person who has been left without a spot is now the new kitty, and the process starts over.

What I find endlessly interesting in this game is the split world it mimics. In one world, a single outcast victim shuffles hopelessly from one hard-hearted "neighbor" to the next. Like a Kafka story, there is no end, no hope, and no purpose to the kitty's quest. To my eyes, this is the way a social problem like homelessness looks in the abstract: generic, overwhelming, and damning. People who are homeless seek shelter—and whether or not they receive shelter for a night, they remain homeless. Housed people point down the road, say *go there* for help: "Go ask my neighbor."

In the other world, a lively dance–race–flirtation is bubbling over. People are alert, highly attuned to one another, bold, creative, flexible. As they listen and speak with their eyes and hurl their bodies across the space, they are fully present. They are improvising. This improvisation is suggestive of the play of democratic power. There is a magic in the eye-to-eye connection that is augmented when the body across from you rises to the moment and leaps from safety into danger for you, trusting you, meeting you. And, wondrously, this magic is not killed when, inevitably, you get stranded in the center and become "it."

This is because the kitty in this other world experiences the deep satisfaction of running on all cylinders. As the kitty, while maintaining my mechanical shuffle and defeated catechism around the circle, I am peeling open the eyes in the back of my head, watching, listening, sensing movement and change. I am managing a tricky balance between the worlds. I see the people who keep sending me away, the "neighbors," for what they are in that moment in their role as "neighbors": empty husks filling up space. Their real awareness is in the electric exchange happening behind my back.

Improv games exercise players' capacities for juggling multiple realities —and the contradictions, confusion, and excitement inherent in this multiplicity. To return to the theme of the pause, theatre games perform a rhythm of accentuated movement and pause—and themselves activate a powerful pause.

From Action to Activation

As a teacher of civic engagement, from experience to experience and from year to year, I am looking for an important element in students' reflections: growth in metacognition. I look out for new questions, evidence of increased self-awareness, and attentive curiosity about the world around them. I do not expect students to "get it." I expect myself and other teachers to listen to students' reflections and learn from them how to build on the nascent questioning we see.

Below is an example of a student reflection that, like the split worlds of Kitty Wants a Corner, articulates two overlapping and conflicting realities. We can see the default mode of efficacy entitlement (usually signaled with words like "take action" and "make a difference"), lacking metacognition—this is frequently the beginning place and default fallback position for our students who come from privileged backgrounds. On the other hand, we can also see the stirrings of self-awareness that we seek to encourage:

> In my group we discussed our constant frustration with our inability to help the women and their families that we have learned so much about. We've gotten the education, we plan on spreading our knowledge, but we want to go further. Jasmin kept telling us to keep working these feelings out, to keep grappling with the concepts that were fresh in our minds. I think some of the frustration we were feeling, and I could tell from the faces of my peers that they were feeling annoyed, was that we were being told to expand on our feelings rather than take action. As restless high school students, we look for instant gratification and worry that we won't be able to make a difference, that we will be stuck in a constant place of learning and absorbing but never helping and acting. We expressed these feelings to Jasmin and she said she agreed with this and understood what we were feeling. After talking to her in our small group she said she was going to do some research on what organizations are out there that we could work with to help the women, in a more tangible manner. While it felt frustrating to get to this point, I feel like this was a step in the right direction. I just have to remember to work on the relationships I'm creating with the students as much as the issues in Mexico because a large part of our community action is creating the basis for positive relationships with people who live in the same city but also in very different situations.

Clara clearly names the expectation of action ("constant frustration with our inability to help"). She also, however, shows that she is starting to question this expectation ("As restless high school students, we look for instant gratification"). The question dissolves for a time in a repeated spike in entitlement: "this was a step in the right direction," Clara peremptorily proclaims of Jasmin's leadership, assuming that the right direction is "action," though she expresses no idea of what that action would be. In this oscillating narrative, Clara then goes on to pronounce a pause that sets the stage for activation: "I just have to remember."

As a teacher, I must pay attention to signs of growth as well as the responses that hinder it. Through the reflection ends promisingly. Clara shows that she has within herself the tools to counter the dangers of efficacy entitlement. She invokes the powerful pause: "I just have to remember." She suggests that *remembering* involves more work, more thought, more resistance, than the expectation of action. *This is activation at work.* When the student is being conscious, she is using words like *wondering*, *questioning*, *remembering*.

Sparks of metacognition can grow into claiming an analysis, an identity, and a set of commitments that defy the status quo. As I discussed in earlier chapters, connections with people outside of one's familiar circles, who will challenge one to become more aware, can lead to a more sophisticated analysis and open up new possibilities for identity and leadership-in-alliance.

Another student, Isabel, articulates what I am calling *activation* in her year-end reflection, where she described how new interactions changed her:

> As a result of my involvement I have been able to develop strong relationships with adults but, most importantly, other students who have grown up in communities that, in many ways, are very different from my own . . . interacting with other individuals is one of the most important aspects of building strong relationships, generating discussion, and creating further opportunities. Through our discussions each student has developed as a youth leader and has understood the difficulties that our communities are facing, whether they be local or in a completely different nation.

Isabel recognizes the danger of misperceptions and disconnections engendered by the expectation of "taking action." Activation involves discernment and introspection. Two years after the TO project, Isabel suggests the significance of the shift from action to activation that this partnership expressed in another reflection:

> No longer was there a feeling in place that we, students of the Francis W. Parker School, were coming with the purpose of establishing a higher power or that we were of a greater authority. To take action and do something good with the sole purpose to finish the work and move forward with one's life is completely useless and against the whole point.

In Isabel's articulation, when people "take action and do something good," it is liable to be self-serving: "to finish the work and move forward with one's life." This unacknowledged selfishness, she argues, corresponds to a similarly unacknowledged sense of superiority: "we were of a greater authority." Isabel is critiquing efficacy entitlement and removing the mask of benevolence from action. While there is some discomfort in "ripping off the Band-Aid," Isabel's reflective move gives her access to a wider range of understanding and relationship.

This takes time though. Through border-crossing connections, by 12th grade, students involved in partnerships like these have had enough experiences—and opportunities to reflect on experiences—that they can articulate activation in more developed terms. For example, as she ends 12th grade, Nora, who spent much of her 10th-grade year unhappy that she was not "taking action," says in a talk to her younger peers,

> Social justice is about recognizing that one person's injustice is an injustice to all. It is about recognizing that the prison industrial complex's mass incarceration of one race perpetuates a capitalist system that takes rights away from more than the stereotypical detainee. Justice is only truly just when it exists within a universal context. My own awareness, my own social consciousness, is the first and perhaps the most important step I can take is to see other people's "problems" as my own. Empathy is the key to entering a socially just work. Taking the time and the responsibility of knowing that I too possess this intangible key has allowed me to see humanity within everyone who society has deemed at fault, including myself.

The more Nora has learned about social issues, the further she has moved from efficacy entitlement. Her activation reflects a deeper understanding of social responsibility, one that manifests in heightened self-awareness, close consideration of others' realities, and scrutiny of oppressive systems.

Dewey, Leadership, Play

I have been emphasizing activation at an individual level; however, border-crossing relationships also generate activation at a *social* level: People experience public space in a transformative way and take part in expanding it. Another student's year-end reflection describes the culminating activity of the TO partnership project between Rudy Lozano and Parker. Phil helped to lead the TO workshop at the Chicago Student Social Justice Expo at the end of the year. He connects the experience to John Dewey's (2008) definition of democracy: "A democracy is more than a form of government; it is primarily a mode of associated living, of conjoint communicated experience" (p. 101). Phil argues that the collaboration between the two schools represented "conjoint communicated experience" at multiple levels. For instance, he writes,

The people stepped into the scenes that we had already made and took on the role as they saw fit. We also opened the floor for discussion, questions, and anything else that the audience wanted to incorporate into the activities. This was probably one of the best moments of the year . . . and it allowed me to better understand Dewey's definition of democracy. Here we were, four kids from Parker, three kids from Rudy Lozano, and 15 other people who ranged in age, gender, ethnicity, and their part of town, yet in the one hour we had, we collaborated together and brought out everyone's take on the situation in Juarez. . . . People whom I had never met before and maybe will never see again were engaged from the start because they were interested in the topic, allowing everyone in the room to feel comfortable with each other even though role-playing and acting may not be their forte. If I remember correctly, almost everyone in the room got up and joined our performance. For example, there was a student in our audience that seemed really shy and talked very quietly; however, when she suggested an idea and performed her take on the situation at hand, it was like she had known us her whole life and she became fully engaged in the activity. . . . The idea of collaborated communication was really shown to me in a way that I had not seen before. While hearing John Dewey's quote before, I never really could apply it to my definition of democracy. With the experiences I had this year, especially at the social expo, I see now why John Dewey defined democracy the way he did because as I stand now, I couldn't picture it any differently.

Phil has developed an inclusive view of democracy, based in social learning. Whereas many leaders would measure the success of a workshop by the number of people attending it, the polish of the presentation (and the presenter), and the amount of applause, instead, Phil's standards for the workshop are the same as the standards for democratic life as he is coming to understand it. He is not looking at how many people are there, but at how many different schools, races, and cultures are represented. His concern with the presentation is not with how it comes off but to what extent it includes everyone, especially the quieter (or less powerful) ones. He is not focused on getting positive feedback—he ends by noting how much he has learned from this experience. In the workshop that Phil and the other student leaders facilitated, together everyone created public space.

Leading a workshop for other students expresses activation, but another important outcome of activation is internalization—finding that the tools developed are useful enough to carry the work/play beyond the bounds of the project. Another student, Tessa, describes a weekend workshop that she participated in a few months after the TO project:

There was this one moment when we were doing the exercises that we all got into partners. Partner A had to first try and keep Partner B's hands from going up. The roles were eventually reversed but it was really interesting to see how people went about this simple exercise, and then the thoughts that the exercise provoked in them. One chick was talking about how when you're a smaller person [she was smaller than her partner] and a weaker person, you need to come up with interesting ways to get around the imposed system, and the group as a whole realized that when people at a lesser advantage do such things, society often deems it cheating. Systems are often made so that those at a disadvantage won't ever be allowed to get around them, or at least not easily.

Tessa's analysis suggests the stakes and the methods involved in what I call *playing with power*. The system is rigged, and like Brer Rabbit, the people without power need to know how to do end runs around the system. TO stimulates ideas, plans, and strategies for activating this subversive power.

Public Space on the Borders

The interactive form of TO helps to illuminate the public relationships that undergird our lives and that we usually take for granted. TO fosters dialogue between people who are born or conditioned into unequal positions; in this way it belongs to the disposition of *dialogic hunger* that I have been following throughout this book. Just as a dearth of public space makes "the outside world" increasingly violent, when dialogic hunger is not explored and honored, it is likely to manifest as conflict. Focusing on conflict, especially as interpreted through artistic and theatrical forms, enables us to think more precisely about public space.

What happens in the National Museum of Mexican Art is that *public* wakes up. It gains being: No longer does it just mean *belonging* to the public. It means *activating* the public, the public *asking who they are as a public*. The activation of the public in this museum space encourages the connection of self and community, including intergenerational and multicultural dimensions of community life. This is place-based education. Shaping thinking, learning, and action around such connections shifts the ground of education. As Woodhouse and Knapp (2000) explain,

> Some critics of place-based education believe that the primary goal of schooling should be to prepare students to work and function in a highly technological and consumer-oriented society. In contrast, place-based educators believe that education should prepare people to live and work to sustain the cultural and ecological integrity of the places they inhabit. To do this, people must have knowledge of ecological patterns, systems of causation, and the long-term effects of human actions on those patterns. One of the most compelling reasons to adopt place-based education is to provide students with the knowledge and experiences needed to actively participate in the democratic process. (p. 2)

Place-based education is not just learning on-site or appreciating a place. It is also considering one's own place as part of the civic ecology of the community. "Place" is not a passive object but a matrix of relationships and a demand that its members risk investing themselves imaginatively, socially, and culturally.

This risk and investment has a political charge. "If place-based educators seek to connect place with self and community, they must identify and confront the ways that power works through places to limit the possibilities for human and non-human others" (Gruenewald, 2003a, p. 7). As the National Museum of Mexican Art's *Women of Juarez* exhibit shows, when international economic pressures and patriarchal systems lead to basic disregard for human life and dignity, they "limit the possibilities"—with cataclysmic consequences. Places like the National Museum of Mexican Art expose forces of inhumanity, creating a sacred space of mourning for loss of life and culture. At the same time, they celebrate human vitality and connection: humanizing, restoring, generating.

Learning based in specific places and contexts challenges universalizing education frameworks. No matter how important the skills and knowledge of global citizenship and career-and-college readiness may be, if they are disconnected from the lived context and values of students, they are trappings of a dehumanizing education.

CLOSING PUBLIC SCHOOLS:
THEATRE OF THE OPPRESSED WITH STUDENTS AND PARENTS AT FRANCIS W. PARKER SCHOOL

The conflict associated with the Juarez murders, though bound up in identity, is broadly political and cultural. In this section I focus on a scene that is local and that involves people in asking questions about their life choices. When people are thinking about their community and how it intersects with their family interests, they are clarifying what solidarity means to them.

Whereas the last scene represented tableaus that emphasized the relationship between body, vision, and art, this scene involves a narrative and a more formalized TO process. The story will center on a heated conflict in Chicago: school closings.

Displacement Versus Democracy in Chicago

> If you close this school, it's like you're taking away a part of this neighborhood. It's just like taking away a child from its mother.
>
> —Chicago Public School Student

School closings in Chicago are a story of divisions, disruptions, and distrust. Since 2002, the mayoral-appointed school board has closed over 100 schools, in a process of making "tough decisions" in the face of widespread protest. School board members, who, as an unelected body, may or may not represent broad Chicago constituencies, cite budget woes, deteriorating facilities, low enrollment, and poor academic performance as the reasons for their decisions. Community members by and large feel disrespected. They see the people making decisions about the lives of thousands of children and their families as unconcerned with community input and driven more by a calculus of profit than by care for children. They point to the initial school closings plan, Renaissance 2010, as a plan created by business-people, not educators, in fact without any consultation of educators, community members, or students. As Pauline Lipman (2008) writes, "Ren2010 is a market-based approach that involves a high level partnership with the most powerful financial and corporate interests in the city" (p. 4).[7]

The board uses school closings as a mechanism for education reform, sweeping away old half-empty buildings and "bad teachers" and opening up more opportunities for "school choice" in the form of charter schools. Many community members believe that land-grabbing, forced relocation of communities of color, and union busting are the real motives behind the school closing agenda. They insist that closing a school removes the one stable thing in many communities, leading to more pain and violence.[8]

In 2013, the Board held hundreds of community hearings in the months before the final vote to close the schools; thousands of testimonials can be found on its website, pleading, arguing, and demanding against the school closings. Andrea Baldwin's testimony is one example:

> You cannot be surprised by the voices of the people in the room. Since I've been here, we've been asking for transparency. We've been asking to really to be able to see what is going on and what your plan is; and year after year, you give us the same thing. And then you look in this room, and you want people to show respect and be happy and joyful about the fact that you want to close our schools.
>
> You're asking our children to walk through crime-infested, drug-infested, gang-infested neighborhoods and act like everything is going to be okay. When you, yourselves, will not put your children or your grandchildren . . . your neighbor's children, and get up at 8 or 7 o'clock in the morning and walk your children through these neighborhoods.
>
> You want to talk about facts. That's just it. The facts is this, the fact of the matter is we know what these neighborhoods are. We know what goes on in this neighborhood. You know what goes on in the neighborhood. Turning a blind eye doesn't make things change, it just means you turn your back. That is all it means. (Washington, 2013)

This parent is questioning the decisionmaking process as much as the decision itself. She charges board members with avoiding, pretending, and ignoring, instead of addressing the concerns of the community. Baldwin's comments suggest that board members' decisions emerge from a deep contradiction that they will not or cannot confront: They will accept dangerous neighborhoods for other people's children but not for their own.

Baldwin complains that the decisionmakers do not see the people in the communities—they are not in the community. However, this is not a matter of simple ignorance. Baldwin gives it direct physical form: *You turn your back:* The people in the community are invisible because you do not want to see them. This is not a good basis for serious decisionmaking. As 9-year-old Asean Johnson declared in his address to Mayor Rahm Emanuel during a massive 2013 protest against school closings, "You should not be walking into these schools, closing these schools, without seeing what is happening in these schools!"

Baldwin is also questioning the decisionmakers' invisibility: "We are asking to really be able to see what is going on and what your plan is." Invisibility makes dialogue impossible and suffocates democratic processes. The "mutual sighting" of equality and respect discussed in Chapter 2 is absent here.

This is a subject that is highly activating for me. I try to be open-minded politically but am utterly partisan when it comes to process. I am neither neutral nor objective on the subject of school closings since the process has been antidemocratic. Since the school closings began, I have been bringing students to school board meetings, rallies, and community organizing forums. Witnessing the antidemocratic ways that decisions about schools are made in Chicago—and knowing what democratic processes in schools can look like—causes anybody watching to question the authority, the decisions, the system that, flanked by the media and dressed up in suits, seem inevitable.

Dominant (middle-class, White) culture does not educate people to expose the calculus of visibility and invisibility—perhaps just the opposite. However, brain synapses start firing when we consider images like Alice in Wonderland's reality check ("Why, you're nothing but a pack of cards!") or the related awakening in the movie *The Matrix* ("It means fasten your seatbelt Dorothy, 'cause Kansas is going bye-bye!"). Such images suggest that freedom comes from the realization that there is a game being played and that people do not have to follow the rules of this game.

In what follows, I will describe a process that engages the calculus of visibility and invisibility through play. I approach the controversial and painful issue of school closings in a setting that is doubly mediated: through a TO workshop on school closings at Francis W. Parker School, in a neighborhood that is notably protected from such community trauma. The workshop reproduced a key dynamic of the school closings that news stories rarely pay attention to: the relationships between parents, students, and neighborhood school. Close consideration of these relationships allows for a broader consideration of the circles of community responsibility for our schools. As Mike Brayndick, who composed the play, commented,

The participants of this workshop have a chance to talk with one another about whether all families will benefit if all children have access to quality education, and whether the community that animates individual neighborhoods serves the larger, interwoven fabric of our society as a whole.

"End Game at Jansen School"

- Can schools be engines of social change?
- In what ways are public schools important to a democratic society?
- What does it mean to be an ally for high-quality education for *all students*?

These are the questions that draw together high school students and parents in a TO workshop on a winter evening at Francis W. Parker School. They pick their way to their seats awkwardly, each family hesitating over whether to sit together or to divide out with parents on one side and students on another. For the most part, the families end up staying together.

A handful of parents and students volunteer to read the script while everyone else listens. The play, "End Game at Jansen School," explores power, loyalty, and resilience against a backdrop of the divisive issue of school closings in Chicago. In the 20 minutes that it takes to read the short play, the "spect-actors" get a strong sense of the conflicts within and between each individual as the characters deal with the crisis of a neighborhood school closing. The play shows clearly the press of external forces, from political scheming to transportation challenges, that surround the decisions that each character must make, and the impossible obstacles she faces as she "tries to do what's right for the kids." The question at the core of the play is *whose kids?*

The play hinges on a scene between Alice, the principal who is unhappily obeying district orders to close the school, and Evette, an activist mother fighting the closing of the school. The principal offers Evette's son Devon, an 8th-grade student, a place at a prestigious magnet school—if Evette will agree to stop organizing the campaign to save the school.

> *Alice:* No. I'm trying to be kind and open a door for Devon. Isn't that what you want?
> *Evette:* But what about all the other kids in this school?
> *Alice:* Evette. This school is going to close and there is not a damn thing you can do about it. Not a damn thing. So be smart. For once in your life, keep your mouth shut, and do the right thing for your son.

Presented with the choice of securing opportunities for my own kid or fighting to ensure access to opportunities for my neighbors' kids, what do I do? This is the dilemma at the heart of the school closings issue for parents, as the closure of neighborhood schools corresponds to the opening of a limited number of spaces at new charter and magnet schools. As a parent, do I fight to keep my neighborhood school open, or do I cut my losses and turn my energies toward getting my child into a "better" school?

The dilemma the play describes is oddly poignant in the setting of this evening's workshop, at a private school where the parents have already made their peace with separating out their kids' fate from that of their Chicago peers.

For the past 10 years in Chicago, the CPS Board has been closing schools at the rate of 10 to 15 schools a year, until 2013 when it closed 50 schools. Charter schools have risen up to take their place. Schools are chosen for closure because they have been classified as Failing or Underutilized. In 2013, the school board stated that closures "will consolidate underutilized schools and programs to provide students with the quality, 21st-century education they need to succeed in the classroom" (http://www.cnn.com/2013/05/22/us/illinois-chicago-school-closures/). However, as I mentioned above, since far more schools in Chicago are rated Failing/Underutilized than the number that are closed each year, there are many questions and much debate about how the choices are actually made, and why, and for whose benefit.

For example, a *Chicago Tribune* editorial declares:

> The teachers may not agree with every closing or any closing. But it will be up to them to make this work. And far beyond that: The teachers will be key to restoring Chicago's focus on building a much better public school system, on graduating students who are prepared to succeed in college and the workplace. That can't be achieved if Chicago's teachers fight every effort at reform, if they are in a perpetual war against those who lead Chicago's public schools. (Editorial: Teachers, perpetual war doesn't help kids, 5/22/2013).

Here, the *Tribune* presumes that the teachers' job is to make district policy work. It accuses the teachers—who are fired en masse when schools are closed—of hurting the students and obstructing the building of a "much better . . . school system." This is part of the "bad teacher" narrative that blames teachers for struggling schools (Kumashiro, 2012).

On the other side, school closing opponents like Jitu Brown, Eric Gutstein, and Pauline Lipman (2009) echo the testimony of community members like Andrea Baldwin's cited above:

> The biggest threat to finally achieving equitable and quality education in Chicago's low-income African American and Latino/a schools is not the individual who carries out the policy but a system of mayoral control and corporate power that locks out democracy. The impact of those policies includes thousands of children displaced by school closings, spiked violence as they transferred to other schools, and the deterioration of public education in many neighborhoods into a crisis situation.

These researchers reject the distracting "bad teacher" narrative and point to a systemic disenfranchisement of low-income communities that underlies policy decisions like school closings. These critics situate the school closings within the context of neoliberal policies that have been on the rise for the past 30 years. "In the effort to construct consent for this policy, state abandonment is framed as public sector failure. The challenges of poverty, urban disinvestment, minimalized curricula, and racism register as low performance on the matrix of performance indicators" (Lipman, 2013, p. 9).

Regardless of their position on school closings, all parties understand that a school closing sends shock waves of accumulating consequences upon a community. Schools slated for closing tend to be in low-income neighborhoods, where students depend on the school not only for education but for meals, safety, and trusted adults. When the school is closed, students and families lose all that. Their lives, already lacking stability, become even more unstable.

Neighborhood schools are where communities shape and grow themselves as communities. Schools' function as classrooms for children is only one part of what they do. In areas that lack the built-in supports that wealthier communities enjoy, the schools hold the keys to community building: a safe place to be and come together, trusted people, encouragement for learning, growth, and change. Some schools also offer family support services such as health care and adult education classes.

People in communities fighting to protect their schools are up against a wealthier class of people who themselves operate under the assumption that school is primarily for academic purposes, who have access to other spaces for social and health supports, and do not value the school's community function. In Chicago, charter schools may in many cases offer better learning conditions, but they pick and choose who they will accept (and keep in their schools), leaving academically struggling students or materially struggling families with even fewer options than before. School staff often come from outside the community and do not know how to support the community.

For these reasons, parents, students, and teachers in low-income neighborhoods have increasingly converged to fight the policy of school closings as well as the closure of individual schools. They have demanded that the board invest resources into neighborhood schools instead of extracting them and funneling resources into charter schools—which have never been proven to be better than the neighborhood schools they replace (Brown & Gutstein, 2009).

Power, Voice, and Visibility

"End Game at Jansen School" is a project emerging from collaboration between private school and public school parents. As a researcher, Parker parent Tania Giordani interviewed Chicago Public Schools parents, and as a playwright, Parker parent Mike Brayndick developed the interviews into a short play.

Giordani and Brayndick drafted the short play as a composite of voices, based on actual events, with the aim of fostering dialogue, debate, and civic involvement on the issue of school closings. The TO format gives the spect-actors the opportunity to think about the choices involved in group conflict and to try out alternative approaches that might transform a story of oppression into a story of liberation, hope, and empowerment. Often TO involves people who are directly affected by an issue in replaying the issue and discovering new ways to approach it. However, the process is also inclusive of people who are not directly affected. The scene here at Parker illustrates how it can play out among such groups.

Giordani has led many groups of parents through this process before; each time it looks different. This is the first time she is leading it in a private school context, among parents and students who have little knowledge— and widely divergent opinions—about the issue of school closings.

To review, in the play, the parent activist, Evette, who has been leading the fight to keep the school from closing, is co-opted by the principal, Alice. Alice has been an ally for school improvement up to this point but has finally succumbed to pressures from the district: Now, Alice is trying to persuade Evette to drop the fight against the school closing. The principal offers the parent a special deal—her child's guaranteed admission to a selective magnet high school—if she will agree to stop organizing. Evette ends up capitulating—then hides her choice from a fellow parent activist who stands to lose even more when the school closes.

The linchpin of the principal's argument is this:

> We all have to make compromises to live in the real world. And our children need to learn from us how to do it. Don't throw this wonderful opportunity away because of sheer stubbornness or false pride or a righteous belief in your own integrity. Believe in [your son]. And give him the chance he deserves to get ahead. What do you say?

The principal's insight into the range of possible considerations and motives that are driving Evette makes her words persuasive. Close attention to the understanding that Alice and Evette have of one another helps the spect-actors to develop a nuanced view of the many sides of each individual and the web of relationships and power dynamics that are part of community life—and its death.

After they have read through the play together, students and parents talk through how each character (the two parents and the principal) is oppressed, noting many layers of oppression. For instance, though the principal is sabotaging parent activism, she is herself oppressed by a district bureaucracy that will shut her out if she fails to rein in community protest around her school.

Alice has been silenced, made invisible, and she now has the touch of invisibility. Evette also succumbs. Whereas Evette entered the play with voice and presence, she ends up ducking out. This leads the spect-actors to wonder how many of the "compromises" that are forced on communities really just come down to somebody ducking out.

The small groups of spect-actors discussing the play also look for each character's strengths. This is crucial for understanding the *human beings* who are on all sides of this issue, and whose outlines the issue taken on its own has a way of erasing. The spect-actors plot out scenarios that might change the outcome of the play. What actions might lead to the school's staying open, the principal's keeping her job, the neighborhood children's staying in the community that supports and knows them, parents' advocating effectively for their children's education, and national media attention's drawing resources to the schools that need them most? These are grand-scale dream endings. The spect-actor groups also discuss alternate endings that involve parents, teachers, administrators, and students forming stronger and more wide-reaching alliances, and parents teaching their kids to speak truth to power—or kids teaching their parents to speak truth to power.

Different small groups of parents and students take the stage and test out their alternate endings. The thoroughly collaborative process ensures that no one feels stage fright—entering the scene is simply a more concentrated moment of the dialogue. No matter what new scenario and approach and argument the spect-actors bring to the play, it is apparent that the story remains the same: a story of oppression and defeat. *Until a new character comes on the scene.*

In some scenarios, a student-as-student enters the scene, and his presence as witness changes the behavior of the adults. Or a parent calls up a reporter, and even as a phoned-in presence, the reporter swiftly changes the terms and stakes of the scene. The most powerful shift in the outcome of the play happens when many parents show up to protest the school closing. Even if they do not succeed in keeping the school open, they strengthen their voices, form stronger bonds with one another, and model commitment and activism to their children. They are building up a reservoir of collective experience and strategy that will be needed for coming fights on behalf of their community. They may lose their schools, but their protection of *the public* remains strong. In the face of district policy that neglects to teach community, the parents will continue to teach the practice of community to their kids.

Questioning Power Builds Community

Teaching community is not about being nice and all getting along. Protecting community is a precise and rigorous art. At its heart is the lesson that protecting the community means standing up to power. It means refusing to remain invisible and to allow the decisionmakers to hide behind screens of words and offices in their own game of invisibility.

The TO process—listening to words and listening with the body, trying out different voices and identities and perspectives, and engaging in deep-reaching public dialogue—is an experience that prepares spect-actors to question power. The experiential nature of this activity is accessible and effective: It offers people from both privileged and disenfranchised groups a context for questioning power that they would not otherwise have had.

Part of this is questioning their own power and problematic assumptions it rests on, such as what I call efficacy entitlement. The TO process creates a powerful pause. It adjusts civic response to a much wider public forum, so that instead of the jump to "How do we fix it?" spect-actors stop and reflect and dialogue. This catalyzes the shift from *action* to *activation*.

The students and parents spect-acting tonight come to understand the importance of *presence*. This group, who comes in large part from a culture where sending a check represents the main form of political action, sees a new role for parents and students in private schools that they had not imagined before: as potential allies, on the scene, in the schools, on the streets. They feel the power of getting involved in complex questions that expose internal as well as interpersonal tensions. Becoming allies who will question power, even when power rests with the group they belong to, is the work of a lifetime. No school or community program can cause the actual transformation that becoming an ally involves. However, they can offer activating experiences that make this transformation possible.

***

In the TO experiences at the National Museum of Mexican Art, focusing on the *Women of Juarez* exhibit, and the school closing play at Francis W. Parker School, place, identity, and community were deeply intertwined.[9] With spect-actors changing from workshop to workshop, each exercise was designed to respond *specifically* to *specific* events and contexts that illuminated intersecting layers of individual and group identity.

Focusing on such contexts makes visible the many dimensions involved in a learning experience that can get ignored in the excessive focus on "what you learn." More and more attention is being paid to "how you learn" and "when you learn," but a focus on "*where you learn*" connects the learning to the person's cultural, social, racial context—and the workings of power. It grounds social responsibility not in ethical or ideological commitment but in the existential bonds of physical place, bodies, and voices. The next chapter will take up this relationship with a focus on the wider community's responsibility for schools.

Chapter 5

On Accountability and the Educating of Counternarrators

Hypocrisy is palpable in an accountability rhetoric that screams out for equalizing student outcomes yet is conspicuously silent on the extraordinary inequities in a still racist and classist society within which we still try to conduct the great American experiment of public schooling.

—Ken Sirotnik

COUNTERNARRATORS:
RUDY LOZANO LEADERSHIP ACADEMY IN CHICAGO

"All my life I've been tracked. I've been told you need to leave your community to be successful. Now I know that's BS. My message is not that I'm intelligent but that *we are intelligent*. Because our *collective* knowledge and abilities are more powerful than that of any individual. And that's powerful, so measure *that*!" The curriculum director of the school hands off the mic and walks down the aisle to the cheers of the students. Administrators and teachers are sharing their stories of academic struggles and achievements, especially surrounding the stress of the ACT test, which some of the students will be taking next week. Each story ends with words that claim intelligence and power. Another teacher speaks into the mic, "I'm intelligent because I'm honest, thoughtful: a reflective person who believes everybody in my community deserves quality education. That's powerful, so measure *that*!"

In this special assembly, the Rudy Lozano Leadership Academy teachers are educating students as "counternarrators," and, like all curriculum at this small alternative public school of predominantly Latino students, this lesson is designed to be liberatory. This is a school that educates students who did not fit or were not accepted in the traditional school system (the term *pushed out* more accurately describes students' experience than the conventional term *dropouts*) and who mostly come from low-income, immigrant families. The faculty has collaboratively developed a Praxis model of curriculum design, based in Paulo Freire's work on liberatory education, to deeply engage the strengths and challenges of the community.

Thus, lessons do not fit within the boundaries of one single discipline; rather, all learning directly relates to students' lives and connects their experiences to a larger social analysis. Learning unfolds in a framework of teacher-designed competencies. The competency this assembly addresses is *Voice vs. Intimidation*—and the contrast with the kinds of knowledge and skills that standardized tests measure is crystal clear. "By claiming your intelligence," the principal tells the students, "you are manifesting what will happen for you." This creative frame ensures that the serious critique at the center of their education is affirming and generative for the students.

Now students take their turn at the mic and share their test-taking stories and related challenges. One student shares, "I am intelligent because I am never ashamed to see errors in my reasoning. That's powerful, so measure *that!*" Another says, "I am intelligent because I have the ability to adapt and adjust to my environment. I practice the virtue of humility; I accept feedback and learn from it, even if it is negative. And that's powerful, so measure *that!*" As I listen, each voice makes me wonder again, well, how *would* you measure that? And is there any reason why students' education should not be based on supporting them in the strengths that they identify and care about rather than information, dictated by people from outside their community, that is irrelevant to their lives?

I learned about the school's "Counternarrators" campaign at a public event, a forum on the problem of over-testing in Chicago. During the forum, Alejandra Frausto, the curriculum director of Rudy Lozano Leadership Academy, held up the T-shirt her students had designed. On the front, it read, "Counternarrator"; on the back was an Einstein quotation: "Not everything that can be counted counts, and not everything is counted that counts." Alejandra spoke about the multiple meanings of "counternarrators." Through this campaign, the students are telling a different story about themselves and their community. The students are transforming the story that casts them as "dropouts" and "gangbangers," and are claiming their creative agency, deeply rooted in community values and support. However, their "Counternarrators" campaign is also drawing attention to the opposing senses of "counting" as a numerical operation and "counting" as *what matters*.

The community counts, critical consciousness counts, solidarity counts. Thus, when confronted by the mandate that they assign the ACT test, the school community takes this emblem of individual competition and success that contradicts their values, and they transform it. They surround the test-takers with the love and wisdom of the community. They put the test in the context of the narratives and counternarratives they study and act on. As Alejandra explains, "The students take the exam, but they are very critical about what's happening." The students at Rudy Lozano know what counts, and they know how to counter intimidation.[1]

This chapter will explore the themes suggested in this scene through the lens of counternarrative. Theories describing counternarrative, and a closely related term, *counterstorytelling*, have been developed by educators who are concerned with drawing attention to the fact that the status quo in America is White and economically, culturally, and linguistically privileged, and that what counts as "normal," "standard," and "good" corresponds to those particular qualities. This is the "master narrative"—also referred to as "essentialist narrative," "official narrative," and other similar terms. It is hegemonic, meaning that it is invisible to the ones whose story it tells, but the people whose stories it does *not* tell see that they are not included in it. People of color, immigrants, people with disabilities, and lesbian, gay, bisexual, and transgender people have been affected and shaped by different circumstances in a reality that the "dominant narrative" does not recognize. When people who have been marginalized tell their stories, it is liberatory not only for them but for everyone who senses that the dominant narrative is one that flattens human energy, relationship, and creativity.

Counternarrative highlights the continuous interaction of what I have been calling *democratic dispositions*. Counternarrative involves interest in the story of one's own group and that of others; in this way, counternarrative expresses both *dialogic hunger* and *self-reflection*. In addition, the word *counter* expresses the image of *turning*, suggesting movement and change, as well as dialogue. These are the operations of *questioning power*, the democratic disposition at the heart of this chapter.

Attention to the structure of story is already a counternarrative. The "meritocratic" narrative of education runs like this: I work hard; my teacher gives me information (and judges me on my acquisition of it); I graduate; I go to college; I graduate; I get a job; I contribute to the country's economy and well-being. The counternarrative questions each part of this master narrative. Work hard for what? What information does my teacher give me, and why that? What does that information have to do with who I am and how I want to be? Who is the I being educated? What is the relationship between this I and other people? Who is my work for? What does it mean to be a contributing member of society? Such questions will underlie this chapter.

Ubicación

At the heart of educational counternarrative are relationships between the people in the school and in the wider community, cocreating a space of trust and respect in which they can intelligently resist pressures of competition, conformity, and judgment that thwart learning. The frame of counternarrative offers a flexible tool for self-reflection, for power analysis, and for connecting with others. Powerful academic growth accompanies resistance; when people remain alert and playful, their intellectual hunger and capacities for drawing connections and thinking in new ways grow. As Valerie Kinloch's student Rosa notes,

> This a new and strange practice, talkin' upfront 'bout power, really listenin' to people to push my thinkin' cause now we gotta make decisions 'bout school work, like what we gonna write, present, or put on the floor for people to pick a part and try to put back together. Pressure's on. (Kinloch, 2012, p. 56)

Playing with power strengthens both individual minds and democratic society (Freire, 2002; Meier, Engel, & Taylor, 2010).

Rudy Lozano Leadership Academy does not buy the dominant narrative of education. It does not tout its test scores or its college acceptance rates. It is too ambitious, and too focused, to accept as its goals the goals of businessmen in Washington—or in downtown Chicago—who know nothing about their community and context. This is a school community that defines success by its effectiveness in building community and empowering students as thinkers and as agents of change. The teachers' Praxis process of curriculum development is animated and sustained by the teachers' study of their students' interests, needs, and lives and by their agile collaboration with one another.

As teacher Miguel Guevara explains, "Everything starts with: What is your connection here?" Rudy Lozano teachers develop competencies that align with Common Core State Standards but connect to students' lives in precise ways. They organize curriculum and assessments around "*Ubicación*": "Where are *you* in what you're learning?" The teachers begin with the themes that students name as important in their lives. Miguel describes a unit the teachers developed in response to the theme of violence. The curriculum involved asking students to "create a counternarrative to oppose violence." In Miguel's classes, students read articles exploring different people's experiences of violence and conduct analysis of oppression. As they read, he asks students, "How does this show up in your life?" This orientation sparks critical analysis that does not exclude emotions, cultural identity, and relationships. He gives the example of a Latino student reading a KKK member's story. The critical pedagogy frame connecting "reading the word" with "reading the world" enabled the student reading the story of a person incredibly different from himself to find points of commonality. These surprising insights, Miguel emphasizes, contributed both to this student's strong academic work and to the school community's antiviolence action.

Students' capacities for empathy, self-expression, and collaboration broaden in praxis at Lozano; so do the capacities of the teachers. At Lozano, the students learn in a community in which the faculty are also learning and publicly sharing their learning, as we saw in the assembly scene above. The students' collaborative work emerges from teachers' collaborative work. "You can't do this alone," Miguel says, "I constantly talk to colleagues, plan and replan."[2]

Rudy Lozano Leadership Academy teaches *counternarrative,* a practice that strengthens democratic capacities. This chapter will connect democratic education as practiced at Rudy Lozano Leadership Academy with education practices at two other schools, June Jordan School for Equity (JJSE) in California and Urban Academy in New York. While these are all excellent schools, I offer them as examples, not as "the best." These are school communities whose competency-based education practices offer alternatives to the test-based accountability that education reform policy has forced upon American public schools. The three schools I study here are public, neighborhood-based (i.e., not charter) schools that are accountable to their students and families and to their corresponding education principles.

These schools take their independence—and the responsibility that comes with it—seriously. This responsibility runs much deeper than the "accountability" models that are pushed on schools with increasing costs to the public (and profit to the testing companies and their allies).[3] This responsibility respects the African American and Latino communities that are set up to lose in the high-stakes testing game. The teachers and students in the schools I describe here show respect epistemologically as well as pedagogically: They do not separate analysis of race, power, and culture in education policies and practices from ongoing learning in all disciplines.[4]

This is education that is place-based, rooted in actual lives. While the Lozano scene described above illuminates the framework of counternarrative, scenes from the other schools will show further directions such pedagogy can take. These are schools that are committed to values by which all aspects of the school are articulated and organized, so looking at one small slice of a day in a class will offer an expression—it is not meant to be an analysis or a summary—of these schoolwide values. For each school, I will describe a classroom scene as it relates to the expressed mission of the school.

The relationship between the school's consciously created stated purpose and approach and the work students and teachers are doing in that school at any given moment, is the heart of authentic educational accountability. This means that the school community has discussed and designed—and regularly reviews and revises—its stated purpose and that it expresses the values and practices that sustain the community and everyone in it. This is in contrast to, and in creative tension with, standards-based accountability, which is designed, mandated, and directed by authorities remote from the school, its neighborhood, and the people in it. Each of the schools I focus on practices portfolio assessments, with models developed by educators at the school.

When the mission, curriculum, and ongoing practices of the school are designed with its specific people in mind, it strengthens local knowledge. This enables a school to resist the problems of external, impersonal evaluation systems (Lipman, 2013). In this chapter I show examples of learning communities that fight the systems of control and surveillance that strangle creative democratic power.[5]

While my discussion of Rudy Lozano Leadership Academy introduced the conceptual frame for this chapter, in the next two sections I will describe my observations of classes at two other schools. In the JJSE section I will look at a scene of students considering the issue of domestic violence. Here I emphasize local knowledge in dialogue with academic knowledge. In the Urban Academy section I show a scene of students wrestling with questions about authority, the law, and consistency, as they prepare to question a police officer about his own drug use. This scene depicts the teacher as a guide in independent thinking, through teaching students precise, subtle, and creative strategies to question power.

These scenes illustrate generative school–community relationships that are deliberately formed and sustained. Schools that prioritize relationships with parents and the neighborhood empower individuals and communities. The schools I focus on stand within the educational system—and successfully respond to its terms. At the same time, these schools teach resistance to the educational system. Such counternarrative work is taking place all over the country; this is work that builds on the work of previous generations and that generates ongoing impetus and resources for education that truly responds to the needs of society. Before proceeding, I need to provide context: what they are up against.

High-Stakes Testing as a Tool of Systemic Racism

> And much of the rhetoric of "rigor" and "high standards" that we hear so frequently, no matter how egalitarian in spirit it may sound to some, is fatally belied by practices that vulgarize the intellects of children and take from their education far too many of the opportunities for cultural and critical reflectiveness without which citizens become receptacles for other people's ideologies and ways of looking at the world but lack the independent spirits to create their own.
>
> —Jonathan Kozol

In her book *Crossing Boundaries*, Valerie Kinloch (2012) recounts an exchange between students reading Jonathan Kozol's (2005) *The Shame of the Nation: The Restoration of Apartheid Schooling in America*. They are studying education in America and in their own community. Kinloch adds an important layer to Kozol's narrative by showing urban African American high school students processing his indictment of American society, which condones the segregation of American schools and the "shameful" inequity that goes with racial isolation. Kozol describes crumbling and overcrowded schools, enforced curriculum, official posters, and school policies that insult the intelligence of students and teachers. He frequently quotes the people in the schools, who know exactly what is going on and why. A principal standing under a garbage bag that keeps the ceiling from leaking tells Kozol,

"This would not happen to white children." A 16-year-old girl remarks that if all the students like her were to suddenly disappear, "people in New York . . . would be relieved." And he quotes those well-intentioned wealthy New Yorkers with children in well-resourced schools who say things like, "'Well, that's how it is. . . . Life isn't fair. . . . We do the best we can, in other ways. . . .' Sometimes, then, a charitable activity is named." Kozol continues his chronicle of hypocrisy, noting that his wealthy interlocutors express "no uneasiness at all about these contradictions and appear to be convinced . . . that money well-invested in the education of the children of their social class makes perfect sense while spending on the same scale for the children of the very poor achieves, at best, only some marginal results, or maybe none at all" (p. 58). One short interchange is representative of Kinloch's students' reading of Kozol's book:

> *Victor:* What kind of society sits back and watch students go to unsafe schools?
> *Hector:* Ain't that these schools not safe. They straight up dangerous for your health and mind.
> *Jasmine:* How you supposed to learn science . . . by looking down empty holes? To sit in a cold class today, a hot class tomorrow?
> *Damya:* Yeah, what kind of society lets that happen? (Kinloch, 2012, p. 66)

Kinloch's students recognize the problem with accountability rhetoric: It is addressing the wrong target. The people creating accountability systems have managed to direct people's concern and blame toward low-performing (more accurately, *under-resourced*) schools, students, and teachers, to keep attention away from the arrangements that set them up to fail. These include environmental conditions (unsafe schools, uncomfortable classrooms) and, just as toxic, learning conditions that contract the mind ("They straight up dangerous for your health and mind"). Worst of all, when the students look at the society that should be caring for them and preparing them for success, they see people who "sit back" and let "that happen."

Kinloch's narrative conveys the pain of young people of color, who have been targeted by the testing policy agenda, watching the adults in our country accept policies that directly lead to the disintegration of their communities and the undermining of their opportunities. The American education system pushes standardized curriculum, tests, and evaluation on students and teachers in the name of "high standards for all," even claiming that high-stakes tests are connected to civil rights. We have had enough generations in this country schooled in obedience that a majority of the American populace—including many parents, students, and teachers—seem to accept this premise. But Kinloch's students know that the bigger question here remains ignored.

Kozol (2005) writes,

There is something deeply hypocritical in a society that holds an inner-city child only eight years old "accountable" for her performance on a high-stakes standardized exam but does not hold the high officials of our government accountable for robbing her of what they gave their own kids six or seven years before. (pp. 53–54)

Kozol describes "the ordering regime" that gives rise to devastatingly stupid practices in the classroom forced by scripted curriculum—signs, charts, and rules are posted everywhere, but human life, curiosity, and thinking are barely allowed. No politician or corporate leader who pushes school reform would want this for his or her own child.

This is racism that our country needs to acknowledge: "Most of these practices and policies are targeted primarily at poor children of color; . . . it is understood that [high-stakes tests] are valued chiefly as response to perceived catastrophe in deeply segregated and unequal schools" (Kozol, 2005, p. 64). A narrative of "bad schools/bad teachers," "violent neighborhoods," and "low standards" justifies stringent discipline and paternalistic condescension. It deflects attention from manufactured crises carried out by flagrant divestment from urban schools and communities. The so-called "achievement gap"—again, the term in common usage blames the victim—is *prescribed* by criminally unequal conditions for students in low-income urban neighborhoods:

Just as educators need to be held accountable, so do policy makers and the public as a whole. A society that is still marked by substantial racism and classism cannot expect just and equitable public schools no matter how much rhetoric is heard about better leadership, better teaching, and "closing the achievement gap." (Sirotnik, 2002, pp. 664–665)

Rather than *achievement gap* terms like *opportunity gap* convey the unequal educational conditions that lower-income students and students from more affluent families experience (Boykin & Noguera, 2011).

Contrary to the opinions of Kozol's wealthy acquaintances who express resignation about the inevitability of inequitable schooling conditions, injustice does not happen on its own. Policy and public response advance in deliberate ways. The relationship between school funding and school testing is tied to the value of public education. There is profit to be made from failing schools and the processes to enable profiteering will continue if the public will not exercise its capacities as a public and for the public. As Larry Cuban notes in his study of accountability in U.S. history, a consequential shift occurred when the accountability narrative moved from a focus on "inputs"—measuring school resources—to "outputs"—measuring student performance—what people are expected to produce. He traces this shift to the 1965 Elementary and Secondary Education Act, at which point schools became accountable to pressures, testing, and authority outside the schools. More important, this event marks a paradigm shift whereby people no longer held government accountable for the "inputs"—the conditions that enabled learning (Cuban, 2004).

This is not just a matter of failing tests. There is a larger issue at work here, one of cultural disconnect:

> From a cultural difference perspective, low-income students and many students of color "are not having academic success" because they experience serious cultural conflicts in school. The students have rich cultures and values, but the schools have a culture that conflicts seriously with those of students from ethnic minority groups. (Banks & Banks, 2004, p. 19)

This conflict can include language many students of color have to "code-switch": shift from their home dialect to the "official," "standard English" dialect of school. With language comes culture—in many cases, the further the cultural distance the student has to travel to get to school, the bigger and more challenging the difference will be in academic language (Dilg, 2003). Students of color have to study White people and change their own ways of speaking, moving, and interacting to meet expectations that many White people do not even know they have.

This work is made particularly hard by the fact that White people do not *want* to know about these expectations and how hard it is to meet them, so students of color have to learn them indirectly, by deduction, watching, and self-monitoring.[6] Even in times or contexts when this is taking place on a subconscious level, the toll this work takes on students of color is tremendous, but often unnoticed by their White peers, teachers, and administrators (Delpit, 2006).

Counternarratives help to express and sustain a more collective identity, which critiques the individualized identity propagated by White middle-class American values. They change the schooling experience to relocate relationships with classmates and with teachers along an axis of affirmation and self-awareness.

Unlike tests and textbook learning, which are part of the "master narrative," counternarrative involves growing, questioning, and seeing different perspectives. While the "master narrative" defines and prescribes, counternarratives are unfinalized, experimental, reflecting the always in-process and always processing nature of human life.

As pedagogic practice, counternarrative enables students and teachers to explore the subject of their lives and develop skills of critical analysis, perspective taking, research, and development of a public voice. To see how this plays out, I bring you into a class at JJSE. The day I visited, the

English class was reading a book that can be considered a counternarrative; my focus, however, will not be on the book but rather on the dialogue that emerged from it.

RESISTANCE AND POWER:
JUNE JORDAN SCHOOL FOR EQUITY IN SAN FRANCISCO

Movie stars are always changing their names, which means they can't sound real, and for sure not Mexican.

—from Carla Trujillo, *What Night Brings*

"Deshawn said something a moment ago that I want to come back to, because there's a contradiction here that we need to talk about. He said that Delia chooses to stay with her abusive husband. And he said that the husband pays the bills. What do you know about the cycle of power and control? How much choice does she really have?"

Twenty-five 9th-graders are deep in a discussion of a novel called *What Night Brings* (Trujillo, 2003). They have been thinking about the question of choice. When a victim of domestic violence does not leave her abuser, is that because she is choosing oppression over liberation? Students keep coming back to the idea that "It's her choice." Their teacher asks them to consider that it may not be that simple.

The issue of abuse draws the class into an analysis of individual motives and social pressures; the more deeply they go into the dialogue, the more they realize how multidimensional are the internal and external forces that shape our behavior. When the abused wife hides from her husband, is she just protecting herself, or is she testing him? Is she practicing leaving because she does not know how? If you think about it, can you see a certain power in hiding?

"She's not in an emotional or psychological state to leave. She's stupid to stay, but it's her choice."

As Daniel says these words, Antonio, another student a few seats away from him, who has been silent and seemingly disengaged throughout the discussion, quietly but distinctly says, "*Stuck.*"

"Is it stupidity or fear?" Ms. Delgado asks the class. Students are quick to answer: fear. She cannot leave if she doesn't have a job. She has to think about her kids. The story is set in the 1950s: The church and the rest of the community would not support breaking up a marriage and would condemn a wife for leaving her husband.

Brian points out that the picture gets even more complicated if you start looking at ways that the abusive husband may himself be oppressed: "Every check he gets he spends on beer. There could be an accident behind that."

Reina says, "I think she hid to get his attention. Like my mom and dad used to fight. My dad used to hit my mom; she would leave but would always go back. People would talk shit about her for leaving."

Ten minutes after Antonio murmured his aside, Ms. Delgado returns to it:

> As Antonio mentioned, she is stuck. Mentally, emotionally, and economically stuck. You know, this is a huge conversation in the domestic violence community—people who have been working on this all their lives are still wrestling with these questions. *Why do people stay in abusive relationships?*

Ms. Delgado knows that the domestic violence literature emphasizes that no hard-and-fast rule can apply to all situations and that filtering all women's experiences through a single lens leads to an overly simplistic resolution: escape. This answer does not apply to every ethnic group, sexual orientation, economic status, and place. The power and control wheel that Ms. Delgado had referenced earlier, a standard tool in the field, is only half of the equation. As the authors of "The Power and Control Wheel" point out, it was developed as the first part of a two-part curriculum (Price, 2012). The first half involves an abuse victim mapping out the forms abuse can take in an individual relationship. The second half widens the focus to drive social analysis: In it, the victim identifies "Cultural and Institutional Supports for Battering." This tool encourages women to situate their abuse within a larger societal analysis of oppression. Through this analysis and acting together on it, women can rise to a level of collective empowerment that is also personally transformative.

Incorporating professional knowledge gained from work with community organizations enables Ms. Delgado to plant students' understanding in a broader range of perspectives than what is available within a conventional classroom context. Engaging perspectives outside of textbook knowledge, like community organizing materials and social theory articles, foregrounds the strong opinions and debate that build knowledge in a field of study. Understanding is rarely universal and noncontroversial—even experts and advocates in the field disagree fervently, and the more people care about a subject, the more dialogue and debate emerge from it (Apple, 2004; Hess, 2009).

For example, to follow the path pointed out by Ms. Delgado, in a critique of the Power and Control Wheel model, one author counters the prevailing approach to domestic violence education, emphasizing that knowledge, analysis, and problem solving must arise out of the particular and local context, rather than a universal format. The wheel model came up out of the Duluth Battered Women's organization, and applying it to all battered women results in a prescriptive approach that is ultimately disempowering and insulting (Price, 2012). Critical analytical models and theories are empowering when they emerge from people's specific lived experiences and address their immediate context.

Ms. Delgado insists that her students look very closely at the context and the multiple dimensions of the issue; she slows down hasty interpretive moves that simplify and generalize. After all, declaring the abused woman stupid for not leaving has direct implications for Reina, who knows very well that without a network of support, a woman has far less capacity to leave. Reina has local knowledge that counters the "single story" (Adichie, 2009) about domestic violence.

Reina's firsthand knowledge, Antonio's insight, Brian's wondering—all perspectives that come into this discussion help to illuminate the social issue of domestic violence. These perspectives have bearing on larger questions of power and relationship dynamics, including gender, age, culture, language, and religion. Sexual orientation is also part of this vibrant mix: The novel the students are reading is part of a growing corpus of Chicana lesbian writing. Ms. Delgado trusts her 9th-graders to be able to engage with complex questions that the adult world struggles with. By including them in this adult conversation, she is educating them for engaging with the world they are part of. She is signaling to them that they are a necessary part of this adult world, not little kids to be tucked away, protected, and babysat until they escape the walls of the school.

The convergence of scholarly engagement with literature, reflection on personal experience, and philosophical and sociological dialogue that unfolded in Ms. Delgado's class is repeated throughout the course of the days and classes at JJSE. Students are working with literature, equations, historical analysis, and other subject matter through the empowering lenses of both theory and real-world experiences. Aligning local context knowledge with academic learning brings depth and charge to both. The teachers constantly foreground students' learning, their cultural heritage, and the terms and resources of their learning. The teachers honor the complexity of a person's inner and outer circumstances. Part of the value of discussions like this—raising questions, letting them stand—is that it enables people to recognize multiple competing voices and tendencies within oneself as well as around oneself.

For young people—often ignored, typecast, or exploited in the master narrative—the displacement of this master narrative is empowering. While academically intense, the students' immersion in theory, analysis, discussion, and action counters conventional school learning, where problems are supposed to have a clear-cut answer (Boykin & Noguera, 2011). Students present thoughtful questions and hypotheses and transfer their learning across classes, contexts, and applications.

Teaching Resistance

Counternarratives enable people in schools to recognize and challenge conventional power relationships in schooling structures. Much as the Power and Control Wheel offers a tool for women to expand their analysis of their own situation to study larger systems of oppression, when students look at the various narratives they have been written into, and ask themselves what narrative they want to write for themselves, they create new ways of knowing that change not only their own lives but their communities too.[7]

However, creative thinking that engages complexity is not the kind of thinking that tests call for, so the JJSE community engages in workshops now and then to deal with the tests. Teachers are up-front in their critique of the tests. Consciously and critically submitting to a practice that they recognize as harmful is part of the ambivalence they live with and navigate, teachers and students, together. It is telling that they navigate it successfully enough for the students to gain some of the city's highest college admission rates although the test scores do not correspond with these rates. The school community is clear about that mismatch.

Faculty and students discuss critical race theory, which provides a political analysis of testing oppression that resonates with students' experience in a society that marginalizes them. According to some critical race theorists, the neoliberal education policies that expand high-stakes testing while eliminating ethnic studies "enforce a color-blind individualistic discourse that excuses (and even celebrates) White domination as the result of individual merit not systemic oppression" (Gillborn, 2013, p. 133). Contrary to the claims of opponents of ethnic studies (and of critical race theory), who view such awareness as negative and anti-White—and thus academically harmful—young people who are thinking about the sociopolitical context of education are *more* successful academically. They are also more agile in navigating the complexities of racial identity (Gillborn, 2013).

Through resistance, through counternarrative, young people can help their older fellow citizens learn to be accountable: to question the master narrative and reimagine themselves. Through their counternarrative, they educate the public in how to be a public.

Unlike many schools, where obedience and conformity are rewarded, JJSE is a school environment that celebrates resistance. The walls are bright with murals and posters of Malcolm X and Occupy posters, and students' work registers the importance of resistance in education. In one classroom, for instance, students had worked in groups to draw up posters outlining "Our Education Priorities." On bright yellow paper, with accompanying drawings, posters included lists like the following:

> Being able to argue against what you don't think is right
> Learning to communicate your ideas in writing
> Getting ready for college
> Preparing to make money
> Liberation
> Learning how to be socially competent
> Learning how to communicate your ideas verbally

Figuring out what you believe in
Learning how to text underneath a desk

Students are learning to prioritize clarity of thinking and of communication—leadership qualities that will take them far. They also see leadership in collective terms—the motivation the students outline here is shared and interdependent. They set a good example for adults: We can see this group-work—yes, especially including the subversive last item!—as a healthy template for democratic life.

JJSE students are learning in an environment where all the activities in the building are consciously designed to express the school's accountability to them. The school's website articulates the centrality of relationships of accountability to its identity. I quote the JJSE vision in full:

> JJSE was founded through a community organizing effort by a group of teachers, parents, and youth, with the explicit goal of providing better educational options for students who were not being served well in traditional schools. One assumption underlying this effort was the idea that real accountability is rooted in relationships rather than bureaucracy.
>
> Accountability in most American public schools today is based on the notion that high test scores mean that the school is performing well and doing a good job. If a school has low test scores, the theory goes, then the teachers must be failing, and thus higher-level educational bureaucrats (either from the district or the state) should more closely direct operations at the school and push for increased performance by the teachers, who will presumably work harder or smarter to please their superiors in the bureaucracy, resulting in higher test scores. While this concept of accountability is a vast improvement over the earlier idea that low achievement was the inevitable result of poverty or race, we believe it is still deeply flawed.
>
> At JJSE, we adhere to the concept of "relational accountability" described in the 2008–2012 SFUSD [San Francisco Unified School District] strategic plan: "We are striving for the genuine accountability you feel when you promise someone you love, or care deeply about, that you will do something that is important to her or him." We believe that teachers are most accountable for results when they have promised those results to families they know and care about, and thus do not want to disappoint.

At every level of the school, from its founding principles through the informational literature, education is framed as dissent, resistance: counternarrative. In the context of a world that dismisses young people, especially low-income youth of color, finding and naming authenticity of place and person is an act of collective creative resistance.

HOLDING POWER ACCOUNTABLE: URBAN ACADEMY IN NEW YORK

The issue of educational evaluation has to do basically with power relationships, which are at the heart of politics: Who has the right to evaluate what and whom? Who decides on criteria and instruments? What degree of consent needs to be sought from those having a stake in the consequences?

—Vito Perrone

"What Students Think and Have to Say"

In Mary Ann Raywid's (1994) account of Urban Academy, she draws attention to words hanging over the desk of Herb Mack, emphasizing the living human connection that undergirds learning at the school:

> I fully realize that I have not succeeded in answering all of your questions. . . . Indeed, I feel I have not answered any of them completely. The answers I have found only serve to raise a whole new set of questions, which only lead to more problems, some of which we weren't even aware were problems. . . . To sum it all up . . . in some ways I feel we are as confused as ever, but I believe we are confused on a higher level, and about more important things. (p. 99)

The sign gushes dialogue: It celebrates the fun of not knowing, the equalizing life of the questions. Raywid scans the wall for further evidence of connectedness in the school and offers a textual collage of what she sees there: notes from students, presumably over the course of years, in a give-and-take that is playful and smart—another mode of dialogue.

> Hola, Herb: There's a leaky pipe in the women's bathroom. Check it out TODAY.

> I hate you, Herb. Love, Bill

> Herb, I feel crabby and/or cranky. I'm sick. Please come and get me in Dance A.S.A.P, —Jean

> Herb, Nancy is driving me crazy. Please help me, Shanti

> Dear Herb, I have been diagnosed with "School Burnout"!!! So I'm going home to sleep it off. P.S.: See you tomorrow. Your hardest working student, Jane

> Dear Herb: i appriciate the fact that you have saved all the letters that i have given you over the years. But you should take them down soon, because i have grown tremendously and find them quite embarassing. . . . Very happily, May (Raywid, 1994, p. 103)

Raywid's article situates these casual notes within a context of the dynamic intellectual discourse at the school. The warmth between students and teachers is part of, not in tension with, the powerful academic work going on:

> The intent to provoke adolescents to use their minds, and to learn to use them well, suffuses literally all that happens in this school—from classes and scheduling to bulletin boards and activities—everything. The priorities at Urban are clear to all involved, and the mission stands as the consistently operative criterion in reaching decisions about everything. (Raywid, 1994, p. 108)

Urban Academy, a small alternative public school with 150 students from mostly low-income, minority families that deliberately includes English language learners and special education students, has a simple mission. It centers the work of the school on regard for students:

> Urban Academy is a small laboratory high school which believes that what students think and have to say are important parts of their learning.

> Our mission is to challenge our diverse student population and to successfully prepare them to handle college-level work.

In the education environment in the United States, for a school to define a mission and hold to it is, paradoxically, a counternarrative, since the prevailing narrative in schools today is set by political, economic, and ideological forces located outside the school. Because the Urban community believes "that what students think and have to say" is important, the school is in dialogue with the world outside of it just as the people within the school are in dialogue with one another. This includes subject matter: engagement with political, social, and cultural questions of the day. It also includes the educational conditions in which the school community finds itself: policy decisions, assessments, and the life conditions that affect students' histories and lives. I will consider each of these areas in this study of Urban Academy as a model of democratic education.

A school community that believes that learning should center around what students think and have to say is taking a philosophical and political stance, as well as pedagogic. Dialogue goes beyond encouraging students in their individual interests and listening carefully to them. The school *creates dialogue* by sustaining an interpenetration of school and world. Like the work of the students, the work of the school's educators takes place externally to the school as well as within it.

In the rest of this chapter, then, I will be exploring dialogue in education, with Urban Academy as the point of reference. I take guidance from the Russian philosopher Mikhail Bakhtin, who describes dialogue as the means by which human beings know themselves and the world:

> The dialogic nature of consciousness, the dialogic nature of human life itself. . . . Life by its very nature is dialogic. To live means to participate in dialogue: to ask questions, to heed, to respond, to agree, and so forth. (Bakhtin, 1984, p. 293)

American educators work with highly developed models and rubrics for sorting and ranking, but approaches to modes of dialogue are not well developed in education. Attention to students thinking and saying enables Urban Academy faculty to develop a sophisticated range of approaches to dialogue, involving real-world connections, exploring difference, and political advocacy.

As I have mentioned in previous chapters, my "dialogic" frame includes both a political understanding of dialogue offered by Paulo Freire and other critical pedagogy writers and an acknowledgment of limits and conditions of dialogue, informed by educators like Lisa Delpit, Nicholas Burbules, and Sophie Haroutunian-Gordon. A far cry from a harmonious, equal exchange that lives more in an ideal world than a real one, dialogue involves a real-time awareness of the power dynamics—including race, class, and privilege—that shape dialogue with or without participants' knowledge. As Lisa Delpit (2006) explains,

> As a consequence of each cultural group having developed its own particular communicative style, miscommunications in ethnically mixed conversations are numerous, including differences in how turns are taken in conversations, use of metaphor and indirect language, organization of talk, and more subtle features such as the rhythmic of tonal patterns of speech. Being able to make accurate interpretations requires either sharing communicative or ethnic background, or having enough communicative experience with the other group to make sense of the alternative styles. (p. 144)

Culture is transmitted in the very breath of language; dialogue is not just about content. Dialogic education affirms and builds on the experiential knowledge that emerges from cultural context.

Proficiencies Versus Testing

Urban Academy students learn within a rigorous and dynamic structure that is carefully observed, calibrated, and revised collaboratively, with input from inside and outside the school. They are learning critical thinking as a social act. A context of public relationships, from project design to enactment to evaluation, frames their work, described in terms of proficiencies. Work that is in public view takes more substantive, real, and valued form than data associated with test scores.

Co-director Ann Cook speaks to Urban Academy's aims: "Proficiencies require students to demonstrate that they can actually do something. . . .

They can write research papers. They can devise and conduct and defend an original science experiment. They can apply mathematical concepts to real situations" (Furger, 2002, p. 2). Cook (2002) emphasizes that the real-world application of students' work includes their relationship to their own education:

> So student voice is a very critical piece of this. I do exit interviews of the students before they graduate. In almost every case over the last fifteen years that I've been doing this, the kids say the same thing. They say, "Well, you were interested in my point of view, you were interested in my ideas; I got an opportunity to express myself and in expressing myself I realized I had an obligation to know what I was talking about. And I had a chance to play with ideas and then figure out what I thought about those ideas." I think that's a critical piece.

What does curriculum look like under such a model, where traditional subject boundaries are crossed and students have such a big hand in their own evaluation? Teachers design inquiry-based classes and curriculum with a strong emphasis on discussion rather than external authorities or textbooks. Access to diverse perspectives on real-world questions cultivates interest in and respect for different opinions.[8]

Urban Academy emphasizes learning through exchange, but not in the usual kind of group projects in which students work together without necessarily seeing and using the assets of their multiple perspectives and different capacities. Students are teaching and learning from one another, and with people from outside of the school, who serve as "outside experts," contributing to classroom learning through reviewing papers or presentations and taking part in evaluating all graduation proficiencies (Furger, 2002, p. 2).

When I visited Urban Academy, I got another view of the school's engagement with "outside experts," in this case not as evaluators but as subjects of study. In most schools, the outside experts are in the textbook companies or research facilities, in school district offices, or in charter school management companies; most students never come into contact with them. At Urban Academy, the "experts" have human faces and voices—and partial, contingent knowledge.

I sat in on Herb Mack's interviewing class. This was the third day that the class was spending preparing to interview their next subject, a police officer. The image of diverse young people, people particularly vulnerable to negative police attention, discussing how to approach a situation in which the usual police–kid interaction-based-in-distrust is overturned, sets the scene for a rich counternarrative, dialogically constructed by the students, teacher, and the police officer.

To highlight what it means to respect "what students think and have to say," I will attend to the process of one class period where students' thinking and saying are in evidence, cognizant that this is true of all their classes at Urban Academy. I am interested in describing this scene on its own, without reference to follow-up work such as the interview itself, reflection on the interview, integration into other areas of the class, or other areas of focus centered on outcomes.

I saw respect for students' thinking in the way the teacher framed and sustained the dialogue, beginning with the subject matter. Herb encourages his students to engage with questions that are urgent, controversial, and charged in the adult world and to collectively refine these questions so that they can bring them into adult discourse and stand them on public ground. He shows respect for students' capacities to think, question, listen, and judge for themselves.

Questions for a Police Officer

November 3, 2012

Yesterday, students generated lists of questions. Today, they are organizing their questions and refining their focus. Herb is helping the students to identify what really interests them and is not just asking questions. Having spent a lot of time myself organizing interview projects for my students—identifying the narrator, scheduling his or her interview, and developing ways for the students to record the interview and connect it with other things they are doing—I am amazed by how much time this teacher spends working through the questions with his students. He pushes them; his questions provoke more questions. At times, he holds them in place on a topic where they want to be moving on; he helps the students ensure that their questions are not arbitrary, disconnected, or insensitive.

From the beginning students are asking about accountability. They are very interested in knowing how the police officer sees his work in the context of the social and political currents of the day. The 2012 elections had just taken place; references to a change in the law decided by yesterday's election will emerge in the course of the class.

The 20 students sit in a large circle; the circle certainly contributes to the dynamic interchange of the group. In the transcription below (this is an excerpt), students' comments are in plain text, Herb's are in italics. Too many students are part of the discussion to name and describe each student; new lines indicate the shift from one voice to another.

Herb asks the students to review their questions. One student starts, and then there is a pause. In this pause, Herb lists the questions the students had generated yesterday.

- Is there a core value all officers hold to? Not all officers go by a code. . . . Before you make a decision, do you think about the code, and follow that?
  Okay. Other questions you generated yesterday:
  "Working in pairs—does that work?"

"What music do you listen to?"

"Do you feel that you're always a cop?"

"Would you want your kids to be a cop?"

"What do you feel when a cop gets shot?"

"How do you feel when you stop and frisk someone and don't find anything?"

"What kind of clothing might lead you to suspect someone?"

- On a slow day, do you take supplements, coffee, things like that?

How about: On slow days, what do you do?

- If we have a cool cop—what do they do at home?

Do cops smoke marijuana?

You have 20 teachers in this school—do you know how many of them have smoked marijuana? How would you find out? How would you ask? . . . There's a question here but it's awkward, because it gets too personal . . .

- Now that two states have legalized recreational marijuana—does that make you less inclined to punish so much for it?

We have a whole set of questions here that can help lead to the question, have you ever smoked marijuana?

- I have a general question. Why do you guys care if a cop smoked marijuana or not? Does that affect how you see him?

- Because they target teenagers—I've seen people stopped for a bag of weed. . . . I want to know if you're going to be a hypocrite about it. If you go home and smoke weed.

- What a teen does in their room at home is their business; isn't it the same for a cop?

- I mean, it kind of humanizes them; makes more of a person, not just a cop. Same kind of mindset as us.

- Do you personally believe in all the rules that you're enforcing?

- Which laws do you think are insignificant?

You could ask . . . there are a lot of things officers have to enforce— which things seem to you more important, which less important? And remember, we're moving toward marijuana.

- How do you feel if a fellow officer breaks the law?

- How do you feel about recreational marijuana being legalized? Are your views on marijuana based on the law, or moral reasons?

- I want to know—when cops feel that stress level, do they use any type of marijuana or anything?

That's a little bit different; is that your question? Get into a question you're really interested in, without shutting the cop down?

- Are you ever off-duty?

- What are your priorities as a cop?

What are you trying to get to here?

- Do you see problems in communities based on marijuana use?

Now you have his views on marijuana. How do you find out if he uses?

- Do you smoke in general . . . ?
- What do you do for stress relief . . . ?

Let me go back to the earlier question—how does a cop spend his day? The marijuana question we haven't solved.

I'm going to write up the questions you've got and put it in homework format so you can play a little more with them.

I am struck by the fact that the discussion has ended with Herb's acknowledgment that what the class has just spent the last 30 minutes discussing has not been "solved." Indeed, it could be that this whole question about drug use will never even come up in the interview with the police officer. For me this is unsettling—I have been conditioned to want to see resolution; to point to measurable progress. What I see is precisely what the school's mission proclaims—*there is an emphasis on students' thinking and on listening to what they have to say.* The students in today's class are not declaring what they have learned; they are not going to be tested on it, but they know the dialogue will continue. All of them, teacher and students, are going to work further on this as homework—to move the conversation further the next day.

Taking the time needed to think through a matter—especially one as complex as drug law enforcement in the United States—makes real sense, but in most schools tightly controlled curriculum and testing prohibit it. The commitment to do so is both a political stance and an educational art.[9]

Like Ms. Delgado at the JJSE, Herb meets his students on real-world ground, composed of real-world questions that adults—politicians, parents, and community members—grapple with. He does not sanitize or avoid the tricky subject of drugs. In fact, he ups the ante to a level the students are not entirely comfortable with when he asks them if they think faculty at the school have used drugs. His point, however, is not to be insurrectionary. He is guiding the students in developing a crucial interviewing skill: getting the subject to talk about something that she or he would rather not talk about but that is of compelling human interest. The students dig deeply into fundamental questions of democratic society as they explore the boundaries of privacy, law, and professional conduct.

In this class, students are working on developing questions that will open up the conversation and create common ground with the police officer. The officer may have values and beliefs that do not line up with the rules and regulations—how does he handle the places of tension? The students have to be able to imagine themselves as the police officer and consider how it might be to respond to difficult questions. They are in the metacognitive space of figuring out how they can create with the police officer the kind of dialogue they are participating in now.

The students' questions show a prevailing interest in consistency: To what extent does the police officer align values with actual practice? How does she or he deal with conflicts between the two? How does she or he set

priorities? Such concerns reflect the educational environment the students
are in at Urban, steeped in thoroughgoing attention to consistency.

The students are asking their interview subjects, "What is the basis
of your work? What does it mean to you personally? How do you deal
with conflicts between who you are and what you do? How do you make
sense of the structures of your work when those structures are changing
(e.g., drug laws)?" These are necessary questions for human beings to be
asking one another. How valuable would it be for everyone to be asking
such questions!

The encounter Herb sets up between the students and the police officer expresses the respect for students that is at the heart of the school.
Herb's students are far more likely than my students are to be targets of the
school-to-prison pipeline: more likely to encounter schools as institutions
that set them up for prison rather than for college (Noguera, 2007). For the
police officer to show up in the students' territory, subject to the questions
they choose to ask him, is to shake up the status quo of the city, whereby
the young people have to mind the police officer's rules. Though this curriculum is not explicitly framed as restorative justice, it shares its focus on
displacement, equalizing, and listening.

This is curriculum that, like Portelli's (1997) discussion of oral history,
discussed in Chapter 2, is practice and dialogue, "both intellectual and social endeavor." It is also live—"each interview is an *experience* before it
becomes a *text*" (pp. xiv–xvii).

Dialogic Curriculum

> Our fundamental educational problem today is not one of turning
> schools into better engines of increased economic productivity and
> growth, or of finding more and more directive ways to inculcate
> students with a body of "basic facts" that we presume they need
> to know. It is in finding ways to involve schools in creating and
> maintaining conditions in which inclusive, democratic, and open-
> ended dialogue can thrive.
>
> —Nicholas Burbules

The Urban Academy class described here depicts knowledge dialogically.
The students' focus is not on textbook knowledge but on what they know
about the world around them, the people with whom they come in contact
in various circles of their lives, and their own perceptions and thoughts.
They are analyzing context—how might a person act differently in one
place than in another? They are studying language—how does one find
out what it is like to walk in someone else's shoes? How do we explore
difference without causing division? They are considering the contingency
of authority—what does it mean about the law if marijuana is legal in one
state and not in another? What does it say about systems of power if one

form of substance abuse is criminalized and not another? These questions are as important to their democratic development as their interest (and, for the 18-year-olds in the class, their participation) in the Election Day voting that had taken place the day before.

Dialogic curriculum involves a dynamic exchange—listening to another person widens imaginative, intellectual, and empathic horizons *and* propels people to reflect on their own situatedness. Such exchange enables people to move in the world with more consciousness, power, and agility.

The differences among the students complement the different voices they are encountering in the course of their interviews. This engagement with different viewpoints is a key democratic practice that goes beyond the default goal of "getting everyone to speak." Careful consideration of different perspectives—those of the person sitting next to you, or of a person of a different race or profession or age or culture—develops the intelligence of both the individual and the group. Consideration of multiple perspectives provides a foundation for political and social analysis that can move nimbly across contexts. It develops capacities for collective problem solving that leads to democratic change (Young, 1996).

Herb's class offers a curricular example of counternarrative: Not only is it handling tricky adult subject matter, but the whole structure of the class proves that knowledge emerges in dialogue, through encounters with stories, multiple perspectives, and questions. In the course of the discussion I witnessed, students were engaged collectively and individually in the project of drawing forth another person's narrative and working with the sensitivities, analysis, self-reflection, and artfulness that attend such a project.

Dialogic Professional Identity

Teachers' experiences and experiments in dialogue impact students' dialogic learning. As I discussed in Chapter 3, democratic education begins in and builds on teacher inquiry. Urban Academy is structured in such a way as to maximize teachers' dialogue. This is not only a topic for faculty meetings and professional development, and it is not contrived for workshop days. It is part of the infrastructure of the school, from physical space to teacher induction to external relationships.

One form that dialogic professional identity at Urban Academy takes is teacher–teacher mentoring. The school invests substantively in new teachers, who learn on the job for a full year with a veteran teacher before taking their own classrooms. The school is realistic about the challenges of teaching and clear about the value of basing teaching directly in learning. This deliberate, thoughtful approach counters the churn-and-burn habit that has besotted so many school districts. Professional identity cannot grow in a field where the norm is to hire barely trained teachers who often leave the teaching profession in bitterness, and leave behind students to handle yet another loss.

English teacher Alex White speaks to his experience as a new teacher at the school, where both the mentoring and the physical layout are conducive to reflection and dialogue. Just as we saw Herb guiding students' thinking, Herb is also guiding new teachers' thinking—through questions, listening, and "a very specific tone":

> It was a little scary to have someone I really respected sit in on my class and watch what I was doing and talk to me specifically about, "Why did you ask James that question that way? Maybe you could have tried asking it this way." And I learned how to teach through that mentoring relationship. My desk is right beside Herb Mack's desk in the office and I can't help but overhear and learn from his way of negotiating with students when there's any kind of a conflict or helping a student who's really having a hard time, either at home or in school. And I think he really sets a very specific tone in the school, one of understanding and really listening to students and knowing how to ask the right questions. (PBS, n.d.)

Through their willingness to be vulnerable and to respect vulnerability in one another, teachers create dialogic classrooms. In urban schools, where many teachers are White, teaching students of color, this means developing both structural analysis and self-reflection—capacities that most teacher education projects, schools, and policies do not support. In dominant culture environments, racial awareness does not develop on its own (Ladson-Billings, 2009). Democratic education requires that racial awareness develop through deliberate reflection and dialogue.

Focusing on student learning apart from the sociological conditions students occupy, and the needs and conditions of democratic society as a whole, perpetuates fragmented, irrelevant, unsound education. Roger Soder points out that

> What learning [in the classroom] is must be considered part of a complex context, a network of relationships. If we as educators believe that there should be no contradictions between what we are teaching, how we are teaching, and how we are structuring our classroom, and if we believe that there are such contradictions, then it is the extent of those very contradictions that need to be assessed, and not just knowledge acquisition. (Soder, 2004, p. 110)

Teachers are serious, deliberate professionals who organize their work around respect for students. They build up the horizontal plane of human life. Democratic education does not target children for inspection without simultaneous and equal evaluation of adult society.

When school structures and discourse about education focus only on student performance or student learning, they are not attending to the formation of the self in community, history, and culture. Oneself in community, and not knowledge of the branches of government or the initiation of a re-cycling program, is the heart of democratic education. Self-awareness, and attention to race, class, and power differentials, enables teachers to support students' affirmation of their own cultures and histories. Teachers must engage in this process to support students engaging in it. It is never finished; students and teachers question, reflect, and imagine in tandem.

Pedagogy centered on youth voice is not only concerned with student engagement: It forces an opening for youth input into public deliberation. Students and teachers at Urban Academy create a counternarrative of young people thinking and saying. This involves a study of assessments. Since assessments are the means by which a school connects student learning to the expectations of the society they are part of, Urban Academy educators develop assessments in very deliberate ways. In so doing, they provide an important example for this country as it deals with the relationship between questions of accountability and democracy.

To reiterate, the educators are not primarily engaged in a pedagogical discussion about what kinds of assessments best serve student learning. Their sights are both broader and more focused. Assessments have been increasingly used as a tool in the dismantling of public education and ac-countability rhetoric crafted to justify the displacement and disenfranchise-ment of families of color in urban schools and neighborhoods (Lipman, 2013). Dialogic education challenges the premises of assessments, on behalf of democratic dignity.

A Dialogic Approach to Assessments

Noneducators have positioned themselves as educational authorities and have sidelined the professional judgment of educators. In this context, lo-cal control of assessments represents a crucial stronghold for quality pub-lic education. Urban Academy participates in a system of educator- and student-designed Performance Based Assessment Tasks, which replace the statewide high-stakes examination. The educators who collaboratively de-sign these proficiencies are themselves engaged in dialogic learning pro-cesses. School leaders Ann Cook and Herb Mack have been engaged in questions about assessment for decades, with colleagues from all over the country and across generations. I will discuss the significance of this span further in Chapter 6. As Cook and Mack wrote in 1975, long before the birth of Urban Academy, education should be based in teacher inquiry, and as-sessments belong in a teacher's study of his or her own class.[10]

Cook and Mack (1975) argue that accountability needs to fit in a framework whereby the teacher is understood as—and required to be—a researcher. As Herb demonstrates in his teaching practice, this means pos-ing questions and framing problems, based on observation of the inter-ests and realities of students' lives. The teachers' goals emerge from these observations—the teachers do not operate by preset goals so much as through a process of developing and refining goals by seeing what the students demonstrate and do not demonstrate of their learning. This is living intellectual work:

> In our search for new, more effective methods of holding teachers accountable for their actions, perhaps we need to judge teachers by the degree to which they show themselves capable of both analyzing their goal and problems, and devising new strategies to solve the problems. We need to encourage teachers who are creative in discovering their actions, so that the resulting information is of use to them in becoming more effective professionals, and of meaningful, immediate value to the children they serve. (Cook & Mack, 1975, p. 22)

The school that Mack and Cook founded, and the educational and political networks they helped connect to the work of the school, provided space for authentic teacher research to unfold.

Urban Academy's institutional approach to developing assessments is also dialogic: In concert with other schools, it makes its own assessments. Urban Academy is part of a consortium of 28 New York State public schools that operate independently of the State Regents Examinations. Started in 1995 by lifelong educators, the New York Performance Standards Consortium is a powerful coalition of schools that, with the backing of university education departments—and in the face of opposition by political, media, and other groups—has designed assessments that directly correspond to student learning, lead to school improvement, and provide the basis for meaningful professional development.

As I mentioned earlier, these assessments deal with performance competencies. Courses, approaches, and curriculum vary, but across the Consortium, schools have in common an inquiry-based approach to learning that supports multiple ways for students to express and exhibit what they know. All the schools use a system of assessment aligned to state standards; teachers and students share an understanding of the criteria by which work is evaluated. Studies have shown that the work students do for these assessments corresponds to 21st-century learning demands whereas the state test assignments do not. Furthermore, the performance assessments correspond with a vastly better rate of teacher retention than in nonconsortium schools.

An exemplar of student work that fulfills the social studies proficiency helps to illuminate what this looks like in practice. A number of exemplar papers can be found on the performance assessment website, but I will focus on just one paper here. The exemplar paper by a consortium school student is a response to the assignment "The Legacy of Robert Moses."[11]

The following are a few of the criteria for the social studies performance assessment:

- Argument draws on, explains, and critiques evidence from alternative points of view.
- Arguments, ideas, and voice reflect a highly informed awareness of the larger historical, political, or cultural context surrounding questions addressed in the paper.
- Broader implications of the central arguments are presented and thoroughly explored.

In the paper, the student considers as an alternate perspective Kenneth T. Jackson's *Robert Moses and the Rise of New York: The Power Broker in Perspective*, a "revisionist" history that challenges Caro's critique of Moses. I will not reproduce the full paper here but will take up a few passages that exemplify alignment with the performance assessments noted above.[12]

The student begins by framing his paper in questions of interest and identity: Right away he makes sure that readers are asking questions about democracy and community. Whose city is New York?

> To debate the life of Robert Moses in a sense, is to debate the values of New York. According to an article by NY Times reporter Michael Powell, when asked, "Doesn't New York need a new master builder? . . . Don't we need a new Robert Moses?" Mr. Caro responded, "We don't need a new Robert Moses because he ignored the values of New York." What are the values? Who represents them? To know the answer, is to know the root of Mr. Caro's perspectives on Robert Moses and politics in general. (New York City History, p. 2)

This student's paper immediately breaks the master narrative. Engaging "alternative points of view" is not just a question of quantity of sources or a pro–con duality. It is asking questions that do not have a single or definitive answer—and challenging expectations that there should be.

This is deeply dialogic work: The student is not just doing research but recognizing that research is far from authoritative and that it carries biases that must be discerned and taken into account. The student goes on to focus on the different research and argumentation methods of the two primary texts he is considering, one of which emphasizes the stories of the people displaced by Robert Moses's city designs and the other emphasizing a more traditionally "objective" data base:

> Throughout *The Power Broker* Mr. Caro's supporting evidence is rooted in the opinions of the people and not only those of the quarter of a million who were dispossessed of their homes but those within the masses who had on a daily basis, to travel on the deteriorating mass transit system, and travel on the miles of congested roadways Moses laid out, in short, people in mainly poor and working classes. Knowing this, it is safe to assume that when Mr. Caro referred to the "Values of New York," he was referring to the values of the poor and

working class, who, might you be reminded, are the majority in the city and in the world.

Kenneth T. Jackson's opinion on Moses is clearly rooted in a different mindset. While reading the article in question it becomes apparent that much of his evidence is comprised mainly of statistics. The balance between statistics data and the quoted opinions of people, let alone from the voices of the working people, is very poor. Furthermore the many statistics he provides, he cleverly molds so that they sound less painful. For instance he claims that 200,000 people were relocated by the city, meaning by Moses. Were they? What does it mean to be relocated? Is it necessarily a good thing? Mr. Caro on the other hand gives the reader much evidence to support that Moses' promise to tenants that "we shall cooperate in every possible way so as to avoid hardships and inconveniences" as part of his "tenant relocation operations," was a dish of bologna. (New York City History, p. 2)

The student's study of the city's design includes political, social, and rhetorical analysis. Not only is he comparing sources and approaches of individual works; implicit in his questions is a fundamental epistemological challenge. He knows that there is no single authoritative source of knowledge; neither is there any neutral ground.

This is a liberatory understanding, which the student further unfolds with another source of knowledge: his own experience. The student is not only concerned with the research and approach of historians but includes his own vantage point (and that of the reader) in his inquiry into the "the legacy of Robert Moses." In this section, featuring his own on-the-ground perspective, the student's style becomes particularly florid—it is both appropriate to this descriptive section and suggestive of the power of settling into one's very own voice. His description of New York City recalls the iconic dichotomy of wealthy and working-class spaces in Fitzgerald's *The Great Gatsby*. The student writes,

If you've ever taken a ferry ride to the Statue of Liberty, gazing south at the mouth of New York's harbor, you would have seen a great silver arc that spans between the two spits of land. The tops of two towers that shoot a climactic burst of thin strands, raining down onto their respective halves of the arc, would probably have kept you temporarily mesmerized. The Verrazano-Narrows Bridge is just one of Robert Moses' many architectural achievements that are pleasure to the eye and lasting monuments to an extraordinary man who built so much in so little time. Of course it was always the case with Moses' architectural creativity, that it was best admired from a bird's eye view of the city. . . . On the ground it's quite a different picture. For example, the Cross-Bronx Expressway is ugly in every sense of the word from any angle of sight. The road is a prime example of the artist's negligence toward the interest of working people. To stand next to it first of all, is to choke on truck exhaust. . . .

The lead and carbon monoxide that sticks to the sides of the road's trench, float up into the neighborhoods that the highways split and destroyed in the first place, and enter the homes of poor and working people. The fumes coat the furniture, the walls, and more importantly the lungs of people in the surrounding area, causing them to suffer all sorts of respiratory diseases, mainly Asthma and Emphysema. (New York City History, p. 6)

The expansive perspective offered to the reader zooms from an ethereal bird's eye view to the insides of neighborhoods, homes, and human bodies. Through this scene, the student emphasizes the problem with making plans and decisions from charts, planes, and skyscrapers: The human (and nonhuman) life is rendered invisible and negligible. This is, the student concludes, Robert Moses's legacy: a city design that served the needs of the wealthy, not the working class, and an approach to planning that perpetuated an unjust status quo.

The student ends by referencing Kenneth Jackson's description of Robert Moses as a visionary who swims with the tides of history. The student writes, "What New York City really needs is not someone brilliant who swims with the tides of history, but someone who swims against it, and possibly changes it completely for the betterment of society. That wasn't Robert Moses" (New York City History, p. 13). The student challenges the legacy he has inherited as a young citizen of New York City. The reproach that has suffused this paper culminates in the charge he levels at the end: *Bring us leaders who will make change.* His analysis, his narrative, and his response models how young people can and do hold power accountable.

This exemplar is reflective of an education marked by much discussion, focused work with multiple texts and conflicting perspectives, literary sensibility, and consideration of the student's own experience. His education facilitates an interpretive playfulness that enables the student to think for himself and to communicate in ways that expand dialogue, critical thinking, and human respect.

Unlike standardized tests, proficiency assessments enable freer range of thought, analysis, and voice—the student's ability to analyze power and envision something better is supported by the assessments. Democratic accountability would mean taking this student seriously.

Coalition-Based Education Design for Real Accountability

Control over and responsibility for schools must be grounded in sound principles of participatory democracy. Accountability systems, therefore, must promote the informed involvement of key actors in the education system: parents, students, educators, and members of the local community first of all. To further strengthen democracy as well as promote equity and overall achievement, government and education systems should be accountable for promoting, expanding and strengthening schooling that is integrated by race and class.

—Monty Neill

Assessing the assessments is also an important part of the Consortium's work. This process helps schools to build research and professional development into school practice, keeping it fresh, informed, and constantly evolving. Teachers visit one another's schools and read and assess the work of their colleagues' students. This exchange is a dynamic means of professional development, whereby teachers learn from one another's feedback and examples. This is a significant time commitment on the part of member schools, "but the results speak for themselves: 91 percent of all students at Consortium schools are accepted to college, compared to a citywide average of just 62 percent" (Furger, 2002). Teachers, for their part, stay in these schools: The turnover rate for teachers with less than 5 years of experience is 15%, in contrast to the 58% of teachers in New York City schools as a whole. As Deborah Meier comments, "That is a telling bit of datum—it means that in these schools, with their teacher-designed and revised assessment system, teachers finally have the professional respect, autonomy, and responsibility to make their schools work for their students" (n.d., "Educating for the 21st Century: Data Report on the New York Performance Standards Consortium," p. ii).

The research base for New York State Performance Standards is multilateral and longitudinal: Rather than encompassing only short-term numbers and limited proficiencies, it has developed metrics pertaining to *sustainable education*. The research follows students not only through high school but into and through college. Consortium schools track graduates' college performance and the rate of African American male and Latino male matriculation. It includes metrics for ELLs and special needs. In every area Consortium schools outperform both the national average and that of New York City schools.

The Consortium was developed in opposition to high-stakes testing. Consortium schools consider students' needs and the actual obstacles they face, developing responsive structures and approaches (Tashlik, 2010). These guide the relationships, principles, and assessments of teachers and students.

As co-director of Urban Academy, Ann Cook (2002) also participates in the Consortium. She explains,

> I think what testing does is change the curriculum. Testing focuses people on the test. The higher stakes you make the test, the more you impact on the curriculum. So you get rid of things like arts. And you get rid of the interesting stuff that's going to engage kids. And you then start attaching penalties if kids don't do well on the tests. Then you need to hold kids back if they don't do well on

the test. And if we look at the data and the research, holding them back once will increase the possibilities that they'll never finish school by 50 percent. If we hold them back twice, based on these tests, we increase the possibilities they'll never finish school by 90 percent.

Unlike the high-stakes tests usually attached to the term *accountability*, Consortium schools see themselves as accountable to their students and families (Foote, 2007).

The Consortium's emphasis on transparency stands in stark contrast to the opaque processes surrounding high-stakes tests, from their development, to how they are used, to their benefit in student learning—the secrecy contradicts the very notion of accountability. Accountability, then, for Consortium schools, includes asking questions about the tests themselves. For educational work to be thorough and effective, it cannot stop at the threshold of the policymakers' door:

> Suspiciously absent from the accountability equation are the tests themselves. Though these tests are the measure by which schools, principals, teachers, students, and even policy makers are publicly deemed successes or failures, many states refuse to release them for public scrutiny. . . . Isn't it time that we hold these tests accountable for what their proponents claim they can do, especially when children's futures and adult livelihoods hang on the results? (Foote, 2007, pp. 360–361)

Claiming and sustaining the authority to carry out their own assessments did not come easily for the Consortium. It was and is an ongoing fight, with challenges, setbacks, compromises, revision, coalition building, and movement. It enacts on a larger scale what I have been arguing needs to be happening in school communities—practices of community organizing, relationship building, and self-reflection.

Part of the work of Consortium schools and their allies is ongoing defense of their autonomy, the system they have created. The leaders know how to build coalitions based on respect for the human being—they have been doing it for decades. Their history networks—and their privilege as educated, majority White people—put them in a position to be able to inform, challenge, and change education policy.

A Continuing Legacy of Political Engagement

From legislative campaigns to lawsuits to media releases, Consortium members work on many public fronts to sustain the principled education policies and practices they have developed. Some of these activities are in response to direct threats to school facilities, funding, and autonomy, and some anticipate challenges that may impact the work of Consortium schools in the future.[13]

One example of this public work is the 2008 "Proposal for Governance of NYC Schools." This document assesses NYC school decisionmaking, from educational, financial, and community perspectives, and, based on evidence that this decisionmaking does not always put the needs of students first, argues for the Consortium to maintain its independent status. The proposal goes far beyond advocacy for the Consortium, however: It outlines a comprehensive model for governance of the schools, based in well-thought-out principles arrived at through long experience, study, and collective deliberation. Like the student exemplar paper discussed above, this public document considers and analyzes multiple sources and asks essential questions of policymakers:

> "With every recommendation concerning mayoral control of schools, legislators must ask themselves this question: does the recommendation restore education to the center of the educational agenda?" (NY Performance Standards Consortium: Testimony to the State Senate Democratic Caucus Task Force on NYC School Governance, September 18, 2008, p. 3)

Consortium leaders turn the lens back on the examiners. The questions they ask help their audience to understand that public education must include standing up for and strengthening *the public*. To be democratic, people must challenge inequalities in decisionmaking power and interrogate the decisions that are made in the name of the people. This testimony goes on to analyze the discourse surrounding accountability. Just as the student paper above analyzed research approaches to the history of New York City planning with a question in mind about whose voices matter, the Consortium asks similar questions about whose voices are heard and whose voices are not heard in creating education policy:

> DOE press releases on accountability, empowerment, improved graduation rates, lowered dropout rates—all of these rhetorical flourishes have been accepted without any real, substantive debate in our communities. We ask you to look beyond the sound bites offered as excuses for a poorly conceived system. Where does the truth lie? What are the consequences of policies on the lives of children? Why has the union become the only voice defending the professionalism of teaching? . . . As proposals are considered for developing a new school governance structure, it is important to take into account questions such as these, and both the intended and unintended consequences of the policies being considered. (New York Performance Standards Consortium: Testimony to the State Senate Democratic Caucus Task Force on NYC School Governance, September 18, 2008, pp. 7–8)

Consortium members question power and hold the power holders accountable. Doing so, they widen democratic space. Government and education systems should be accountable not only for their policies but for the means by which they arrive at and evaluate these policies. Without such accountability, the school system undermines democracy in this country.[14]

Part of the reason the consortium has the power it does is that it is rooted in longlasting relationships that have weathered political storms before. While powerful individuals are part of this coalition, what makes it so strong is the collective commitment that drives it. Collective power is the counternarrative to the individualism, isolationism, and heroism that dominates education rhetoric today. Many members of such coalitions came of age as educators during the Civil Rights Movement and continued not only the commitments to justice that drove the movement but also the commitment to collective over individual leadership. The next chapter will look at this national network spanning generations, educational eras, and philosophies, as a story of sustainable educational change.

***

Learning, like community organizing, is strongest when people are actively constructing counternarrative: It is a frame for heightening consciousness, creativity, and challenge. The dominant narrative, the meritocratic narrative, is about "I"—individual success, earnings, and profit. Counternarrative questions those values: Who are they really for? Who do they really serve? Do they make it any more likely for me to get mine? Or are they, for most of us, a mirage?

Each of the three schools studied here offers a different counternarrative. At Rudy Lozano Leadership Academy, we saw students and teachers claiming the knowledge of their lives in the face of testing systems that devalued them. JJSE classes showed curriculum centered in community knowledge, culture, and creative resistance. The teachers and students at Urban Academy unfolded the power of questioning, both within the classroom and in the wider public world. These three schools grow trusting and powerful school–community relationships in educating for collective identity, knowledge, and action. This focus emerges from and honors the cultural values of Latino, African American, Asian, White, and other families who oppose individualist and meritocratic schooling models promoted by most American schools. These families and these values offer support for teaching for the common good, for the collective responsibility that our schools greatly need. The next chapter will pick up this strand of education for collectivity, focusing especially on the coalition model of the North Dakota Study Group.

Chapter 6

Building Sustainable Education

A Dissenting Democratic Countertradition

> I have felt it important from time to time to reaffirm some of the pieces of the fabric that has bound us over these many years, to suggest again that regardless of the circumstances that surround us, no matter how difficult, or discouraging it might seem, those large understandings need to be held, the cracks found, possibilities kept alive.
>
> —Vito Perrone

When it comes to education in America, there are a lot of well-meaning people and innovative directions in the mix, with answers to the $60,000 question of democratic education: *How does this country provide quality education to all children?* Throughout this book I have sought to show that democratic education demands that people in schools take the lead in addressing this question publicly. Students and teachers need to learn multiple perspectives, practice self-reflection, and dare to question power, so that they focus this question to the appropriate target: the society behind the schools. While people in schools cannot solve the problems of poverty, violence, and environmental and health concerns, they are well positioned to call out the powers that both undermine and limit access to high-quality education.

The act of calling out inequality in education is democratic education. It is not an avoidance of teachers' accountability but an appropriate use of it. It stands in the noble tradition of dissent in the United States: It is enriched by the diversity of voices that make up this country and grounded in the brilliant capacities for collective self-reflection of American thinkers from Twain to Greene.

As Guinier and Torres (2003) note, "New forms of social change will emerge if more people are aware of those ways in which power subtly shapes the rules of the game and the ways in which we tacitly accept those rules without question" (p. 301). What people understand as *play* needs to be vastly expanded—both to make play more accessible to people in their lives and to recognize its power in the public realm. For democracy is not a single action, a strong campaign, or a method. Democratic life has to be built day to day; it is never done. Jay Featherstone's (2003) term captures its complexity and its historicity: *a dissenting democratic countertradition.*

Holding the Space

> Schools provide individuals with the intellectual strength to be able to make up their own minds, to stand against false persuasions, and to unleash their idiosyncratic imaginations.
>
> —Ted Sizer

In this book I have shown what the day-to-day dynamic, imperfect work of democratic education can look like in a number of contexts. In this final chapter, my focus is on the people who hold the space for democratic work, in individual schools, in policymaking, and in resistance movements. In each of the preceding chapters we encountered people who hold this space, who illustrate the manifold ways conditions can be created to affirm human dignity and enable collective powers to bloom. Like Tayo, who holds the space of ceremony, they are witnesses. Like Brian Schultz, who helped his students connect their struggle for education justice with the Civil Rights Movement, they are allies. Like Adam Heenan, who studies his students' work and listens to them studying one another's work, they are curators. Like Jasmin Cardenas, who encourages students and teachers to explore how power impacts identity and relationships with their bodies and voices, they are storytellers. Like Ann Cook, who collaborates with other educators to develop and advocate for systems of teaching and assessing that respect young people, they are protectors.

Democratic educators inside and outside of classrooms hold space for young people, for the power and insight they bring to the world. They have to be deft and resourceful in holding this space—it is far more active work than conventional teaching. The activity of democratic education is kaleidoscopic; it moves, forms new combinations, and changes perspectives, always with people—past, present, future, near, and far—at the center. Practicing social learning, and standing up for it, is deeply sustaining for educators.

The people who sustain democratic education are not heroes; they are not on the news, and teaching methods and grants are not named after them. They are ordinary people who are committed to working for democratic education together. Democratic education grows in the relationships between them, in what Maxine Greene (1988) calls in-between space, referring to Hannah Arendt's example of French Resistance fighters: "They had become 'challengers,' had taken the initiative upon themselves and therefore, without knowing or even noticing it, had begun to create that public space between themselves where freedom could appear" (p. 15).

Our democracy requires that our educators keep a steady eye on the systems that shape their students' lives, that they understand their work in both global and local contexts. Democratic education is a commitment that unfolds over the long haul: It means, as Linda Darling-Hammond (1997) emphasizes, building the profession, mentoring, and sharing responsibility for those who enter teaching. Democratic education

> calls on us to work to surmount the walls that have separated us in our own institutions—across department, division, and union lines. And it calls for all of us to be as concerned with educating policymakers and the public as we are about educating our students. (p. 52)

Democratic educators need to be crossing boundaries in their own practice through the activating work of questioning power, self-reflection, and dialogic hunger. Professional teaching practice is continuously extended and refined by the larger public work of crossing boundaries between schools and statehouses and streets: It is in this dynamic in-between space that the power of young people learning enters the public.

When educators and students cross borders between schools and real life and challenge hierarchical divisions by age, race, and culture, they are taking part in the democratic work of *coalition building*. This is a community organizing method that has been for too long underused in education practice and induction: Financial and political interests have been allowed to run roughshod over students' education rights.[1] In this chapter I offer a brief sketch of a group that has resisted these forces, engaging in democratic coalition building continuously over the course of generations, and between generations. Throughout this book I have drawn on the work of individual members of this group, but in this chapter I focus on the exchange *between* them. By choosing to fight for the dignity of every child in every community, following the lead of the families in these communities while remaining aware of their own identities, these democratic educators step outside of prescribed roles and foster a new kind of freedom.

The long-standing professional community and committed community organizing on the part of leaders like Joan Bradbury, Pat Carini, Ted Chittenden, Ann Cook, Louisa Cruz-Acosta, Brenda Engel, Helen and Jay Featherstone, Francisco and Miguel Guajardo, Mike Klonsky, Deborah Meier, Vito Perrone, Joseph Suina, Lillian Weber, and many other educators helped in the formation of educational philosophies and practices uniquely capable of standing up to political pressures and gamesmanship. They enact the progressive mandate put forth by Robert Raup in 1933, urging teachers to take on the work for better societal conditions for their students: "When the type of character desired by the school is so dependent for support upon conditions in the whole culture," Raup wrote, "and this support is not forthcoming, the educator's responsibility moves out into society to agitate and to work for that support" (Cremin, 1976, p. 7).

This commitment has taken the shape of generative work ranging from political advocacy to creating policy to education practices in teacher education and teacher professional development. The numbers and directions of these projects are too vast to list here, so I will confine myself to a brief note on North Dakota Study Group on Evaluation (NDSG), one of the spaces that gathers and supports these educators and their work and that is representative of the power of cross-context coalitions in education. While this group is not the only such coalition-building group and these educators are not the only such educators, I focus on NDSG to highlight approaches that are sustainable and sustaining in education today.

"Experiment Station"

> Broad citizens organizations success seemed to me to depend crucially on a bold conceptual act: they deprofessionalize politics.
>
> —Harry Boyte

A brief historical note: Vito Perrone assembled the NDSG in North Dakota in 1972; since that time educators from around the country have been meeting every year for 2–3 days in February to compare notes on education and social change, in a fluid structure of large and small groups. Between meetings and over the years, these educators make their work public in their local contexts. A regular flow of this work was collected in the Monograph Series (now on the NDSG website: ndsg.org). A recent book, *Holding Values: What We Mean by Progressive Education* (Engel & Martin, 2005), brings together the writing of many NDSG leaders, all of whom have written books and articles individually as well.

The combination of intellectual work, personal fellowship, political involvement, play, self-reflection, and dialogue that NDSG participants engage in together makes it a sturdy model of the social learning called for by the original progressive educators like John Dewey, Jane Addams, Neva Boyd, Francis Parker, and Flora Cooke. These diverse activities sustain connections within and around educators, empowering them to create the same kind of connective framework for their students. I see NDSG as a modern incarnation of the Settlement House Movement, embodied in places like the Hull-House, in which people come together to confront inequity and injustice. As Harriet Vittum of the Northwestern settlement in Chicago noted, settlements "understand that they are experiment stations and they are willing to help people who are just beginning to think, think aloud, and that they will not be afraid" (Carson, 1990, p. 186).

NDSG is an "experiment station" in fostering community among people questioning power. The mobile, inclusive, research-intensive nature of their work makes NDSG a vehicle of democratic education. By building up the vibrant "in-between space" of good collaborative thinking and action, groups like NDSG broaden public space.

Public space is not only a physical place. It is a disposition and a hope. The public spaces I have been referencing throughout this book,

Hull-House and Highlander, represent such public spaces in our democratic consciousness. "Hull-House," Jane Addams (2002) writes, "endeavors to make social intercourse express the growing sense of the economic unity of society" (p. 14). Addams emphasizes that what is important about Hull-House is the coming together. The *how* of mutuality is the key—not *what* one person does to or for another. Pat Carini calls this "alongside learning," where "change is multiplied: Everyone is changed—teacher and student, advisor and teacher, experienced teacher and novice" (Engel & Martin, 2005, p. 9). The dance of reciprocity fosters circulation between school and community, with the great bridging help of the arts, and trust in children's own capacities. The outcome of this democratic play is not high test scores but public presence.[2]

As matrices of the connections made within them—between people of different cultures and classes, between different functions of society—public spaces organize democratic energy to counter oppression. NDSG nurtures relationship building in schools and communities and universities, such that they also are part of public space and contribute to its ongoing expansion. In an era of growing privatization of schools and other foundations of society, the widening of public space is a matter of survival for democratic life.

Public spaces illuminate a deeper meaning of "free education," connected to human experience rather than to money. Freedom grows in spaces where people from different backgrounds, contexts, and situations come together to change the systems that unjustly limit people from some groups and promote others. In the "free spaces" of this public work, people reinvent themselves in more connected ways. Democratic education makes space for healthy interchange among diverse people. Dialogue frees people from narrow functions and opens up to them a collective identity that draws on more parts of the individual, in connection with ever-widening circles of community.

People who participate in NDSG (which can be anyone; there is no formal membership, staff, or budget) understand that social learning is not just having fun together and getting along. NDSG generates counternarratives: As a collective, it resists power, challenges the dominant narrative, and continually creates new narrative. As Jay Featherstone writes, "The progressive emphasis on schools as democratic communities is important and necessary in its own right as an ideal in opposition to many of the reigning market, corporate, and consumerist visions of education; it ought to figure more prominently in a nation and world facing unprecedented immigration, dislocation, and the movement of peoples around the planet" (2005, p. 43). Democratic community means committing to the struggle for human dignity; schools should be explicitly teaching, modeling, and learning through this struggle.

Part of this living counternarrative is engaging conflict within the group itself. NDSG began as a mostly White, middle-class group of education professors, who had much to learn about dynamics of power and privilege within the progressive education movement—within themselves. Younger people, colleagues of color, and people with less education access challenged the educators to analyze and change these dynamics. Over the course of its 50-year history, NDSG has not only become more diverse in age, profession, race, language, and geography, but it has also learned to put dialogue, reflection, and study of diversity squarely at the heart of education. In ever-widening circles of learning, this dialogic work takes place among the educators themselves, in their home education contexts from California to New York, and in the development of teacher education and education policy.

A strong history of community organizing in social justice movements enables NDSG participants—who include leaders from SNCC and Freedom Schools and other civil rights groups—to recognize and nurture organic connections between the different constituencies in and around schools. Parents, policymakers, and community organizations are all part of this coalition for democratic education. NDSG is a national organization that affirms the *local* contexts of its members, strengthening the "free space" of politics in the hands of ordinary people. As one of many "hives" for NDSG participants, a great deal of cross-pollination takes place; NDSG is an educational form of community organizing. "Organizing begins with the culture, history, and past work of change in any setting. It has, as its first premise, a respect for the intelligence and talents of ordinary, uncredentialed citizens. It taps diverse self-interest, understanding self-interest in terms of the passions, life histories, relationships, and core values that motivate people" (Boyte, 2005, p. 35). By connecting the hopes and capacities of ordinary people, grassroots organizing holds space for democracy.

Like community organizing, democratic education recognizes the work people have already been doing. It sustains and builds that work in ongoing cycles of experimentation, reflection, and visioning. NDSG holds space for these processes by organizing meetings around "Works in Progress," in which a few people share with a larger group a project they are working on, with a strong emphasis on local context. The emphasis on the local within this national setting grounds thinking about educational change in the living stories and realities of students and teachers and community members. Change is, however, ongoing, not a stopping point. As Pat Carini emphasizes, "Struggle itself has positive value, is indeed itself a worthy work, and more than that, a work indispensable to the well-being of society . . . there isn't going to be a time when advocacy and struggle can be set aside" (Martin & Schwartz, 2014, p. 177). The counternarrative of democratic education challenges the fixation on efficiency that perennially dominates education policy.

"The Communal Nature of Our Work"

> If you want to walk faster, you walk by yourself. If you want to walk longer, walk with company.
>
> —African proverb

I will highlight two texts that represent this group, the oral histories project (on the NDSG website) and a collection of essays by NDSG participants, *Holding Values* (2005), edited by Ann Martin and Brenda Engel. These texts express NDSG's focus on documentation instead of testing (I discuss documentation practices in Chapter 3). Both of these texts ground the progressive education movement in collective identity developed over generations, especially as educators were shaped by and continued the legacy of the Civil Rights Movement.

Civil Rights Movement organizing fostered self-reflective group leadership representing people from many different generations, races, regions, and educational levels. Educators who were active in the Civil Rights Movement continued this momentum in building their educational work together. NDSG texts emphasize the collective nature of social justice leadership, as opposed to the qualities and achievements of charismatic individuals.

To convey the diverse voices, local knowledge, questions, and listening that make up the dialogic work of this group, I begin with a few moments in the NDSG Oral Histories. I will then turn to the written voices included in the book, many of which overlap with the oral history narratives.

Jay Featherstone introduces the oral history site with these words:

> The democratic argument here is that, through practices acquired over the push and pull of the last forty years, understandings gleaned from multi-cultural and multi-generational experiences, and values that have been generated thereby— coaxed into being, nourished, and held—we have more to work with than is ordinarily acknowledged. (www.ndsg.org/oralhistory/index.html)

As much as they are individuals' life stories, oral histories are reflections that help us to understand groups and relationships between groups. They are less about historical accuracy than about gaining greater perspective on the present moment.

The NDSG Oral Histories create a picture of education that is based in the exchange of many voices, the intersections of many histories, and ongoing questioning, conflict, and growth. Here, educators are human beings, not talking heads. The conversation between Arthur Tobier ("AT") and Alice Seletsky ("AS") on the Oral Histories site expresses the group's emphasis on collective work and suggests how it helps to shape democratic education. Here is a small excerpt from that conversation:

> *AS:* The communal nature of our work was really very important. Throughout it was always collective and shared, and that was enormous support.
>
> *AT:* The general public looks at the test scores and has no notion of the collective effort that's being made, not only on behalf of their own kids, but on behalf of a larger meaning of our society. Where's the public for that?

Unlike many educational approaches, the work AS and AT refer to is collective: created in groups, practiced in communities, evaluated in coalitions. *Public.* Like Neva Boyd's efforts to address social problems through social methods, the work of these educators emphasizes social learning in education for democracy. The Oral Histories suggest that the diversity and diffuseness of the NDSG contribute powerfully to its longevity. Its initial impetus in countering the testing industry expanded to exploration of multicultural education, development of constructive models of partnership between schools and community organizations, and wide-ranging philosophical and political work.

"AT" and "AS" continue:

> *AT:* Diane Mullins, who had been an elementary school teacher in Greenwich Village, said something similar in her interview. She felt that what was most meaningful for her at these meetings were all the different voices from around the country.
>
> *AS:* Yeah, right.
>
> *AT:* Different sounds, different tones of voice, different ways of talking American speech.
>
> *AS:* Well, also different experiences. I mean there were people, like Joe [Suina], whose whole teaching world—I mean, we're all teachers, more or less, so we had that common ground; but then everybody's individual, personal story was sort of unique and distinctive. [There were] people from different worlds, and it was wonderful to be able to meet with them and talk to them. Our meetings weren't so much about the issues in education, as far as I was concerned, although those issues—testing for one, and certification for another—were always the subtext. The goal was eventually to develop strong critiques of standardized testing. But every year testing increased and so there was an inverse relationship between what the goals were and what the results were. As the group expanded, over the years, it took in other issues. Testing was always dreadful, but it

seems like we were never ever going to succeed in dismantling it, and we didn't. And so for some part of the time, we sort of worked around it . . . we did an end run.

Like the sandcastle metaphor Guinier and Torres (2003) use in *The Miner's Canary*, the group's work is not just about "constructing the sandcastle," accomplishing specific goals. Its work is made more powerful by its reflexive quality; like people building a sandcastle that they know will wash away, NDSG participants value working together even when they do not see immediate success. They actively analyze and craft their collaborative processes together in order to continue collaboration in all their many education contexts, locally and nationally.

In this interview, Seletsky touches on a crucial strength of educators like those in the NDSG. Coming together across differences, and the accompanying dialogues—back-and-forth, tensions, support—give the group an agility, a wiliness, that Seletsky puts in terms of play when it comes to the group's relationship to power, specifically represented by tests. That they could do an "end run" around the tests does not mean they were just dodging them. NDSG folk were in the game, and they stayed in the game.

The importance of the difference in voices is not just in what people have to say, but how they say it—in other words, who they are. Democratic dialogue does not happen in the abstract, but unfolds in specific places with specific people who bring with them their traditions, their language, their view on the world. They are interested in other specific people who also stand in their culture. Attention to how things are said has ramifications beyond the face-to-face dialogue between people; the arts of democratic education must be practiced as much in response to tone, timbre, and gesture as to the content of words.

Learning in Community Partnerships

> Instead of trying to bully young people to remain in classrooms isolated from the community and structured to prepare them to become cogs in the existing economic system, we need to recognize that the reason why so many young people drop out of inner-city schools is because they are voting with their feet against an educational system that sorts, tracks, tests, and certifies them like products of a factory because it was created for the age of industrialization. They are crying out for the kind of education that gives them opportunities to exercise their creative energies because it values them as whole human beings.
>
> —Grace Lee Boggs

I will touch on a moment from my own experience at an NDSG meeting to provide an example of how such exchange leads to greater understanding of student learning. Every time I attend one of these meetings, I hear stories of young people taking leadership and exchanging wisdom with elders in their home contexts, whether that be in Texas or New Orleans or Hawa'ii. The young people describing artfully designed partnerships with older generations have deeply influenced my thinking about education.

The 2014 meeting was in Detroit, at the invitation of Grace Lee Boggs, a powerful social justice leader almost 100 years old, who along with other Detroit community organizers and educators introduced NDSG to the work Detroiters were doing "reimagining and restorying" the city. Before coming to the conference, participants read assigned articles like James Boggs's (2011) "Community Building: An Idea Whose Time Has Come," which argues,

> our first priority must be the rebuilding or the regeneration of our communities because it is in community that human beings have always found their personhood or their human identity as persons. You can't find your human identity out there by yourself. It is in the community that our human identity is created because it is in the community that love, respect, and responsibility for one another are nurtured (p. 334).

Educating citizens for equity and justice requires a strong focus on community power, especially the conflicts and transformations involved when community power is engaged. For democracy exists in the ongoing work of specific human beings analyzing and changing systems of power. Grace Lee Boggs describes the growth of local community power as an "organically evolving cultural revolution." Detroit, like thousands of other local communities fighting for social justice, is "growing the soul" of interdependence and resistance to dehumanization. "In 'this exquisitely connected world,'" Boggs writes, quoting Margaret Wheatley, "the real engine of change is never 'critical mass'; dramatic and systemic change begins with 'critical connections'" (G. L. Boggs & Kurashige, 2011, p. 50).

At the 2014 meeting of the NDSG, participants continued a many-year inquiry into the relationship between education and sustainability. One of the community sites that participants had an opportunity to visit on this bright February morning was the Eastern Michigan Environmental Action Council (EMEAC). At EMEAC's beautiful site, a Gilded Age–era mansion called the Cass Corridor Commons, which houses several social justice organizations, leaders talked to a small group of educators—not about plants and pollution but about learning, relationships, and personal growth as environmental issues.

At Cass Corridor Commons, young adult leaders from the community engage teenagers only a few years younger than them in "hip-hop literacy." This community organization is not the kind of external partner that imposes top-down change from outside of students' experience; rather, it supports critical analysis people in the schools may not have access to, such as structural analysis of race and power and interpersonal relationship building.

The young EMEAC leaders explained the educational premises of this literacy pedagogy to the assembled educators, who were mostly teachers a generation or two older and uneducated in the meaning of hip-hop. Hip-hop literacy, we learn, presents the conditions and issues that are most real in young people's lives, within a critical framework that enables young people to construct meaning and to connect with values that affirm them culturally and linguistically. In hip-hop art, "maturity and power can be triggered through vocabulary," Todd Ziegler, one of the young EMEAC leaders, explains. Hip-hop is a deeply democratic art, an expression of healing and hope: "Hip hop," Todd narrated, referring to histories of violence in urban communities that drove people into isolated and fearful private spaces, "came out of people bringing people back on the street . . . bringing music outdoors . . . the message was, 'stop staying indoors, come together!'" The hip-hop modality of sampling is also democratic education: By setting iconic musical "texts" in new relations to one another and connecting them with contemporary rhythms and beats, hip-hop music traces knowledge and histories that span generations. In this way, young people connect to the cultural legacy of musical traditions of older generations like jazz and blues; hip-hop puts them in dialogic relationship to cultural knowledge and power that they can build on.

Because they were so recently teenagers themselves, and were themselves mentored in empowering ways, these young community educators have powerful insights about liberatory educational relationships. Through dialogue, conversation that invokes values and recognizes capacities, drawing on what both adults and students know and do not know, a learning exchange unfolds between educators and students. In this reciprocal exchange, it is not "students' learning" or "teachers' learning," but learning as the field that connects them.

As I listened, it seemed to me that this approach was more natural—and thus more possible—with young African American leaders in educational relationships with African American youth. When I asked how this exchange might translate for White teachers of students of color, EMEAC leader Will Copeland responded with the story of a young White teacher who came to teach in the neighborhood school. The first thing she did, he said, was learn where the young people spent their time out of school, and go there. Even though she did not live in the community, she spent her free time in the community spaces where her students were. She knew that she did not walk in the door with the kind of relational capital that a colleague who is a person of color might and that she faced a steep learning curve. By respecting students in their neighborhood environment, trust developed that could nurture strong reciprocal learning relationships. This White teacher was doing her part in the "restorying" of Detroit, by basing her teaching in the close company she kept with her African American students, in their neighborhood.

I highlight the educational work of EMEAC not as an exceptional program with exceptional people (though they *are* exceptional!), but as an example of the kind of local knowledge and democratic practices that thousands of ordinary people all over the country (and the world) are engaged in. The social knowledge that blooms in grassroots organizations is a transformative resource for our schools, as the scores of schools in Detroit who partner with such organizations understand.

A speaker at the NDSG meeting later that day underscored what was so important in the approach the White teacher took in the Cass Corridor neighborhood. Former Black Panther Ron Scott talked about the unacknowledged racial tensions that poison education in America. Of education reformers who claim to transform kids and communities, he said, "We never put ourselves in uncomfortable situations to transform ourselves." "The charity model," he continued, "created a dynamic we can't handle. It's crippling. You want to come into an area and you don't want to respect the indigenous knowledge that's already there—a wall goes up." Unlike the White teacher Will had talked about earlier, many educators as well as education policymakers assume that they are doing good without taking the time to learn how to enter a space respectfully. In this way, a White supremacist master narrative remains unchallenged.

Longtime NDSG member Deborah Meier raised a perspective closely related to Scott's analysis at a Progressive Education Network conference, composed in large part of majority White educators in private and charter schools thinking together about equity in education. To the suggestion that private schools should build support for neighboring public schools into their budget and their mission—a forward-thinking progressive idea—Meier, the founder of several public schools in New York, responded, "I find your proposal insulting." Her students "shouldn't have to thank anyone" for having access to materials that are their educational right, Meier continued. "How about you put this in your mission: Tell rich people to pay more taxes. Our society honors people who have a lot of money and give away a lot of money—but it doesn't honor people who pay a lot of taxes. We see the government as a resource of last resort, not as a strong economic force." Meier and other NDSG members challenge progressive educators to resist market-based reforms such as privatization of the public school system, pushed by wealthy funders of progressive schools.

Progressive education has long held that the child is at the center of the learning, not the external standards and content. However, current education reform subordinates the students in the toughest conditions to the most standardized and least holistic education. If it is to truly be democratic, progressive education must publicly challenge the unspoken assumptions about race, class, and ability that underlie both education policy and education reform. Neoliberal systems manifest a belief that low-income communities of color do not have the capacity to improve on their own but need predominantly White, privileged people to solve their problems. Whether this happens through creating new schools or new standards, systems that approach education achievement separate from the social conditions that shape children's experiences stifle the heart of democratic life.

"Looking at Education in a Democratic Context"

NDSG meetings offer educators opportunities to wrestle with the legacies of dominant culture education on people of color. In another interview on the oral history site, Joseph Suina discusses why considerations of race and culture have become so central to the work of NDSG.

AT's interview with "Joe," referenced in Alice Seletsky's reflection, highlights looking closely at differences and understanding identity in education. Suina, a Native American educator, describes NDSG's work from its beginnings in 1972 as "looking at education in a democratic context":

> Looking at more than just reading but reading between the lines. What it means to be "educated" as a democratic citizen . . . I started looking at schools with an eye out for more than just achievement. I started teaching with a greater emphasis on social justice issues, and that worked well in my bilingual education classes. Materials development became important because there was so little of it for specific minority groups. How did you, as a teacher, extend yourself to have more materials? One of the problems with materials, of course, particularly here in the Southwest, was the lack of Indian-ness in classrooms. There was not a whole lot of material even for the Hispanics in the Albuquerque schools. They were using materials developed in Dade County, Florida, for the Cuban population, which was inappropriate for our area.

Suina's attention to language, appropriate texts, and culture evolved into his study of the learning environment in education (Loughlin & Suina, 1982). Affirming the local environment and cultural and familial relationships counters dehumanizing abstraction in education.

Later in the interview, Tobier asks Suina about "hidden messages" in the curriculum and in schools. Suina responds,

> Messages which are ever so subtle, yet very powerful. The textbooks I had as a child, for example, that pictured only pitched roofs and straight walls, sidewalks and grass. My world was quite different; it was one of adobe homes, dirt floors, the bare ground, and not a whole lot of vegetation in the yard that I was growing up in. It was a different way of life, a different lifestyle that was presented clearly as one to be valued over anything else. But because these materials were produced by very educated people, in high gloss, and in the context of being central to the curriculum, they communicated very strongly "the ideal

life." As if to say, "This was what you become and get when you get educated, when you finally get civilized! What you have at home now is not good enough!" And although it was not true, as a child I began to take in that message.

There was always this measuring of self and the past, and of self and the future. Even a simple thing, like this couch behind us here, was framed as something you lived to have in the future. In the meantime, the sheepskin, the Indian blankets, the things that we rolled up during the day and used as a couch, what you already had, were demeaned. . . . The message was that you become, and when you reach for it well, one day you will have it . . . if you will only become educated and let go of the past. And for a good while, I actually had that dream in my head. (www.ndsg.org/oralhistory/index.html)

The hidden messages of disrespect that did violence to tribal culture are continued into the present in standardized curriculum and testing. Education based in "measuring" devalues the local knowledge that every human being has access to in his or her own family story and community. Suina took an undemocratic education legacy and worked to integrate into it value for different cultures. This kind of respect for human dignity and justice permeates NDSG.

The group's evolving understanding of itself over generations is dialogic. It takes note of strengths and weaknesses in its history, trajectory, and present. Suina highlights Lisa Delpit's (2006) incisive critiques of NDSG, for its assumption that progressive child-centered pedagogy is universally appropriate, without recognizing the contexts of many African American (and Native American) students for whom this pedagogy does not connect. The essays included in *Holding Values* express the potency of collective self-reflection.

"A Dissenting Democratic Countertradition"

Holding Values presents strands of dialogue that NDSG participants engage in with educators and policymakers and with progressive forerunners like John Dewey and Jane Addams. These voices embody the constructive power of democratic dissent: They confront political power, experiment with new approaches, and engage in honest self-reflection. In her Introduction, Brenda Engel (Engel & Martin, 2005) tells the story of the group's evolution over generations, the story of a network of individuals and groups that resist education injustice continuously and thoughtfully. Engel articulates the democratic question that NDSG writings address:

The issue of educational evaluation has to do basically with power relationships, which are at the heart of politics: Who has the right to evaluate what and whom? Who decides on criteria and instruments? What degree of consent needs to be sought from those having a stake in the consequences? (p. 13)

When evaluation is divorced from practice, learning, and human beings in relationship, it cannot be an instrument of education; it is more likely to serve the ends of profiteers.

The NDSG founders came out of the Civil Rights Movement, in conjunction with the progressive education revival of the early 1960s: "They were trying to maintain the connection between classroom reform and egalitarian political reform." Jay Featherstone explains what this means in today's context:

> Within education, democracy has to mean not only the participation of all children intellectually and socially in school subjects, but also a renewed fight for equal access and racial justice. We need a fresh new struggle to equalize the scandal of unequal funding on education, and new scrutiny of the role of schools in reinforcing inequities of class and race and gender. It is also obvious that schools alone cannot take us to a better democracy, though clearly they have a role to play. (Engel & Martin, 2005, p. 45)

A deep and ongoing commitment to struggle courses through the work of NDSG educators. The public struggles NDSG has been part of over the years have been shaped and refined by struggles within the group itself, to understand itself. Members learn by working with one another's differences in terms of generation, educational experience, race, culture, political perspective, economic status, sexual orientation, and gender. Honesty about racial inequality and integrating racial awareness into education means accepting unresolvable questions, uncertainty, uncomfortable self-reflection—the organs of progressive education, as George Hein points out in his piece, "A Progressive Education Perspective on Evaluation":

> Perhaps nothing is as important in articulating a progressive stance on evaluation as Dewey's concept that the world is an uncertain place, that actions need to be guided by and respect actual experience—the human condition in constant flux—and that the nature of any human enterprise needs to be examined continually and modified to respond to the consequences of previous decisions and actions. (Engel & Martin, 2005, p. 177)

The dialogic work of reflection, action, and change has allowed the group to evolve and gain power and breadth. Testing remains at the center of the struggle that NDSG has convened around since it is a linchpin in the push and pull between centralized, one-size-fits-all education control and education freedom, based in respect for teachers, students, and parents.

"The Progressive agenda," Vito Perrone argues, must take on the pivotal historical moment for education policy marked by the 1983 report *A Nation at Risk*, widely used as the definitive statement of education in crisis in America. Noting that the report was methodologically ill-founded and politically motivated, he asks, "How could such a document with so little social-cultural-education evidence have played so well in the media?" He goes on to tell the story of NDSG's response to the impact of the report:

> In those complicated, backlash years, members of the Study Group challenged the directions, continued to write about more powerful possibilities for the schools, found allies in parents, and convinced many state legislators that some space needed to be provided for a different vision of education. (Engel & Martin, 2005, p. 32)

An important part of the "different vision of education" NDSG members fought for was actualized in the fight itself: not just implementing progressive education practices in the classroom but keeping a constant eye on and hand in the "larger work" of education.

NDSG sustains a living memory of generations of education policy, and many members understand standardized testing as part of a conservative narrative initiated decades ago, designed to push back social programs and the local control of schools. According to Harold Berlak's (2003) history of education policy, corporate interests and government powers developed standardized testing as a political and economic weapon, to counter the rise of Black Power, La Raza, and other movements of people of color asserting their power. New waves of reform and different tests simply screen the fact that

> substituting the current crop of standardized tests with a new breed of "authentic" standardized tests is not an advance because they do not challenge the centralization of power. Standardized testing is the key issue because it is the essential tool for centralizing control. (pp. 64–65)

Testing-dominated education is the polar opposite of the respect for indigenous knowledge that Suina puts at the heart of democratic education.

There is power in resisting the systems of authority that operate by means of testing—and in creating alternatives: "Unity of thought and action leads toward freedom of the individual—whenever a person acts in obedience to someone else's thinking, he is giving up a measure of independence" (Engel & Martin, 2005, p. 15). Depersonalized, disconnected information imposed on people in schools through standardized tests and curriculum degrade the dignity of the individual human being.

Though progressive education developed to counter mechanized systems of schooling, it has succeeded only in creating small refuges for some students; too many students are still subject to education that represses their full range of power and growth. Like Jay Featherstone (2003), who criticizes the antipolitical strain in progressivism that makes educators avoid confrontation, conflict, and resistance, Berlak warns that "progressive" does not take into account the fight needed for improvement of the social order. Berlak emphasizes that progressive educators need to learn from their experiences, their mistakes, and their failures—pedagogically *and* politically:

Many progressive educators depoliticized progressive education, viewing it narrowly as a children's rights and pedagogical movement to the exclusion of a wider vision of economic and political democracy. If a new reinvigorated national progressive education movement is to take shape, it must see itself also as a political movement, as an integral part of the broader struggle for human rights, social and economic justice. And progressive educators must deal with cultural parochialism, classism, and racism within our practices and organizations. These are deeply rooted in history and remain as formidable barriers to collective action and achieving democracy and equality. (Engel & Martin, 2005, p. 65)

Focusing on student learning apart from not only the sociological conditions students are in but also apart from the needs and conditions of democratic society as a whole perpetuates fragmented, irrelevant, unsound education.

People in schools are resources for social improvement, and perceptions about them need to change correspondingly. The schools are not "the problem." Fixation on evaluating, reforming, and improving the schools distracts people from dealing with the real problem of democracy: identifying the economic, cultural, and political processes by which the strong fortify themselves against inroads for equality. The more people in and around schools challenge these processes, the stronger the schools and society will be.

Adult society needs to learn to take young people seriously, not only respecting their agency in their own lives but also recognizing them as leaders who have an important role to play in democratic progress. Instead of pinning them to individual measures on a standardized scale, schools should be nurturing youths' understanding of themselves as part of a vibrant collective leadership. They should be helping students learn the language and methods of collective power. We have the ability to change the rules that make up the structures of our individual and collective lives—and thereby change the structures themselves. By focusing on intellectual development, cross-cultural relationships, and intergenerational activism, people in schools and communities sustain education for democratic life.

Notes

Introduction

1. Indeed, many observers suspect that current test-based accountability structures are a smoke screen to, as Ken Sirotnik (2004) writes,

> divert public attention from other explanations that call for substantial investments in educating urban and rural poor and minority children before they come to school, reducing class size, securing qualified and experienced teachers, instituting a full employment policy, and reducing rural and urban poverty. (p. 31)

Externally imposed measurements confound the central premise of citizenship: independent thinking.

2. As Gloria Ladson-Billings (2009) and Lisa Delpit (2006) argue, if progressive education does not deliberately and consistently concern itself with the academic success of students of color, it perpetuates injustice. At the same time, I believe that W.E.B. DuBois's emphasis on the social and political vocation of the teacher of African Americans students is fundamental to addressing their social context. DuBois writes in 1933 that the teacher

> has got to be able to impart his knowledge to human beings whose place in the world is today precarious and critical; and the possibilities and advancement of that human being in the world where he is to live and earn a living is of just as much importance in the teaching process as the content of the knowledge taught. Teachers . . . have got to be social statesmen and statesmen of high order. (DuBois, 2001, p. 105)

3. Sheldon Berman (1997) points out that the development of social responsibility in young people depends not on instilling particular qualities or skills in young people but recognizing behaviors of social responsibility as they emerge. He writes,

> Our conception of the child as egocentric, morally immature, uninterested in the social and political world, and unable to understand it has effectively deprived young people of the kind of contact they need to make society and politics salient. Young people's distance from politics and their lack of interest may be an effect of our misconceptions, our ignorance of their potential, and our protectiveness. (p. 193)

4. Alexander (2010) writes,

> The valiant efforts to abolish slavery and Jim Crow and to achieve greater racial equality have brought about significant changes in the legal framework of American society—new "rules of the game," so to speak. These new rules have been justified by new rhetoric, new language, and a new social consensus, while producing many of the same results. This dynamic . . . is the process through which white privilege is maintained, though the rules and rhetoric change. (p. 21)

5. This includes struggle for the terms themselves. As many thinkers have observed, "democratic education" has been claimed by opposing sides. In Apple and Carlson's (1998) words,

> recent rhetorical shifts to concerns about consumer choice, diversity, democracy, etc. within current neo-liberal education policy . . . cover the fact that these "reforms" may simply be new ways of reproducing older class and race hierarchies. . . . "Democracy" may be talked about as "enhancing individual choice," but it may also be a code word for increased conditions of what might better be described as something like apartheid. (p. 9)

I agree with these thinkers in prioritizing "a fully political and educative notion of democracy that recaptures the collective struggle by citizens to build institutions in participatory ways" (1998, p. 9). People do this locally, thoughtfully—the more change is "done" by external players and with the aim of maximum scalability, the less democratic it will be.

6. See Semel and Sadovnik (1999) for extensive study of the contradictions presented by progressive schools for the wealthy.

7. As Connie North (2008) notes,

> When some students are struggling to find food and shelter while others are debating the merits of this advanced placement class over that one, we cannot expect a single approach to social justice education to be effective for all students in all contexts. (p. 1200)

8. Harry Boyte (2005) emphasizes that ordinary people taking up political work is critical to democracy:

> Politics is the master language of decision-making and power-wielding in complex, diverse societies. When politics becomes increasingly professionalized, the property of professional politicians, activist lobbyists, or ideological mobilizers of the people, most people are shut out of the serious work of deciding about and creating the world. Citizens are reduced to righteous demands, complaints, or peripheral acts as helpers. (p. 31)

9. More recently, constructivist theories of learning (such as those put forth by Lev Vygotsky, 1978) developed progressive education practices with understandings of how people construct knowledge through interaction with other people and with the world around them. Constructivist frameworks intersect with the experiential learning described in this book.

10. Dewey (2008) describes democratic education as developing the "capacity to live as a social member so that what (the person) gets from living balances with what he contributes. What he gets and gives as a human being, a being with desires, emotions, and ideas, is not external possessions, but a widening and deepening of conscious life—a more intense, disciplined, and expanding realization of meanings" (p. 369).

11. Foucault's analysis of power and knowledge is too vast to treat substantively here. For the present I will just note that my discussion of the individual–collective relationship in democratic education is influenced by Foucault's observation that freedom is undermined by unseen controls (the less they are recognized, the more powerful they are). These controls shape the individual's conception of selfhood, but when individuals together confront these controls, they discover freedom and democratic power:

> the political, ethical, social, philosophical problem of our days is not to try to liberate the individual from the state and from the state's institutions but to liberate us both from the state and from the type of individualization which is linked to the state. We have to promote new forms of subjectivity through the refusal of this kind of individuality which has been imposed on us for several centuries. (Foucault, 1982, p. 785)

12. Noting the consequences of progressive educators' reluctance to take the political stand necessary to protect public education, Counts (1934) writes,

> . . . the fact cannot be stressed too strongly that in capitalistic society, where large areas of life are reserved to the operation of business enterprise, a sharp line divides public from private interest. It is this line that educators have been unable to pass. As a consequence, the school is forced into an artificial world and organized education is pushed out upon the periphery of existence. (p. 561)

13. Evans and Boyte emphasize that public space illuminates relationships among differences: "Public spaces . . . exist on the borders, connecting as well as differentiating community and public arena. Their democratic character grows out of the fact that they are both located in community and look outward toward the larger world" (p. xii).

14. Evans and Boyte (1992) refer to these dynamics as "drama":

> If power relationships in many settings are sharply unequal, they are also always contested and mutually transformative. One never simply "acts on" another— any process of action always has reciprocal moments, changing both partners in the drama. Groups of people in society are never simply or completely "powerless"; there are always resources, stratagems, and social and cultural maneuvers available to and used by even those who seem at first appearance most unambiguously victimized. Out of the density and complexity of power dynamics, in ways rarely explored, relatively autonomous popular activity— what can be called "free spaces"—can be sustained over long periods. (p. xvii)

15. Boyd explains with significant stimulus the individual has in himself potentially a new person and the group a new collective life. This is another way of saying that, given dynamic environment, the individual has within himself the possibilities for a fulfillment that is both preventive and corrective of problem behavior. Fulfillment for the individual lies in the development of sufficiently varied types of powers and vital interests to maintain balanced living. (Boyd, 1971, p. 148)

16. I am interested in a wide-ranging dialogue of educators that challenges traditional hierarchies in education institutions:

> Teachers of all kinds (at universities and colleges, elementary, middle, and secondary schools, community and cultural activists, and so on) can mutually teach each other about how more democratic policies and practices can be developed and how to talk about them in ways in which all can participate. (Apple & Carlson, 1998, p. 29)

17. As Deborah Meier (2003) notes of democratic education, habits of social responsibility "cannot, on the whole, be taught didactically; but the way we organize schooling will contribute to or negate the development of such inclinations" (p. 19).

18. George Counts (1934) discusses this issue in his analysis of the social composition of school boards. Pointing out that school boards are often populated with highly educated people, he questions the assumption that people who have had the most access to education should be the ones who control access to education.

19. Practices of deficit-based education are based more in political than philosophical theory: "The deficit-thinking model is a theory that blames the victims of school failure for their own lack of success in a system that was designed to serve the interests of the wealthy and powerful" (Riester, Pursch, & Skrla 2002, p. 282).

20. In focusing on the wide field of democratic relationships beyond the space of the classroom, I purposely (and unhappily!) omit discussion of the fundamental educational relationship of teacher and student. Other writers discuss this significant relationship in transformative ways: cf. Rodgers and Raider-Roth (2006); Ladson-Billings (2009); Duncan-Andrade (2011); Noguera and Boykin (2011); Ayers, Ladson-Billings, and Michie (2009).

Chapter 1

1. In describing analytical work that leads to social change, Linda Christensen (2007) points to her student Omar's comment, "When we read children's books, we aren't just reading cute little stories, we are discovering the tools with which a young society is manipulated" (p. 8). Once students began to engage in this kind of critical inquiry, Christensen emphasizes, "they couldn't stop analyzing the rest of the world" (p. 13).

2. See Cremin (1964) and Benson, Harkavy, and Puckett (2007) for critiques of Dewey for retreating from the complexities and controversies that social learning provokes.

3. Derek Woodrow (1996) challenges the assumption often made by progressive educators that student-centered education serves all students equally and leads to social progress:

student-centered learning rarely involves real sharing of control but, by focusing on the individual learner, directs attention away from societal and institutional forms of disempowerment, for example due to inequalities of class, ethnicity, or gender. In particular there is an unquestioning acceptance of the social, political, and economic status-quo—blaming the individual victim for their educational failures. (p. 48)

Noting that student-centered education works well for students from more privileged families, Woodrow urges that we ask how progressive it really is to empower students who are already empowered.

4. See Rodgers (2006) for the compelling story of the Putney School.

5. A short list of these foundational texts includes Ayers, Hunt, and Quinn (1998); Levinson (2012); Gutstein (2006); North (2009); and Westheimer and Kahne (2004).

6. Experiential educator Salvatore Vascellaro (2011) notes that when teachers and children move beyond the school building and beyond the book, learners

experience the deep connections that exist between the physical and social worlds around them and understand how these connections affect their lives; how human existence is dependent on a complex weave of people's work, people whose lives and work too often remain invisible. (p. 9)

By coming into physical contact with the realities of other people's lives, people begin to experience interdependence of place and person, word and identity.

7. In their outline of "counterstories" as a foundation of critical race theory, Solorzano and Bernal (2001) explain that

counterstories can serve several theoretical, methodological, and pedagogical functions, including the following: (a) They can build community among those at the margins of society by putting a human and familiar face to educational theory and practice; (b) they can challenge the perceived wisdom of those at society's center; (c) they can open new windows into the reality of those at the margins of society by showing the possibilities beyond the ones they live and to show that they are not alone in their position; (d) they can teach others that by combining elements from both the story and the current reality, one can construct another world that is richer than either the story or the reality alone; and (e) they can provide a context to understand and transform established belief systems. (pp. 327–328)

8. For a fuller history of this educational colonization—whose effects are far from ended—see Deloria and Wildcat (2001).

9. Native American educator Joseph Suina uses the physical reality and cultural symbol of the fence to describe the American schooling system from his perspective as a 5-year-old Pueblo Indian entering school: "A prominent barbwire fence to keep out both the cows and our native tongue completely insulated the school" (Engel & Martin, 2005, p. 88). The campaign against his Keres language and many other Native American tongues forced assimilation by separating the children from their Native identities; in the process, Suina

mourns, the American schooling system pillaged the language, traditions, and continuity that sustains Native American cultures.

10. The term *toxic tour* is problematic. Community-based environmental groups like LVEJO use the term to heighten awareness and concern over the pollution imposed on people's homes and lives, but when people from outside the neighborhood accept language like *toxic tour*, instead of grappling with the violence of the concept, it can contribute to cynicism rather than solidarity. A related critique is associated with the term *poverty tourism*: When well-meaning people go to other neighborhoods or countries "to see how the other half lives" or "to help," they strengthen rather than counter an unjust status quo of exploitation regulated by charitable enterprises rather than by the oversight of an intelligent and active public. Place-based education evokes political analysis grounded in heightened awareness of race, class, and gender identity.

11. See Illich's (1968) "To hell with good intentions," for critique of unconscious cultural imperalism.

12. My students' responses fit the patterns of privilege that Sharon Welch (1990) describes in *A Feminist Ethic of Risk*: "It is easier to give up on long-term social change when one is comfortable in the present—when it is possible to have challenging work, excellent health care and housing, and access to fine arts. When the good life is present or within reach, it is tempting to despair of its ever being in reach for others and resort merely to enjoying it for oneself and one's family" (p. 41). When people from affluent communities faced with social problems refuse to persist in struggle, when they withdraw into cynicism, they weaken democracy.

13. Gruenewald (2003a) writes, "A critical pedagogy of place is thus a response against educational reform policies and practices that disregard places and that leave assumptions about the relationship between education and the politics of economic development unexamined" (p. 3).

14. In her study of social justice education, Connie North (2009) observes,

> I have yet to meet someone who learned solely through textbook knowledge or conscious reasoning the courage to dissent publicly, the humility to examine continuously one's own blind spots, or the ability to witness the physical, material, and psychological suffering of others. (p. 75)

The messiness of experiential learning exposes the messiness of inequality and racism in society.

Chapter 2

1. Iris Marion Young writes about the importance of diverse relationships for democratic society: "Expressing, questioning, and challenging differently situated knowledge . . . adds to the social knowledge of all the participants. This greater social objectivity increases their wisdom for arriving at just solutions to collective problems" (p. 128).

For an important challenge to this vision, see Alison Jones's (2006) argument that democratic dialogue is an exercise in self-deception for people of privilege and an added burden on marginalized people:

Dialogue and recognition of difference turn out to be access for dominant groups to the thoughts, culture, lives of others. While marginalized groups may be invited—with the help of the teacher—to make their own social conditions visible to themselves, the crucial aspect of the dialogic process is making themselves visible to the powerful (Boler, 2006). In facilitating dialogue across differences, it is crucial to keep in mind such challenges.

2. In retelling the story, I follow Guinier and Torres's lead. They name the public school but not the private one.

3. In related work, Janet Helms's (1990) description of White racial identity development emphasizes that the process of becoming aware of one's Whiteness leads to internalizing "a realistically positive view of what it means to be White" (p. 55). In Helms's model, the White protesters Guinier and Torres describe might be in the "pseudo-independence" stage, when their response to injustice takes the form of wanting to "help" people of color, but not to challenge systems of dominance.

4. Guinier and Torres borrow the term *charismatic community* from Marshall Ganz.

5. Amina Knowlan (forthcoming) explains that awareness of group identity is central to social equity work:

> The invisibility of privilege is culturally encouraged when dominant group members are systematically taught to see themselves as individuals, not as members of a group, and to view privileges as distinct entities that are effects of individual merit. . . . To truly understand *systems of oppression and privilege,* the first requirement is that we shift our focus from *individuals* to belonging to *groups* of individuals that are defined by sharing a common *identity.* Any one individual can maintain that he or she is not racist. As members of a dominant group in our U.S. culture we are trained to see *racism* or *sexism* or *homophobia* as individually mediated acts of unconsciousness, meanness or even violence. Most of us are not trained to see the privileges that we are given to us simply because of an *identity* we share with others.

6. Paul Loeb (2010) also emphasizes the collective leadership obscured by the conventional narrative of Rosa Parks: "Her tremendously consequential act, along with everything that followed, depended on all the humble, frustrating work that she and others had undertaken earlier on, and on the vibrant, engaged community they had developed in the face of continual hardship and opposition" (p. 2). The "vibrant, engaged community" certainly includes Highlander, where political training was informal, evolving, and relationship-based. Loeb questions why Highlander, a studio for democratic change over most of the last century, remains little known; he suggests that this historical omission corresponds to weakness in democratic skills and understanding in this country.

7. For a discussion of social justice curriculum weakening students' commitment to social justice, see Seider (2008).

8. Immersion programs can be transformative, but these are special programs for selected kids. Most students are priced out of such opportunities. Furthermore, these

"boutique" programs often offer life-changing experiences that can be character building, but there is a danger that instead of leading to continued and growing social justice work, students can be demoralized back home, where the glamorous opportunity of building a village or saving a species is not proffered to them.

9. Elizabeth Ellsworth (1989) articulates a paradigm for building understanding that is built in reflection and dialogue:

> If you can talk to me in ways that show you understand that your knowledge of me, the world, and the "Right thing to do" will always be partial, interested, and potentially oppressive to others, and if I can do the same, then we can work together on shaping and reshaping alliances or constructing circumstances in which students of difference can thrive. (p. 25)

10. Indeed, many civic educators caution that focusing on service and philanthropy rather than systems analysis and collective action can distract from efforts for social change (Boyte, 2005; Levinson, 2012; Westheimer & Kahne, 2004).

11. Organizations that encourage cross-cultural connections abound in urban centers especially. Other Chicago-area organizations that have contributed to the development of this model of democratic education in our school and other schools include Mikva Challenge, Circesteem, Kuumba Lynx, Chicago Grassroots Curriculum Taskforce, Young Chicago Authors, and many others.

12. For a powerful story of the pain that can arise in partnerships between schools that express the inequality in American society, see "550: 3 Miles," http://www.thisamericanlife.org/radio-archives/episode/550/three-miles.

13. The term *White flight* suggests neutral economic forces driving segregation in Chicago and other urban areas. As Ta-Nehisi Coates (2014) shows, however, "white flight was not an accident—it was a triumph of racist social engineering" (p. 64).

14. Christine Bennett Button offers an important example of a curricular context for "teaching for political efficacy." She describes a class that incorporated systemic analysis into an action civics framework. The four key elements of the curriculum include (1) students analyzed their own political socialization and how their political attitudes were shaped, (2) students studied the distribution of political power in America ("The students explored such questions as: Who rules America? What political linkages exist between those who hold power and those who do not? And, how does institutional racism operate in the political system?"), (3) study of historical and contemporary models for political involvement and change, and (4) political fieldwork. The development of political efficacy in Button's heterogeneous class depended on multiple supports for critical analysis and reflection—social action did not, and should not, stand alone (Berman, 1997, pp. 147–149).

Chapter 3

1. In the Teaching Tolerance movie *The Children's March*, referring to what is usually called "The Children's Crusade," historical footage, re-enactments, and

present-day interviews with participants intertwine to tell the story of the young people who galvanized the Civil Rights Movement and inspired the March on Washington. In an interview, Gwen Webb, who had participated in the march as a teenager, reflects, "A lot of people thought the kids were going to get hurt, but the reality was that we were born black in Alabama, and we were going to get hurt if we *didn't* do something." The film is a counternarrative to the stock story told of the Civil Rights Movement led by a few charismatic (male, middle-class) leaders. It focuses on the undertold story of collective youth leadership and the strategic support of adult allies in the growth of the movement.

Images of children being attacked by police dogs and shot with water hoses entered the living rooms of America and provoked a sea change:

Millions of Americans who had been seeing demonstrations for years and saying, "Well, there's something wrong about that and we should do something but it's not for me, it's for somebody else," that broke down those emotional barriers. When they saw those children suffering . . . millions of people said, "I need to do something about this." (Stewart, 2013)

2. In their study of the Elsa-Edcouch walkout of 1968, Francisco and Miguel Guajardo comment on the relationship between "macro and micro social and political developments" illuminated when Latino youth from a rural Texas community challenged ongoing segregation in the schools. The Guajardo brothers conclude, "The Edcouch-Elsa Walkout of 1968 teaches us that youth citizen action can create community change, perhaps even the kind of change that nurtures sustainable communities" (2004, p. 523).

3. Mass marches of Chicago teachers against school closings demonstrated to many Chicago families that the teachers were willing to challenge city authorities and risk their jobs for their students. Trust between teachers and families took on a more political face when families joined teachers on the picket lines for the Chicago Teachers' Union strike of 2012 (Wheeler, 2013). When the mayor then closed 50 schools, in a move that was widely understood as both revenge for the teachers' strike and an attack on low-income communities of color, he set the stage for the power struggle at the heart of the 2015 mayor's race. In this historic race, teachers and African American and Latino communities wielded tremendous political muscle through the coalition they had built over years of struggle.

4. In a commentary on the conflict between the teachers and the mayor that the Chicago teachers' strike carried out, Giroux (2013) suggests that the mayor's hostility toward the teachers emerges from his awareness of their power as civic leaders:

What scares Emanuel and other neoliberal reformers is that pedagogy is a moral and political practice that is always implicated in power relations because it offers particular versions and visions of civic life, community, the future, and how we might construct representations of ourselves, others, and our physical and social environment.

Indeed, the Chicago teachers' strike showed teachers outside of their classrooms, and suggested the power that comes when ordinary people step out of bounds, outside of their expected contexts. Coalition building is an important means of, and venue for, strategic emergence from separated contexts.

5. Correspondingly, Harry Boyte (2005) argues for reversing the expected sequence of civic engagement, from inquiry-then-action to action-then-inquiry: Living experience provokes more learning and deeper research.

6. As Maxine Greene (1988) writes, "the point of cognitive development is not to gain an increasingly complete grasp of abstract principles, it is to interpret from as many vantage points as possible lived experience, the ways there are of being in the world" (p. 120). Oral histories multiply the voices and perspectives available for consideration.

7. Charles Payne (2010) emphasizes how the emotional and social climate of adults in schools affects education, noting, "The essential problem in our schools isn't children learning; it is adult learning" (p. 179). Payne is not talking about standards-based deficiencies, but about the structures needed for adults—administrators as well as teachers—to teach effectively. This includes the freedom to develop curriculum and assessments based on experience and professional judgment.

8. Bearing in mind Lisa Delpit's (2006) critique of progressive educators' unintentional reinforcement of White privilege, I emphasize the importance of *balance*, not the elimination of individual learning. Delpit points out that dismissing the importance of individual academic success in promoting alternative learning methods can be seen as a way of withholding access to the language and culture of power that many families of color expect schools to provide.

9. Relatedly, Reggio Emilia educators apply artistic seeing to the work of students and teachers. Educators at Reggio Emilia, a set of schools in Italy, have developed processes of documentation of students' work involving reimagining teacher–student relationships in democratic ways: "Documentation is largely about building connections—temporal, relational, and conceptual—and communication. When documentation serves these purposes, it blurs the lines between who is inside or outside the learning group and when learning experiences begin and end" (Krechevsky, Mardell, Rivard, & Wilson, 2013, p. 75). Unlike traditional assessments, documentation is not evaluative but exploratory. For more information about Reggio Emilia's documentation processes, see Gandini et al. (2005) and Rinaldi (2005). Since I have more experience with Descriptive Inquiry processes, here I focus on them rather than those of Reggio Emilia. All of these processes were important in the development of more widely known processes such as Project Zero's Visible Learning and Critical Friends.

10. Carini borrows the phrase "poets of our own lives" from Jay Featherstone.

11. As Lynn Strieb describes the process,

Because the Descriptive Review of Practice occurs in a collaborative setting which offers multiple perspectives on her work, [the teacher] may uncover new ways of fulfilling the visions of teaching that inspired her to be a teacher in the first place. A teacher may have a particular concern about her practice and may use this process to address that concern. . . . For the participants, a Descriptive

Review of Practice will add to their understanding of the nature of teaching, what in the person is being fulfilled, and what is central and indispensable to the work of teaching. (Strieb, Carini, Kanevsky, & Wice, 2011, p. 53)

12. For more information on Mikva Challenge and Action Civics, see *Democracy in Action Curriculum:* http://www.mikvachallenge.org/educators/center-for-action-civics/.

13. Writing about Descriptive Inquiry processes, Cecelia Traugh (2000) argues that inquiry

interrupts some of the forces that block us from seeing: disdain for children; a problem-solving emphasis; a content emphasis; evaluation via testing; experiences of being overlooked and unrecognized; familiar practice; expert knowledge. Because inquiry aims to create this tension, it necessarily moves the inquirers into untracked territory. For this reason it can be viewed as daring and even dangerous. (p. 104)

14. Perhaps even more problematic, educators are isolated from their own sources of power. bell hooks (2003) reminds us of the importance of sustaining physical, mental, and spiritual integrity as we model learning for our students:

Democratic educators show by their habits of being that they do not engage in forms of socially acceptable psychological splitting wherein someone teaches only in the classroom and then acts as though knowledge is not meaningful in every other setting. When students are taught this, they can experience learning as a whole process rather than a restrictive practice that disconnects and alienates them from the world. (p. 44)

Chapter 4

1. Reinhold Niebuhr (1932/1960), whose philosophy influenced many Civil Rights Movement leaders, takes Boyd's analysis a step further, arguing that dominant powers in society have a vested interest in *preventing* the social learning Boyd and other Progressives call for:

The physical sciences gained their freedom when they overcame the traditionalism based on ignorance, but the traditionalism which the social sciences face is based upon the economic interest of the dominant social classes who are trying to maintain their special privileges in society. (p. xiv)

2. Other related forms of social theatre also emerge from this space of inequality consciousness. Michael Rohd's dynamic image theatre work, for instance, grew out of school-community theatre with Sidwell Friends School students and AIDS patients in Washington, DC.

3. Both Boal and Freire directly address the problem of well-meaning people unaware of their power and their privilege. Freire (2002) calls it "false generosity":

Any attempt to "soften" the power of the oppressor in deference to the weakness of the oppressed almost always manifests itself in the form of false generosity; indeed the attempt never goes beyond this. In order to have the continued opportunity to express their "generosity," the oppressors must perpetuate injustice as well. An unjust social order is the permanent fount of this "generosity," which is nourished by death, despair, and poverty. (p. 44)

4. See Narayan (1988) for elaboration on the understanding that "good-will is not enough"—or, in Ilich's (1968) words, "To hell with good intentions."

5. In addition to Meira Levinson's comprehensive study of civic education in *No Citizen Left Behind* and Westheimer and Kahne's (2004) foundational "What Kind of Citizen," it is important to consider Beth Rubin's (2007) study of differing civic attitudes among students from low-income and higher-income communities. She concludes,

White students in a homogenous, wealthy setting tended to be complacent in their stance toward civic participation, positing that voting and paying taxes would be enough for them to fulfill their civic duties as adults. Youth in a racially and socioeconomically integrated setting which emphasized analyses of social inequality had a strikingly different approach, expressing the desire to become actively involved in social change. Urban youth of color in a poor community showed both a sense of empowerment that hinged on their intentions to work for social change, and, at times, discouraged resignation when faced with the daily discrepancies between what was and what should be. These youth credited teaching practices with revealing the possibilities of action, but these were not always enough to bridge the disjunctures. (p. 478)

6. For instance, Mercedes Olivera (2006) quotes the response of the authorities of Chihuahua to the murders:

It is important to note that the behavior of some of the victims does not correspond with those established characteristics of the moral order, being there has been excessive frequenting into the late hours of the night of entertainment establishments not appropriate for their age in some cases, as well an inadequate care and abandonment of the family unit in which they have lived. (p. 3)

Olivera sees the patriarchal blame-the-victim approach as directly complicit in the murders—both evince a profound disrespect for women.

7. This local analysis is part of a wider concern about neoliberal growth nationally and globally:

School reform strategies, especially the emphasis on charter schools, currently enjoy powerful backing and good press in the U.S. Less attention goes to critiques of school reform and its place in wider patterns of neoliberal growth. So, I highlight such critique here, in hopes of promoting wider dialogue on questions about education in democratic society. (Barton & Coley, 2009)

8. In Stephen Haymes's (1995) analysis of the racial politics of urban spaces, school closings as a function of urban development contribute to the dismantling of Black urban spaces and Black civil society:

> Within a white supremacist culture, such as in the United States, the concepts "private" and "public" now act as racialized metaphors; the private is associated with being "good" and "white," and the public with being "bad" and "black." . . . It is the symbolic construction of "white places" as civilized, rational, and orderly and "black places" as uncivilized, irrational, and disorderly that allows for police occupation and the removal of black people from their public spaces. (pp. 20–21)

9. As David Gruenewald (2003a) writes of place-based education,

> In place of actual experience with the phenomenal world, educators are handed, and largely accept, the mandates of a standardized, "placeless" curriculum and settle for the abstractions and simulations of classroom learning. Though it is true that much significant and beneficial learning can happen here, what is most striking about the classroom as a learning technology is how much it limits, devalues, and distorts local geographical experience. Place-based education challenges all educators to think about how the exploration of places can become part of how curriculum is organized and conceived. It further challenges educators to consider that if education everywhere does not explicitly promote the well-being of places, then what is education for? (p. 8)

Chapter 5

1. Similarly, Christine Sleeter (2007) describes teachers who educate their students about the history and politics of standards-based reform efforts, such as Xitlali:

> Referring to the standards as part of "the culture of power," she set out to equip her students with the skills and knowledge necessary for survival in mainstream America. . . . She argues that students additionally need to understand the role that standards and standardized tests play in sustaining dominant power structures. (p. 18)

Teachers like this are defying the systems that lie behind the tests, in part through clarifying how they themselves navigate the standards—not accepting and reproducing them blindly but using them "strategically"—for their own purposes, critically, imaginatively, intelligently.

2. Miguel's account of pedagogy at Rudy Lozano Leadership Academy takes place within a Teachers' Inquiry Project seminar, which, bringing together educators from museum and school contexts throughout the community, represents a broader expression of the kind of collaboration he describes.

3. Recent work (e.g., Lipman, 2013; Ravitch, 2013; Sirotnik, 2002) challenges the testing industry's domination over schools and education policy and argues that it

serves corporate and financial interests, not the interest of students. The assumption that business models (accountability) and language (scaling up) are an improvement on educational practice threatens people in schools: "The business-corrupted approach is shot through with distrust. We do not trust teachers to act responsibly, and so we insist that they must be held accountable. How? For what exactly? We are using language that belongs to another game" (Noddings, 2013, p. 156).

However, the issue is far from recent—educators have been concerned about the policymakers colluding with business interests for over a century (see, for instance, Sadovnik & Semel, 2002, for an account of Ella Flagg Young's battles with the school board and their textbook company friends in the early 1900s).

4. Thinkers like Nel Noddings urge the more relational and democratic term *responsibility* over *accountability*:

> Responsibility digs deeper and carries further than accountability. When we are moved by accountability, we are concerned with what may happen to us, what penalties we may suffer, what rewards we may gain. In contrast, when we are moved by responsibility, our concern is with *others*; it is not focused on ourselves. Probably most people who choose teaching as a profession feel their responsibility keenly. The current emphasis on accountability may actually undermine the moral/emotional state of mind that supports the best in teaching. (Noddings, 2013, p. 156)

5. Books like Cammarato and Romero's (2014), Kessler's (2000), and others offer in-depth guidance for designing curriculum and school structures around local knowledge and indigenous practices.

6. Lisa Delpit (2006) argues that educators need to understand the following:

1. Issues of power are enacted in classrooms.
2. There are codes or rules for participating in power; that is, there is a "culture of power."
3. The rules of the culture of power are a reflection of the rules of the culture of those who have power.
4. If you are not already a participant in the culture of power, being told explicitly the rules of that culture makes acquiring power easier.
5. Those with power are frequently least aware of—or least willing to acknowledge—its existence. Those with less power are often most aware of its existence (p. 24).

7. For example, Cammarota and Romero (2014) offer examples of young people changing the narratives in their communities, as when they challenge English-only policies in their schools and their parents begin then to challenge such policies in their workplaces.

8. Furger (2002) describes the real-world learning contexts at Urban:

> In a constitutional law class, for example, students break into teams that are charged with the task of arguing a case before the U.S. Supreme Court. Another group of students serves as the distinguished panel of judges, asking questions, poking holes in arguments, and challenging their classmates to use

the law, not their own personal opinions, to defend their positions. Joining in the critique—and the discussion—is a group of attorneys from a Manhattan law firm. Their presence provides a real-world connection for students and sends a powerful reminder that their opinions, their analysis, and their perspective matters. (p. 2)

9. Postman and Weingartener (1971) point out that conventional measurements of student learning are inept in comparison to assessments based in inquiry learning:

The inquiry teacher measures his success in terms of behavioral changes in students: the frequency with which they ask questions; the increase in the relevance and cogency of their questions; the frequency and conviction of their challenges to assertions made by other students or textbooks . . . ; the increase in their tolerance for diverse answers; their ability to apply generalizations, attitudes, and information to novel situations. (p. 36)

10. Cook and Mack (1975) attach the design and study of their own assessments to teachers' professional responsibility:

Generally speaking, outside evaluators do not concern themselves with the goals of the teacher or the growth points of students. Rather, their assumptions are conclusions based on what they, not the teacher, think is important . . . the institution doesn't demand that they take on the critical responsibility of determining what needs their students have and of figuring out what strategies to use. (pp. 15–16)

11. The assignment reads:

As a culminating assignment for the work of this semester, your final paper on the legacy of Robert Moses should reflect the issues we have discussed in class; references to our main text, *The Power Broker* by Robert Caro; and additional research that you have done on a topic of your choice. Citations must be included. Your paper should reflect the opposing views of Moses and his work while providing a clear argument for your perspective.

12. However, in offering these assessments and exemplars, the Consortium leaders explain that their assessments emerge from dialogue, not in strict adherence to the rubrics, since "Cookie cutter results would not be a true mirror of the students Consortium schools serve." Rather, the educators emphasize the consideration of the students' work in a wider frame of educational inquiry and dialogue:

The task was not to align each paper precisely with the indicators on the rubric. When rubrics dominate a discussion, they have the potential of limiting discussion to the indicators already enumerated. Instead, the goal was to read the students' papers closely discuss and share response with colleagues, and reach a consensus on the characteristics of outstanding work. (New York Standards Consortium: Exemplars of Consortium student work, n.d., p. 1)

13. For a fuller story of many challenges the Coalition faced over the years, see Cook and Tashlik (2005).

14. For more commentary on accountability for education policy, see the FairTest website, for example, the report "Failing Our Children" (by Monty Neill, Ed.D., Lisa Guisbond and Bob Schaeffer with James Madson and Life Legeros, May, 2004).

FairTest provides the latest research, analysis, and news updates on accountability, assessments, and models and advocacy strategies for alternative assessments.

Chapter 6

1. In recent years, education and community organizers have found common cause in cities like Chicago, New York, and Los Angeles, dramatically shifting the political landscape. Their political gains prove that coalition building is a vital strategy for reclaiming educational rights for children who have been traditionally neglected and oppressed.

2. Highlander Folk School is also a model for the democratic work of holding space for democratic relationships. Folk school educational philosophy is based in the conjoint struggle for human dignity:

> The individual was seen whole only as a part of a community, connected to a time, place, and culture. This education was for the purpose of responding to the needs and struggles of the common people, and knowledge and enlightenment was to be found in the common people. This education was to happen collectively and would embrace the heart, mind, and body. And perhaps most importantly, the basis of this learning was the living word—that word spoken by and between teachers and students. (Ribble, 2002)

References

Abram, D. (1997). *The spell of the sensuous: Perception and language in a more-than-human world*. New York, NY: Vintage Books.

Addams, J. (2002). The subjective necessity for social settlements. In J. Elshtain (Ed.), *The Jane Addams reader* (pp. 14–28). New York, NY: Basic Books.

Adichie, C. (2009). *The danger of a single story* [Video file]. Available at www.ted.com/talks/chimamanda_adichie_the_danger_of_a_single_story?language=en

Alexander, M. (2010). *The new Jim Crow: Mass incarceration in the age of colorblindness*. New York, NY: The New Press.

Allen, D. (2004). *Talking to strangers: Anxieties of citizenship since Brown v. Board of Education*. Chicago, IL: University of Chicago Press.

Allen, P. G. (1992). *The sacred hoop*. Boston, MA: Beacon Press.

Anfara, V. A. (1999). Urban schools and liminality. *National Forum Journals, 10,* 1–7.

Anzaldúa, G. (1999). *Frontera/borderlands: The New Mestiza*. San Francisco, CA: Aunt Lute Books.

Apple, M. (2004). *Ideology and curriculum*. New York, NY: Routledge.

Apple, M., & Carlson, D. (Eds.). (1998). *Power, knowledge, pedagogy: The meaning of democratic education in unsettling times*. Boulder, CO: Westview Press.

Arendt, H. (1958). *The human condition*. Chicago, IL: University of Chicago.

Ayers, W., Hunt J. A., & Quinn, T. (1998). *Teaching for social justice*. New York, NY: The New Press.

Ayers, W., Kumashiro, K., Meiners, E., Quinn, T., & Stovall, D. (2010). *Teaching toward democracy: Educators as agents of change*. Boulder, CO: Paradigm.

Ayers, W., Ladson-Billings, G., & Michie, G. (2008). *City kids, city schools: New reports from the front lines*. New York, NY: The New Press.

Bakhtin, M. M. (1984). *Problems of Dostoevsky's poetics* (C. Emerson, Ed. & Trans.). Minneapolis, MN: University of Minnesota Press.

Bakhtin, M. M. (1993). *Toward a philosophy of the act* (V. Liapunov, Trans.). Austin, TX: University of Texas Press.

Bakhtin, M. M. (2009). *Rabelais and his world* (H. Iswolsky, Trans.). Bloomington, IN: Indiana University Press. (Original work published 1965)

Ball, S. J., & Larsson, S. (Eds.). (1989). *The struggle for democratic education: Equality and participation in Sweden*. New York, NY: Falmer Press.

Banks, C. (2007). The more things change, the more they stay the same: Lessons from the past on diversity and teaching. In C. Sleeter (Ed.), *Facing accountability in education: Democracy and equity at risk*. New York, NY: Teachers College Press.

Banks, J. (1990). A curriculum for empowerment, action, and change. In C. Sleeter (Ed.), *Empowerment through multicultural education*. Albany, NY: State University of New York Press.

Banks, J., & Banks, C. (2004). Multicultural education: Historical development, dimensions, and practice. In C. Banks & J. Banks (Eds.), *Handbook of research on multicultural education* (2nd ed., pp. 3–29). San Francisco, CA: Jossey-Bass.

Barber, B. (1997). Public schooling: Education for democracy. In J. Goodlad & T. McMannan (Eds.), *The public purpose of education and schooling* (pp. 21–32). San Francisco, CA: Jossey-Bass.

Barrett, X. (2013). Yes, I was fired and still we will win [Web log]. Available at chiteacherx.blogspot.com/

Barton, P. E., & Coley, R. J. (2009). *Parsing the achievement gap.* Available at www.ets.org/Media/Research/pdf/PICPARSINGII.pdf

Benson, L., Harkavy, I., & Puckett, J. (2007). *Dewey's dream: Universities and democracies in an age of education reform.* Philadelphia, PA: Temple University Press.

Berlak, H. (2003). Education Policy 1964–2004: The No Child Left Behind Act and the Assault on Progressive Education and Local Control. In B. S. Engel & A. C. Martin (Eds.), *Holding values: What we mean by progressive education* (pp. 58–65). Portsmouth, NH: Heinemann.

Berman, S. (1997). *Children's social consciousness and the development of social responsibility.* Albany, NY: State University of New York Press.

Boal, A. (1985). *Theatre of the oppressed* (M. L. McBride & C. A. McBride, Trans.). New York, NY: Theatre Communications Group.

Boal, A. (1995). *The rainbow of desire: The Boal method of theatre and therapy* (A. Jackson, Trans.). London, UK: Routledge.

Boal, A. (2001). *Hamlet and the baker's son: My life in theatre and politics* (A. Jackson & C. Blaker, Trans.). New York, NY: Routledge.

Boal, A. (2002). *Games for actors and non-actors.* New York, NY: Routledge.

Boggs, G. L., & Kurashige, S. (2011). *The next American revolution: Sustainable activism for the twenty-first century.* Oakland, CA: University of California Press.

Boggs, J. (2011). *Pages from a Black radical's notebook: A James Boggs reader.* Detroit, MI: Wayne State University.

Boler, M. (Ed.). (2006). *Democratic dialogue in education: Troubling speech, disturbing silence.* New York, NY: Peter Lang.

Bowles, S., & Gintis, T. (1977). *Schooling in capitalist America.* New York, NY: Basic Books.

Boyd, N. (1934). Play—A unique discipline. *Childhood Education, 10*(8), 414–416.

Boyd, N. (1971). *Play and game theory in group work: A collection of papers by Neva Leona Boyd.* Chicago, IL: Jane Addams Graduate School of Social Work at the University of Illinois at Chicago Circle.

Boykin, A. W., & Noguera, P. (2011). *Creating the opportunity to learn: Moving from research to practice to close the achievement gap.* Alexandria, VA: Association for Supervision & Curriculum Development.

Boyte, H. (2005). *Everyday politics: Reconnecting citizens and public life.* Philadelphia, PA: University of Pennsylvania Press.

Brown, J., Gutstein, E., & Lipman, P. (2009). Arne Duncan and the Chicago success story: Myth or reality? *Rethinking Schools.* Available at http://www. rethinkingschools.org/restrict.asp?path=archive/23_03/arne233.shtml

Brown, L., & Gutstein, E. (2009). *The charter difference: A comparison of Chicago charter and neighborhood high schools. A Collaborative for Equity and Justice in Education Report.* Chicago, IL: University of Illinois–Chicago, College of Education.

Burbules, N. (1993). *Dialogue in teaching: Theory and practice.* New York, NY: Teachers College Press.

Burbules, N. (2006). *Democratic dialogue in education: Troubling speech, disturbing silence.* New York, NY: Peter Lang.

Cammarota, J., & Romero, A. (2014). *Raza Studies: The public option for educational revolution.* Tuscon, AZ: University of Arizona Press.

Carini, P. (2001). *Starting strong: A different look at children, schools, and standards.* New York, NY: Teachers College Press.

Carson, M. (1990). *Settlement folk: Social thought and the American Settlement Movement, 1885–1930.* Chicago, IL: University of Chicago Press.

Christensen, L. (2007). Unlearning the myths that bind us. In W. Au, B. Bigelow, & S. Karp (Eds.), *Rethinking our classrooms: Teaching for equity and justice* (pp. 3–7). Milwaukee, WI: Rethinking Schools.

Coates, T. (2014, June). The case for reparations. *The Atlantic.* Available at http://www. theatlantic.com/features/archive/2014/05/the-case-for-reparations/361631/

Cochran-Smith, M. (2004). *Walking the road: Race, diversity, and social justice in teacher education.* New York, NY: Teachers College Press.

Coleman, J. (1991). *The Compass: The improvisational theatre that revolutionized American comedy.* Chicago, IL: The University of Chicago Press.

Cook, A. (2002, February 11). *A view on performance-based assessment.* Available at www.edutopia.org/ann-cook-performance-based-assessment?page=18

Cook, A., & Mack, H. (1975). *The word and the thing.* North Dakota Study Group Monograph. Available at ndsg.org/monographs/NDSG_1975_Cook_and_Mack_ The_Word_and_the_Thing.pdf

Cook, A., & Tashlik, P. (2005). *Making the pendulum swing: Challenging bad education policy in New York State.* Available at http://archive.essentialschools. org/resources/317.html.

Cooke, F. J. (1912). *The social motive in school work. Francis Parker Yearbook, Volume 1.* Chicago, IL: The Francis W. Parker School.

Counts, G. (1934). *The social foundations of education.* New York, NY: Scribner.

Counts, G. (1978). *Dare the school build a new social order?* Carbondale, IL: Southern Illinois University Press.

Cremin, L. S. (1964). *The transformation of the American school.* New York, NY: Vintage.

Cremin, L. S. (1976). *Public education.* New York, NY: Basic Books.

Cuban, L. (2004). Looking through the rearview mirror at school accountability. In K. Sirotnik (Ed.), *Holding accountability accountable: What ought to matter in public education,* (pp. 18–34). New York, NY: Teachers College Press.

Darling-Hammond, L. (1997). Education, equity, and the right to learn. In J. Goodlad & T. McMannon (Eds.), *The public purpose of education and schooling*. San Francisco, CA: Jossey-Bass.

Delgado, R. (2011). Storytelling for oppositionists and others. In R. Delgado & J. Stefancic (Eds.), *The Latino/a condition: A critical reader* (pp. 229–240). New York, NY: New York University Press.

Deloria, V., & Wildcat, D. R. (2001). *Power and place: Indian education in America*. Toronto, Canada: Fulcrum.

Delpit, L. (2006). *Other people's children: Cultural conflict in the classroom*. New York, NY: The New Press.

Dewey, J. (1902, October). The school as social center. *The Elementary School Teacher, 3*(2), 73–86.

Dewey, J. (1902/1987). *The later works of John Dewey, Volume 2, 1925–1953*. Carbondale, IL: Southern Illinois University Press.

Dewey, J. (2008). *The middle works of John Dewey, Volume 9, 1899-1924: Democracy and education, 1916 (The Collected Works of John Dewey, 1882-1953)*. Carbondale, IL: Southern Illinois University Press.

Dewey, J. (1934/2008). The need for a philosophy of education. In J. A. Boydston (Ed.), *Later works* (Vol. 9, pp. 194–204). Carbondale, IL: Southern Illinois University Press.

Dewey, J. (1954). *The public and its problems*. Athens, OH: Swallow Press.

Dilg, M. (2003). *Thriving in the multicultural classroom*. New York, NY: Teachers College Press.

Polanski, R. (Director). (1994) *Death and the maiden* [motion picture]. United States of America: Fine Line Features.

Dubois, W.E.B. (2001). *The education of Black people*. New York, NY: Monthly Review Press.

Duncan-Andrade, J., & Morrell, E. (2008). *The art of critical pedagogy*. New York, NY: Peter Lang.

Duncan-Andrade, J. (2011). *Roses in concrete TED talk*. https://www.youtube.com/watch?v=2CwS60ykM8s

Ellsworth, E. (1989). Why doesn't this feel empowering? Working through the repressive myths of critical pedagogy. *Harvard Educational Review, 59*, 3; Research Library Core.

Engel, B. S., & Martin, A. C. (2005). *Holding values: What we mean by progressive education*. Portsmouth, NH: Heinemann.

Evans, S. M., & Boyte, H. C. (1992). *Free spaces: The sources of democratic change in America*. Chicago, IL: University of Chicago Press.

Featherstone, J. (2005). Progressive, democratic education: A primer. In B. S. Engel and A. C. Martin (Eds.). *Holding values: What we mean by progressive education*, (pp. 41–46). Portsmouth, NH: Heinemann.

Featherstone, J. (2003). *Dear Josie: Witnessing the hopes and failures of democratic education*. New York, NY: Teachers College Press.

Fitzgerald, F. S. (1925/1994). *The Great Gatsby*. New York, NY: Scribner.

Flinders, C. (1999). *At the root of this longing: Reconciling a spiritual hunger and a feminist thirst.* San Francisco, CA: HarperOne.

Foote, M. (2007). Keeping accountability systems accountable. *Phi Delta Kappan, 88*(5), 359–363.

Foucault, M. (1982). The subject and power. *Critical Inquiry, 8*(4), 777–795.

Freire, P. (2000). *Pedagogy of freedom: Ethics, democracy, and civic courage.* Lanham, MD: Rowman & Littlefield.

Freire, P. (2002). *Pedagogy of the oppressed* (30th anniversary ed.). New York, NY: Bloomsbury Academic.

Friend, N., & Mullen, K. (2012). *No place for kids.* Available at vimeo.com/44171498

Funders' Collaborative on Youth Organizing/Movement Strategy Center. (2012). *The power of transformative youth leadership: A field analysis of youth organizing in Pittsburgh.* Available at www.heinz.org/UserFiles/File/PghYouthLeadership.pdf

Furger, R. (2002). *Testing is anything but standard at the Urban Academy.* Available at www.edutopia.org/urban-academy-testing-anything-standard?page=2

Gadamer, H.-G. (1987). *The relevance of the beautiful and other essays.* Cambridge, UK: Cambridge University Press.

Gadamer, H.-G. (1994). *Truth and method* (J. Weinsheimer & D. Marshall, Trans.). New York, NY: Continuum.

Gandini, L., Hill, L., Cadwell, L., & Schwall, C. (2005). *In the spirit of the studio: Learning from the atelier of Reggio Emilia.* New York, NY: Teachers College Press.

Ganz, M. (2010). Leading change: Leadership, organization, and social movements. In N. Nohria & R. Khurana (Eds.), *Handbook of leadership theory and practice.* (pp. 509–550). Cambridge, MA: Harvard Business School.

Garrison, J. (2006). Ameliorating violence in dialogue across differences: The role of *eros* and *logos.* In M. Boler (Ed.), *Democratic dialogue in education: Troubling speech, disturbing silence,* (pp. 89–104). New York, NY: Peter Lang.

Gerzon, M. (2006). *Leading through conflict: How successful leaders transform differences into opportunities.* Cambridge, MA: Harvard University Press.

Gillborn, D. (2013). The policy of inequity. In M. Lynn (Ed.), *Handbook of critical race theory in education,* (pp. 129–139). New York, NY: Routledge.

Giroux, H. (1988). *Teachers as intellectuals: Toward a critical pedagogy of resistance.* Santa Barbara, CA: Praeger.

Giroux, H. (2005). *Border crossings: Cultural workers and the politics of education.* New York, NY: Routledge.

Giroux, H. (2013, May 7). Marching in Chicago: Resisting Rahm Emanuel's neoliberal savagery. *Truthout.* http://www.truth-out.org/opinion/item/16478-marching-in-chicago-resisting-rahm-emanuels-neoliberal-savagery.

Goodman, D. (2001). *Promoting diversity and social justice: Educating people from privileged groups.* Thousand Oaks, CA: Sage.

Greene M. (1988). *The dialectic of freedom.* New York, NY: Teachers College Press.

Greene, M. (1998). Introduction. In W. Ayers, J. A. Hunt, & T. Quinn (Eds.), *Teaching for social justice: A democracy and education reader.* (pp. xxvii–xlvi). New York, NY: The New Press.

Gruenewald, D. A. (2003a, May). The best of both worlds: A critical pedagogy of place. *Educational Researcher*, 3–12.

Gruenewald, D. A. (2003b). Foundations of place: A multidisciplinary framework for place-conscious education. *American Educational Research Journal*, *40*(3), 619–654.

Guajardo, F., & Guajardo, M. (2004, Fall). The impact of *Brown* on the Brown of South Texas: A micropolitical perspective on the education of Mexican Americans in a South Texas community. *American Educational Research Journal*, *41*(3), 501–526.

Guajardo, F., & Guajardo, M. (2013, Fall). The power of Plática. *Reflections*, 159–164.

Guinier, L., & Torres, G. (2003). *The miner's canary: Enlisting race, resisting power, transforming democracy*. Boston, MA: Harvard University Press.

Gutierrez, G. (1973). *A theology of liberation: History, politics, and salvation* (15th anniversary ed.; C. Inda & J. Eagleson, Trans.). Maryknoll, NY: Orbis. (Original work published 1971)

Gutstein, E. (2006). *Reading and writing the world with mathematics: Toward a pedagogy for social justice*. New York, NY: Routledge.

Haymes, S. N. (1995). *Race, culture, and the city: A pedagogy for Black urban struggle*. Albany, NY: State University of New York Press.

Helms, J. E. (1990). *Black and White racial identity: Theory, research and practice*. New York, NY: Greenwood Press.

Hess, D. (2009). *Controversy in the classroom: The democratic power of discussion*. New York, NY: Routledge.

Hess, D., & McAvoy, P. (2015). *The political classroom: Evidence and ethics in democratic education*. New York, NY: Routledge.

Hoffman, N. (Ed.). (1991). *Women's "true" profession: Voices from the history of teaching*. Old Westbury, NY: Feminist Press.

hooks, b. (1990). *Yearning: Race, gender, and cultural politics*. Boston, MA: South End Press.

hooks, b. (1994). *Teaching to transgress*. New York, NY: Routledge.

hooks, b. (2003). *Teaching community: A pedagogy of hope*. New York, NY: Routledge.

Horton, M., Kohl, H., & Kohl, J. (1997). *The long haul: An autobiography*. New York, NY: Teachers College Press.

Howard, G. (1999). *We can't teach what we don't know: White teachers, multiracial schools*. New York, NY: Teachers College Press.

Illich, I. (1968). *To hell with good intentions. Conference on Inter-American Student Projects*. Cuernavaca, Mexico. Available at www.swaraj.org/illich_hell.htm

Ingersoll, R.M. (2003). *Who controls teachers' work? Power and accountability in America's schools*. Cambridge, MA: Harvard University Press.

John Paul II. (1979, January 28). Address of His Holiness John Paul II. Puebla, Mexico. Available at http://w2.vatican.va/content/john-paul-ii/en/speeches/1979/january/documents/hf_jp-ii_spe_19790128_messico-puebla-episc-latam.html

Jordan, J. (1985). *On call: Political essays*. Cambridge, MA: South End Press.

Kessler, R. (2000). *The soul of education: Helping students find connection, compassion, and character at school*. Alexandria, VA: ASCD.

King, M. L. (1963, June). Letter from a Birmingham jail. *The Atlantic.*

Kinloch, V. (2012). *Crossing boundaries: Teaching and learning with urban youth.* New York, NY: Teachers College Press.

Knoester, M. (2012). *Democratic education in practice: Inside the Mission Hill School.* New York, NY: Teachers College Press.

Knowlan, A. (forthcoming): *Matrix leadership: The art and science of creating sustainable organizations and communities.*

Kozol, J. (2005). *The shame of the nation: The restoration of apartheid schooling in America.* New York, NY: Crown.

Krechevsky, M., Mardell, B., Rivard, M., & Wilson, D. (2013). *Visible learners: Promoting Reggio-inspired approaches in all schools.* San Francisco, CA: Jossey-Bass.

Kreisberg, S. (1992). *Transforming power: Domination, empowerment, and education.* Albany, NY: State University of New York Press.

Kumashiro, K. (2012). *Bad teacher! How blaming teachers distorts the bigger picture.* New York, NY: Teachers College Press.

Ladson-Billings, G. (2009). What is critical race theory and what's it doing in a nice field like education? In E. Taylor, D. Gillborn, & G. Ladson-Billings (Eds.), *Foundations of critical race theory in education,* (pp. 17–36). New York, NY: Routledge.

Ladson-Billings, G. (2009) *Dreamkeepers: Successful teachers of African-American children* (2nd ed.). San Francisco, CA: Jossey-Bass.

Levertov, D. (2001). *Poems, 1972–1982.* New York, NY: New Directions.

Levinson, M. (2012). *No citizen left behind.* Cambridge, MA: Harvard University Press.

Lewis, J. (1998). *Walking with the wind: A memoir of the movement.* Orlando, FL: Mariner Books.

Lipman, P. (2003). *High stakes education: Inequality, globalization, and urban school reform.* New York, NY: Routledge.

Lipman, P. (2008, April). *Making sense of Renaissance 2010 school policy in Chicago: Race, class, and the cultural politics of neoliberal urban restructuring.* Paper presented at the Annual Meeting of the American Educational Research Association, New York.

Lipman, P. (2013). Economic crisis, accountability, and the state's coercive assault on public education in the USA. *Journal of Education Policy, 28,* 557–573.

Loeb, P. (2010). *The soul of a citizen: Living with conviction in challenging times.* New York, NY: Macmillan.

Loughlin, C. E., & Suina, J. H. (1982). *The learning environment: An instructional strategy.* New York, NY: Teachers College Press.

Lynn, E., & Wisely, S. (2006). Four traditions of philanthropy. In E. Lynn & A. Davis (Eds.), *The civically engaged reader: A diverse collection of short provocative readings on civic activity.* (pp. 201–217). Chicago, IL: Great Books.

MacDonald, E., & Shirley, D. (2009). *The mindful teacher.* New York, NY: Teachers College Press.

Martin, A., & Schwartz, E. (2014). *Making space for active learning.* New York, NY: Teachers College Press.

Mayotte, C. (Ed.). (2013). *The power of the story: The Voice of Witness teacher's guide to oral history*. San Francisco, CA: Voice of Witness.

Meier, D. (2003, September). So what does it take to build a school for democracy? *Phi Delta Kappan, 85*(1), 15–21.

Meier, D., Engel, B. S., & Taylor, B. (2010). *Playing for keeps: Life and learning on a public school playground*. New York, NY: Teachers College Press.

McLaren, P. (2007). *Critical pedagogy: Where are we now?* New York, NY: Peter Lang.

Michie, G. (2009). *Holler if you hear me: The education of a teacher and his students*. New York, NY: Teachers College Press.

Miéville, C. (2009). *The city & the city*. New York, NY: Del Rey Ballantine Books.

Monárrez Fragoso, J. (2002, April). Serial sexual femicide in Ciudad Juárez: 1993–2001. *Debate Femenista, 25*, 279–305.

Morrison, T. (2007). *The bluest eye*. New York, NY: Vintage.

Murowski, M., & Cordova, R. (2012). Sharing vision/transforming practice. *Journal of Museum Education. 37*(2), 52–55.

National Commission on Excellence in Education (1983). *A nation at risk: The imperative for education reform*. Washington, DC: Author.

Narayan, U. (1988, Summer), Working together across difference: Some considerations on emotion and political practice. *Hypatia, 3*(2), 31–47.

Nichol, C. (2014). *Waiting for the electricity*. New York, NY: The Overlook Press.

Niebuhr, R. (1960). *Moral man and immoral society: A study in ethics and politics*. New York, NY: Scribner. (Original work published 1932)

Noddings, N. (2013). *Education and democracy in the 21st century*. New York, NY: Teachers College Press.

Noguera, P. (2007, October 16). Renewing and reinventing Freire: A source of inspiration in inner-city youth education. *In Motion Magazine*.

North, C. (2008). What is all this talk about "social justice"? Mapping the terrain of education's latest catchphrase. *Teachers College Record, 110*(6), 1182–1206.

North, C. (2009). *Teaching for social justice? Voices from the front lines*. Boulder, CO: Paradigm.

Ochoa, V., Benavides Lopez, C., & Solorzano, D. G. (2013). Toward a critical race case pedagogy: a tool for social justice educators. In J. K. Donnor & A. D. Dixson (Eds.), *The resegregation of schools : education and race in the twenty-first century*, (pp. 194–212). New York, NY: Routledge.

Olivera, M. (2006). Violencia femicida: Violence against women and Mexico's structural crisis. *Latin American Perspectives, 33*(104), 104–114.

Ong, W. (1991). *The presence of the word: Some prolegomena for cultural and religious history*. Minneapolis, MN: University of Minnesota Press.

Parker, F. W. (2001). *Talks on pedagogics*. Chicago, IL: Francis W. Parker School. (Original work published 1937)

Parker, W. (2002). *Education for democracy: Contexts, curricula, assessments*. Charlotte, NC: Information Age.

Payne, C. (2010). *So much reform, so little change*. Cambridge, MA: Harvard Education Press.

Portelli, A. (1997). *Battle of Valle Giulia: Oral history and the art of dialogue*. Madison, WI: University of Wisconsin Press.

Postman, N., & Weingartner, C. (1971). *Teaching as a subversive activity*. McHenry, IL: Delta.

Price, J. (2012). *Structural violence: Hidden brutality in the lives of women*. Albany, NY: State University of New York Press.

Ransby, B. (2005). *Ella Baker and the Black Freedom Movement: A radical democratic vision*. Chapel Hill, NC: University of North Carolina Press.

Ravitch, D. (2013). *Reign of error: The hoax of the privatization movement and the danger to America's public schools*. New York, NY: Knopf.

Raywid, M. (1994). A school that really works. *Journal of Negro Education, 63*(1), 93–110.

Reagon, B. (1991). Interview with Bill Moyers. Available at billmoyers.com/2013/05/03/moyers-moment-1991-bernice-johnson-reagon-on-this-little-light-of-mine/

Rinaldi, C. (2005). *In dialogue with Reggio Emilia: Listening, researching, and learning*. New York, NY: Routledge.

Ribble, M. (2002). *A brief history of folk education*. Available at http://www.peopleseducation.org/history/folk-education/

Riester, A. F., Pursch, V., & Skrla L. (2002). Principals for social justice: Leaders of school success for children from low-income homes. *Journal of School Leadership, 12*(3), 281–304.

Rodgers, C. R. (2006). "The turning of one's soul"—Learning to teach for social justice: The Putney Graduate School of Teacher Education (1950–1964). *Teachers College Record, 108*(7), 1266–1295.

Rodgers, C. R., & Raider-Roth, M. B. (2006). Presence in teaching. *Teachers and Teaching: Theory and Practice, 12*(3), 265–287.

Rohd, M. (1998). *Theatre for community, conflict, and dialogue*. Portsmouth, NH: Heinemann.

Rose, M. (1996). *Possible lives: The promise of public education in America*. New York, NY: Penguin Books.

Rubin, B. C. (2007). "There's still not justice": Youth civic identity development amid distinct school and community contexts. *Teachers College Record, 109*(2), 449–481.

Sadovnik, A. R., & Semel, S. F. (2002). *Founding mothers and others: Women educational leaders during the Progressive Era*. New York, NY: Palgrave Macmillan.

Schill, M., & Austin, R. (1991). Black, Brown, poor, and poisoned: Minority grassroots environmentalism and the quest for eco-justice. *Kansas Journal of Law and Public Policy, 69*, 69–82.

Schultz, B. (2008). *Spectacular things happen along the way: Lessons from an urban classroom*. New York, NY: Teachers College Press.

Seider, S. (2008). "Bad things could happen": How fear impedes social responsibility in privileged adolescents. *Journal of Adolescent Research, 23*(6), 647–666.

Semel, S. F., & Sadovnik, A. R. (Eds.). (1999). *"Schools of tomorrow," schools of today: What happened to progressive education?* New York, NY: Peter Lang.

Silko, L. M. (1986). *Ceremony.* New York, NY: Penguin.

Sirotnik, K. (2002). Promoting responsible accountability in schools and education. *Phi Delta Kappan, 83*(9), 662–673.

Sirotnik, K. (Ed.). (2004). *Holding accountability accountable: What ought to matter in public education.* New York, NY: Teachers College Press.

Sleeter, C. (Ed). (2007). *Facing accountability in education: Democracy and equity at risk.* New York, NY: Teachers College Press.

Smith, G. (2002). Place-based education: Learning to be where we are. *Phi Delta Kappan, 83*, 584–594.

Soder, R. (2004). The double bind of civic education assessment and accountability. In K. A. Sirotnik (Ed.). *Holding accountability accountable: What ought to matter in public education,* (pp.100–115). New York, NY: Teachers College Press.

Solorzano, D. G., & Bernal, D. D. (2001). Examining transformational resistance through a critical race and Latcrit theory framework: Chicana and Chicano students in an urban context. *Urban Education, 36*(3), 308–342.

Spolin, V. (1999ing). *Improvisation for the theater: A handbook of teaching and directing techniques.* Evanston, IL: Northwestern University Press.

Steele, C., & Aronson, J. (1995). Stereotype threat and the intellectual test performance of African Americans. *Journal of Personality and Social Psychology, 69*(5), 797–811.

Steinbeck, J. (2002). *The grapes of wrath.* New York, NY: Penguin Books.

Stewart, D. (2013, May 1). Children's March 1963: A defiant moment. *The Root.* Available at www.theroot.com/views/childrens-march-1963-defiant-moment

Strieb, L., Carini, P., Kanevsky, R., & Wice, B. (2011). *Prospect's descriptive processes: The child, the art of teaching, and the classroom and school.* North Bennington, VT: The Prospect Archives and Center for Education and Research.

Suina, J. H. (2005). Tongue-tied again: Policy, schooling, and American Indian tribes. In B. S. Engel & A. C. Martin (Eds.), *Holding values: What we mean by progressive education,* (pp. 87–92). Portsmouth, NH: Heinemann.

Sutton, S. (1996). *Weaving a tapestry of resistance: The places, power, and poetry of a sustainable society.* Westport, CT: Bergin and Garvey.

Swalwell, K. (2013). *Educating activist allies: Social justice pedagogy with the suburban and urban elite.* New York, NY: Routledge.

Tashlik, P. (2010). Changing the national conversation on assessment. *Phi Delta Kappan, 91*(6), 55–59.

Teaching Tolerance & HBO. (Producers). (2004). *The Children's March* [video]. United States of America: Teaching Tolerance.

Terkel, S. (1983). *American dreams: Lost and found.* New York, NY: The New Press.

Terkel, S. (1992). *Race: How blacks and whites feel about the American obsession.* New York, NY: The New Press.

Terkel, S. (2003). *Hope dies last: Keeping the faith in troubled times.* New York, NY: The New Press.

Terkel, S. (2008). *Touch and go: A memoir.* New York, NY: The New Press.

Thoreau, H. D. (2008). *On the duty of civil disobedience.* Rockville, MD: Arc Manor. (Original work published 1849)

Traugh, C. (2000). Using descriptive inquiry in school settings. In M. Himley (Ed.), *From another angle* (pp. 150–181). New York, NY: Teachers College Press.

Traugh, C., Kanevsky, R., Martin, A. C., Seletsky, A., Woolf, K., & Strieb, L. (1986). *Speaking out: Teachers on teaching.* North Dakota Study Group. Available at http://www.ndsg.org/monographs/NDSG_1986_Traugh_et_al_Speaking_Out.pdf.

Trujillo, C. (2003). *What night brings.* Willimantic, CT: Curbstone Press.

Turner, V. (1995). *The ritual process: Structure and anti-structure.* Piscataway, NJ: Transaction. (Original work published 1977)

Turner, V. (2001). *From ritual to theatre: The human seriousness of play.* New York, NY: PAJ.

Vascellaro, S. (2011). *Out of the classroom and into the world: Learning from field trips, educating from experience, and unlocking the potential of our students and teachers.* New York, NY: The New Press.

Vygotsky, L. S. (1978). *Mind in society: The development of higher mental processes.* Cambridge, MA: Harvard University Press.

Wachowski, L., & Wachowski, A. (Directors). (1999). *The matrix* [motion picture]. United States of America: Warner Bros.

Washington, D. (2013, May 12). *The mathematics of civic injustice. Every Chicago public school is my school: 133 schools, 133 stories* [web log]. Available at everyschoolismyschool.org/2013/05/12/marconi/.

Weiner, L. (1993). *Preparing teachers for urban schools: Lessons from thirty years of school reform.* New York, NY: Teachers College Press.

Weiner, L. (2012). *The future of our schools: Teachers unions and social justice.* Chicago, IL: Haymarket Books.

Welch, S. (1990). *A feminist ethic of risk.* Minneapolis, MN: Fortress Press.

Westheimer, J., & Kahne, J. (2004). What kind of citizen? The politics of educating for democracy. *American Educational Research Journal, 41*(2), 237–269.

Wheeler, J. (2013, May 28). Building teacher–parent unions. *In These Times.* Available at http://inthesetimes.com/article/14711/building_parent_teacher_unions

White, P. (1996). *Civic virtues and public schooling.* New York, NY: Teachers College Press.

Woodhouse, J. L., & Knapp, C. E. (2000). *Place-based curriculum and instruction: Outdoor and environmental education approaches.* Charleston, WV: ERIC Clearinghouse on Rural Education and Small Schools.

Woodrow, D. (1996, February). Democratic education—Does it exist—especially for mathematics education? British Society for the Research of Learning Mathematics. *BSRLM Proceedings, 16*(1).

Young, I. M. (1996). Communication and the other: Beyond deliberative democracy. In S. Benhabib (Ed.), *Democracy and difference* (pp. 120–136). Princeton, NJ: Princeton University Press.

Young, I. M. (2004). Five faces of oppression. In L. Heldkem & P. O'Connor (Eds.), *Oppression, privilege, and resistance,* (pp. 37–36). Boston, MA: McGraw-Hill.

WEBSITES:

jjse.org/
urbanacademy.org/
performanceassessment.org/consortium/calternatives.html
timeoutfromtesting.org/MC_SenateFinal.pdf
www.fairtest.org/
www.pbs.org/onlyateacher/today14.html
www.teachingchannel.org/videos/inquiry-based-teaching-roles

Index

Note: Page numbers followed by "n" indicate numbered endnotes.

217

About the Author

Shanti Elliott directs civic engagement at the Francis W. Parker School in Chicago. She also co-leads the Teachers' Inquiry Project and teaches in the School of Education and Social Policy at Northwestern University. Previously, Shanti taught Russian and Arabic literatures at UC Berkeley. Her work focuses on education for social change, through community–school partnerships, cross-disciplinary antiracism pedagogy, and deepening political awareness. Shanti is part of diverse collaborations, from the U.S.–Russia Social Expertise Exchange to the Interfaith Committee for Detained Immigrants, to education activist coalitions. Shanti has written for a wide range of publications, from *Folklore Forum* to *Dostoevsky Studies* to *Schools Journal*.